**A STEP-BY-STEP GUIDE TO YOUR
NEW HOME SEWING MACHINE**

OTHER BOOKS IN THE CREATIVE MACHINE ARTS SERIES, AVAILABLE FROM CHILTON

Robbie Fanning, Series Editor

The Button Lover's Book, by Marilyn V. Green

Claire Shaeffer's Fabric Sewing Guide

The Complete Book of Machine Embroidery, by Robbie and Tony Fanning

Creative Nurseries Illustrated, by Debra Terry and Juli Plooster

Creative Serging Illustrated, by Pati Palmer, Gail Brown, and Sue Green

Distinctive Serger Gifts and Crafts, by Naomi Baker and Tammy Young

The Expectant Mother's Wardrobe Planner, by Rebecca Dumlao

The Fabric Lover's Scrapbook, by Margaret Dittman

Friendship Quilts by Hand and Machine, by Carolyn Vosburg Hall

Innovative Serging, by Gail Brown and Tammy Young

Innovative Sewing, by Gail Brown and Tammy Young

Owner's Guide to Sewing Machines, Sergers, and Knitting Machines, by Gale Grigg Hazen

Petite Pizzazz, by Barb Griffin

Sew, Serge, Press, by Jan Saunders

Sewing and Collecting Vintage Fashions, by Eileen MacIntosh

Simply Serge Any Fabric, by Naomi Baker and Tammy Young

Twenty Easy Machine-Made Rugs, by Jackie Dodson

Know Your Sewing Machine Series, by Jackie Dodson

Know Your Bernina, second edition

Know Your Brother, with Jane Warnick

Know Your Elna, with Carol Ahles

Know Your New Home, with Judi Cull and Vicki Lyn Hastings

Know Your Pfaff, with Audrey Griese

Know Your Sewing Machine

Know Your Singer

Know Your Viking, with Jan Saunders

Know Your White, with Jan Saunders

Know Your Serger Series, by Naomi Baker and Tammy Young

Know Your baby lock

Know Your Pfaff Hobbylock

Know Your White Superlock

Other Books in the Teach Yourself to Sew Better Series by Jan Saunders

A Step-by-Step Guide to Your Bernina

A Step-by-Step Guide to Your Sewing Machine

A Step-by-Step Guide to Your Viking

Teach Yourself to Sew Better

A STEP-BY-STEP GUIDE TO YOUR NEW HOME SEWING MACHINE

Jan Saunders

Chilton Book Company
Radnor, Pennsylvania

Copyright © 1992 by Jan Saunders

All Rights Reserved

Published in Radnor, Pennsylvania 19089, by Chilton Book Company

No part of this book may be reproduced, transmitted, or stored
in any form or by any means, electronic or mechanical,
without prior written permission from the publisher

Illustrations by Pamela Poole

Photography by Lee Philips and Jim Conroy

Manufactured in the United States of America

Library of Congress Cataloging-in-Publication Data
Saunders, Janice S.
    A step-by-step guide to your New Home sewing machine / Jan
Saunders.
        p.   cm.—(Teach yourself to sew better)
    Includes bibliographical references and index.
    ISBN 0-8019-8115-8 (pbk.)
    1. Machine sewing. 2. Sewing machines. I. Title. II. Series:
Saunders, Janice S.   Teach yourself to sew better.
TT713.S2574   1991   90-55325
646.2'044—dc20   CIP

1 2 3 4 5 6 7 8 9 0   1 0 9 8 7 6 5 4 3 2

CONTENTS

by Robbie Fanning

Part One:

Have you wanted to know how your New Home works without having to go to school to become a mechanic? What about those gadgets that came with your machine? This is a crash course to clear up misunderstandings you may have about threading your machine, tension adjustments, and needle and thread selection. You will also find simple care and maintenance information and learn how to use the basic presser feet and stitches. Also see how various tools can make sewing easier and a lot more fun.

Part Two:

Learn the proper stitches and presser feet to sew woven and knit fabrics by making a pair of woven pull-on shorts and a knit top with ribbing. Once you complete this project, you'll have the basic skills to tackle more challenging ones.

Practice the basics of machine appliqué and embroidery by making an embroidered tote bag. Embellish a pocket for your shorts and knit top made in Chapter 2.

Make Envelope Placemats and matching "Lapkins" to master buttonholes, mitered corners, and professional edge finishes.

Contents

FOREWORD

It had been a long, hard, hot day at work—interruptions, backtracking, emergencies, deadlines. I came home at 6 pm, pooped. But within an hour, I was rejuvenated, relaxed, peaceful. Why? Because I was machine-piecing a quilt for my daughter. You see, I truly love to sew. Like a kid's blankie, sewing is my Best Thing. (And best of all is to listen to recorded books as I sew.)

But I was lucky. My mother sewed as we grew up and we learned by osmosis. Later came seventh grade home ec. and some sewing classes at the local fabric store.

Today, people are not as lucky as I was. Sewing is rarely taught in home ec., and many stores do not have classes. (Thank heavens for 4-H, where teaching sewing is still strong.) While fabrics have improved, machines have become easier to use, and speedy techniques have revolutionized sewing, fewer people know how to sew.

Jan's book should help. She gives step-by-step instructions for simple projects for any age. She then explains how the skills learned in each chapter can be transferred to more ambitious projects. The experienced sewer will appreciate Jan's Encyclopedia of Stitches and Presser Feet (Part III).

Still, I propose you take one further step: share your love of sewing with someone else. You don't need teaching credentials to do this. Simply challenge yourself to help someone else learn to sew. It may be as simple as inviting a neighborhood child in to help you thread your machine. If he or she wants to run the machine, use the warm-up exercises in Chapter 1.

There are many other imaginative ways to share our mutual love of sewing. Set up a machine at work and let interested people use it on lunch breaks. Join 4-H and learn to teach sewing. Take your machine to a local school and show the students what you have made. Volunteer to teach how to sew costumes at a community theater. Demonstrate sewing at the church bazaar or county fair. Spend a day in the children's ward of a hospital, machine-embroidering patients' initials on bean bags.

As Diana Davies, a member of the Minneapolis chapter of the American Sewing Guild, suggested, "Each one teach one."

Jan and I would like to hear about your experiences. Please write us at the address below.

Robbie Fanning
Series Editor, Creative Machine Arts

Are you interested in a quarterly newsletter about creative uses of the sewing machine, serger, and knitting machine? Write to The Creative Machine, PO Box 2634, Menlo Park, CA 94026.

PREFACE

In most sewing books the word "sewing" means making garments. Such books spend pages showing you how to measure yourself, choose patterns, lay out fabric, cut, and mark.

This book is different. I approach a project by considering the fabric and how to use the stitches, presser feet, and techniques I've learned on my New Home to create something unique—unlike most sewing books that approach sewing with the emphasis on everything but the sewing machine.

To me, the word "sewing" implies using your New Home to its fullest potential. You may want to use your machine to make garments, but that's only part of the World of Sewing. In this book you'll learn to use your New Home wisely not only for making clothing, but also for appliqué and embroidery, home decoration, quilt making, toys and games, and gifts.

For this reason, *A Step-by-Step Guide to Your New Home Sewing Machine* takes a broad look at sewing. In Part I, Meet Your New Home, you will take a look at the parts of the machine, at tools necessary for respectable results, and at basic stitches. You will also preview the way the projects in Part II are constructed by completing three simple exercises.

Part II, The World of Sewing, is divided into six chapters—like spokes in a wheel, with the sewing machine at the hub.

> Sew Fashion
>
> Sew Embellishments—Machine Appliqué and Embroider
>
> Sew for Your Home
>
> Sew Quilts
>
> Sew Toys
>
> Sew Gifts

You may wonder how the World of Sewing can be covered in one book. I don't pretend to cover each area in infinite detail. But just as you don't need to know every landmark to follow directions to a place you've never been before, you don't need to know everything about one area of sewing to complete a project. Each chapter covers how to use some part of your New Home and guides you step by step through a project. The projects were selected and designed to appeal to almost anyone, regardless of age or gender. Instructions for many projects are written as a "master recipe." The variations for each project should enable you to tailor it to your needs. Even if you don't plan to make a project, read through the directions and make the project in your mind. You will learn many valuable techniques that can be transferred to other projects. At the end of each chapter look for Transferable Learnings, a section that provides a checklist of what you have learned by making the project and acts as a chapter review.

Also look for the Sew-How tips sprinkled throughout the book. I think of them as a sewing smorgasbord: keep what you like and discard the rest. Sew-How tips are designed to give you insight into a particular technique—a kind of "did you know?" or "don't forget" department. Other Sew-How information should enhance your knowledge and understanding of sewing.

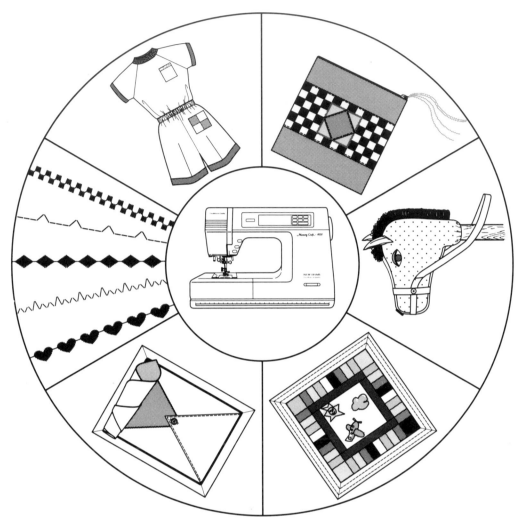

The World of Sewing—six spokes, with your New Home sewing machine at the hub.

Don't think I've ignored the benefits of using the serger for fast, professional results. However, I couldn't cover everything about sewing in this book. If there is a particular technique or step that could be completed as well on the serger as on your conventional sewing machine, you will see a serger symbol in the margin.

Part III is an encyclopedia of the undiscovered treasures available for your machine— stitches and presser feet. Each major stitch and foot is illustrated. The text explains settings and uses, and the projects in Part II are cross-referenced to both stitch and presser feet encyclopedias in Part III.

This book is for anyone who wants to sew . . . better. Whether you're a beginner or have been sewing for years, whether you need a refresher course or an advanced look at your machine, this book shows you how to sew more efficiently by learning to use your New Home better. Some of the information you may know already; some may be enlightening. My hope is that you'll sew more (and encourage others to do the same) by enjoying your machine, stitches, and presser feet as much as I do.

Jan Saunders
Columbus, Ohio

ACKNOWLEDGMENTS

When you read a book, you remember the subject matter and maybe the author—and you may even recognize the names of those quoted on the back cover and of the editors—but there are many other people who selflessly lend their knowledge and expertise so a book can be the best it can be.

I thank the following people, who are very much a part of this book: Audrey Griese, Marsha Fredrickson, Ron and Barbara Goldkorn, Janet Penwell, Kathy Thompson, and Ann Williams for their candid comments on their businesses and their retail customers; and Carol Ahles, Sue Bagley, Sandra Betzina, Gail Brown, Clotilde, David Coffin, Louise Garigk, Lois Gotwals, Audrey Griese, Sue Hausmann, Carl Jorden, Kathy Embry, JoAnn Pugh, Nancy Rice, Cheryl Robinson, Ann Wallace, and Nancy Zieman for their insightful comments on our industry at large and for their interest and love for sewing in their own lives.

Also a big thanks to the McCall Pattern Company for use of their patterns and pattern graphics. Thanks also to the New Home Sewing Machine Company for the use of its machines, and to Pam Stabler, who was so generous with her knowledge and made sure I had everything I needed to complete this book.

A special thanks to Pam Poole for her willingness to make each drawing as clear and understandable as possible, even at the expense of many corrections. Thanks also to Jeff Smith of the Sewing Center Supply Company, Inc., who answered Pam's questions and made the equipment available so her drawings could be as technically correct as they are beautiful.

As always, thanks to Robbie Fanning for crafting this book, polishing my writing style, and helping me when I really needed it.

MEET YOUR NEW HOME

Chapter One: Meet Your New Home

Part I

MEET YOUR NEW HOME

1 MEET YOUR NEW HOME

Every time I sit down to sew, I want my New Home to perform perfectly. But it can't take care of itself. This chapter will acquaint you with the common parts of your New Home and briefly explain their function. You will also brush up on how to take care of your machine so it takes care of you. You will also make stitch samples, so have on hand a variety of fabrics such as cotton kettle cloth, T-shirt knit, and light- and medium-weight wovens, cut into 7″ (18cm) squares. To keep your samples organized, buy a large three-ring binder and clear, pocket-type pages to document your successes and failures. Why keep your failures? So you don't make the same mistake twice.

Your New Home *Instruction Book* is well written and illustrated to help you understand the basics of your machine. I've designed this chapter to accompany your *Instruction Book*. If it has disappeared, call your local dealer to get another one (or see the Sources of Supply).

Step One:
IDENTIFY THE PARTS OF YOUR NEW HOME

Regardless of the model or sophistication, New Home sewing machines have many parts in common. Review Figs. 1.1 (computerized New Home 8000) and 1.2 (mechanical New Home 3023) and compare them with your machine.

Fig. 1.1
New Home Memory Craft 8000 computerized sewing machine.

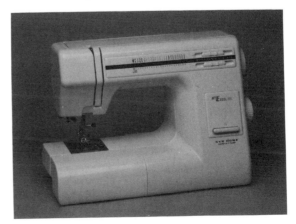

Fig. 1.2
New Home 3023 (My Excel 23L) mechanical sewing machine.

Table 1.1 Fabrics, Needle, Thread, and Presser Foot Guide								
Type of Fabric		Machine Needle			Thread				Presser Foot
		U.S. Size 15 x 1	Eur. Size 130/705	Style	Mercerized Cotton	All-purpose Cotton-covered Polyester	Long-staple Polyester	Nylon	
Knits	**Lightweight:** Tricot	8-10	60 H, 65 H, 70 H	Universal	Yes	Yes	No	Yes	Zigzag (A) or tricot
	Medium Weight: Interlock, Qiana, swimsuit fabric, Spandex	11-14	75-90 HS	Stretch or Blue Tip	Yes	Yes	Yes	Yes	Zigzag (A)
	Heavyweight: Double knit, velours	12-14	80-90 H or HS	Universal or Blue Tip	Yes	Yes	Yes	No	Zigzag (A) or satin stitch (F)
	Fake Furs & Furlike Fabrics	14-16	90-100 H, 90HJ	Universal or Denim	Yes	Yes	Yes	No	Roller or walking foot
Wovens	**Very Sheer:** Lace, net, chiffon, voile	8	60 H	Universal	Yes	Yes	No	Yes	Zigzag (A) or tricot
	Sheer: Qiana, lawn, taffeta, gingham, crepe, organdy	10-11	65-70 H	Universal	Yes	Yes	Yes	No	Zigzag (A)
	Medium: Wool, linen, piqué, brocade, velvet, velveteen, terry cloth, nylon (outerwear)	12	80 H	Universal	Yes	Yes	Yes	No	Zigzag (A) or satin stitch (F)
	Heavy: Denim, heavy corduroy, sailcloth, duck	14	90 HJ	Denim	Yes	Yes	Yes	Yes	Zigzag (A), roller, or Teflon
	Extra Heavy: Canvas, upholstery, awning, drapery fabric	14-16	90 HJ, 90-110 H	Denim or Universal	Yes	Yes	Yes	Yes	Roller or walking
Leather	**Ultrasuede, Ultraleather**	11	75 HS	Blue Tip	Yes	Yes	Yes	No	Teflon foot
	Vinyls	Leather 14-18	HLL 90-110	Wedge-point	Yes	Yes	Yes	No	Roller or Teflon
	Light to Medium Weight: Leathers and suedes	Leather 14	HLL 90	Wedge-point	Yes	Yes	Yes	No	Teflon, roller, or walking
	Vinyl Fabric with Knit Backing	14	90 HS	Stretch or Blue Tip	Yes	Yes	Yes	No	Teflon or roller
	Heavy	Leather 14-16	HLL 90-100	Wedge-point	Yes	Yes	Yes	No	Teflon or walking
Decorative Stitching	**Machine Embroidery**	14	90 HS	Stretch or Blue Tip	Yes*	No	No	No	Satin stitch (F) or appliqué (F)
	Topstitching with Heavier Thread	14	Topstitching 90 N	Universal large eye	No	Yes	Yes	No	Zigzag (A) or straight stitch
	Twin Needles Distance btwn. needles: 1.6mm 2.0mm 2.5mm 2.5mm 3.0mm 3.0mm 4.0mm 4.0mm 4.0mm 6.0mm	Distance btwn. needles: 1.6mm 2.0mm 2.5mm 2.5mm 3.0mm 3.0mm 4.0mm 4.0mm 4.0mm 6.0mm	Size: U.S./Eur. 10/70 H 12/80 H 11/75 HS 12/80 H 12/80 H 14/90 H 11/75 HS 12/80 H 14/90 H 16/100 H	Universal Universal Stretch Universal Universal Universal Stretch Universal Universal Universal	Yes " " " " " " " " "	Yes " " " " " " " " "	Yes " " " " " " " " "	No " " " " " " " " "	Satin stitch (F) or pintuck foot
	Twin Wing Needles	2.5mm	16/100 H	Wing/Univ	Yes	Yes	No	No	Satin stitch (F)
	Triple Needles	2.5mm 3.0mm	12/80 H 12/80 H	Universal Universal	Yes Yes	Yes Yes	No No	No No	Satin stitch (F) or pintuck foot
	Wing Needle	—	16/100 H	Universal	Yes	Yes	No	No	Satin stitch (F)

*Use 100% cotton mercerized embroidery, 100% rayon, or acrylic machine embroidery thread in size 40, 50, or 60. See Sources of Supply.

The **needle** is the most important part of the machine.

*Sew-How: To prevent skipped stitches and snagging, **change the needle once a garment or project.** Use a fine needle for fine fabric, heavier needles for heavier fabric (see Table 1.1).*

The **needle plate,** sometimes referred to as a stitch plate, rests on the bed of the machine over the feed dogs and has an oblong hole for the needle to pass through.

The **bobbin** and **bobbin case** are necessary to make a stitch. The bobbin holds thread necessary for sewing; the bobbin case, which may be removable or built in, holds the bobbin and is positioned in the front of the machine in the hook/race area (see page 23). When top and bobbin threads lock, a stitch is formed.

Feed dogs are the teeth under the presser foot that move the fabric through the machine. New Home sewing machines have a unique feeding system called a box feed. The advantage of the box feed is that the feed dogs have extended contact with the fabric as it moves under the presser foot. This ensures uniform stitch quality and enables you to sew through heavy thicknesses without stitch distortion or needle breakage.

Sew-How: Keep the lint cleaned out from under the feed dogs to prevent skipped stitches (see Care and Maintenance later in this chapter).

The **presser foot,** sometimes incorrectly referred to as the "pressure foot," holds the fabric firmly against the feed dogs for proper stitch formation. There are many types of presser feet, each designed for a specific purpose (see Chapter 9, Encyclopedia of Presser Feet).

Sew-How: To determine the use of a presser foot, examine its underside. Even if you have lost your Instruction Book, you may be able to figure out the intended use of the presser foot just by looking at it.

The **free-arm,** often called an open arm, enables you to stitch tubular areas, such as cuffs, armholes, or pant legs, without ripping out a seam.

Stitch length used to be calibrated in stitches per inch (spi). Now it is more commonly calibrated in millimeters (mm), and it is described this way in the Machine Readiness Checklists throughout this book. The following chart shows you what stitch length really means:

setting in mm	stitches per inch (spi)
0.5	60
1	24
2	13
3	9
4	6
5	5

*Sew-How: Instead of adjusting thread tensions, remember this rule for selecting the proper stitch length: If the fabric **puckers** when you sew, **shorten** the stitch length. Shortening the length adds thread to the stitch, allowing the fabric to relax and eliminating puckers. If the fabric **waves out of shape** as you sew, **lengthen** the stitch. Lengthening the stitch eliminates thread from the stitch, preventing the thread from pushing the fabric out of shape.*

Stitch width is what gives the sewing machine its creative possibilities. Vary the width of utility and decorative stitches to create different effects.

The **flywheel,** also called a hand wheel or balance wheel, is found on the right end of the machine and turns as you are sewing. The flywheel either helps drive the machine or coordinates needle swing with the action of the feed dogs to create a stitch. Move the flywheel by hand to place the needle exactly where you want it for stitch-by-stitch control. On the Memory Craft models, simply push the up/down key to stop sewing with the needle in or out of the fabric.

The **pattern selector** indicates stitches available on your machine. Rather than creating a variety of stitches manually, you can select built-in stitches with a lever, push button, or touch on a visual touch screen.

Top thread tension is one of the most misunderstood parts of your machine. I prefer the term "thread control." Thread control is necessary on both top and bobbin for proper stitch formation. Both can be changed without damaging your New Home to create many interesting effects (see Part II, The World of Sewing). The Memory Craft models have computer thread control, which has been programmed for the amount of bobbin thread necessary for each pattern. Although the top tension can be adjusted manually, set it at "auto" unless indicated in the Machine Readiness Checklist (see more information under Thread Control later in this chapter.)

The **take-up lever** is what pulls the thread through the upper tension as the stitch is being formed.

The **reverse button** is touched to back-stitch with a straight stitch at the beginning and end of a seam. On the 8000, it is also used as a lock-off stitch at the end of utility and decorative stitches.

Sew-How: Prevent your mechanical New Home from unthreading the needle by stopping with the take-up lever at the highest position. Newer computerized models automatically stop with the needle in the highest position.

The **feed balancing dial** enables you to fine-tune buttonhole density and reverse cycle patterns. Check your *Instruction Book* for model-specific information. Turning the feed balancing dial to + causes the reverse cycle stitches to lengthen so there is more space between them. Turning the dial to − makes the stitches closer together. You can also use the feed balancing dial to fine-tune the darning stitch (7500, 111; 8000, 9) so stitches are exactly next to each other (see *Instruction Book*).

The **needle threader** makes it easier to thread the needle. Simply pull it down into position, lay the thread across the guide, and push the button. When you push the threader up into its original position, the thread pulls through the eye.

FEATURES AND COMPUTER TERMINOLOGY

If you have a New Home Memory Craft 6000, 7000, 7500, or 8000, you have computerized features and functions on your machine. The following explanations should help you understand and identify the functions and the symbols used in the Machine Readiness Checklists found throughout this book.

The forward cycle utility, reverse cycle utility, decorative stitches, alphabet, and numbers have a **programmed width and length.** If you want to adjust or fine-tune the width and length for specific uses, you can override the programming by touching the + and − keys under the manual stitch width and stitch length indicators (Fig. 1.3). Some stitches will totally distort if lengthened or shortened too much. The computer automatically limits the stitch length for those stitches to prevent this distortion.

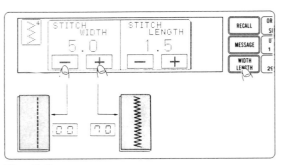

Fig. 1.3
Manual stitch width and length key.

Sew-How: *Preprogrammed width and length settings aren't shown on the manual stitch width and length indicators until you push the width or length keys or the width/length pad on the visual touch screen (see below for more information on the visual touch screen).*

The **speed setting lever** enables you to slow the sewing speed to half speed even when the foot control is being pressed all the way down. Use this feature when sewing accuracy is crucial, for stitch-by-stitch control without having to turn the flywheel by hand, and to eliminate acceleration surges.

Sew-How: *A hand-held speed control accessory (Fig. 1.4) is available for New Home models 7500, 7000, 6000, and 2122. The ring and control fit in the palm of your hand, leaving both hands free to guide the work. This accessory is especially helpful for people who have difficulty using a foot control. On the 8000, the* **start/stop** *button can be pushed to achieve the same result.*

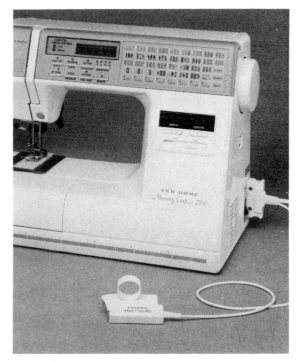

Fig. 1.4
Hand-held speed control accessory and the Memory Craft 7500 control panel.

The **visual touch screen** is an exclusive feature on the New Home Memory Craft 8000 (Fig. 1.5). The screen is sensitive to the touch and contains everything you need to select and adjust a stitch.

Fig. 1.5
Memory Craft 8000 visual touch screen.

Sew-How: *When selecting a pattern or function on the screen, just touch the screen with your finger.* Do not press the surface with a hard sharp object such as a pencil or screw driver.

When you turn the machine on, the first seven stitches appear. After you touch (select) the stitch you want, the screen will change to tell you what presser feet are recommended for that stitch. Touch the **message** pad, and the screen tells you where the tension and pressure should be set. The information on the screen also includes a recommendation for the needle type and size for your fabric.

Within the visual touch screen are other pads. To select utility or decorative stitches, push the **utility** or **decorative** pad to bring the stitches up on the menu. **Recall** retrieves a stitch or program in memory. If you do something incorrectly, the screen tells you what to do.

Another computerized feature of the Memory Craft 8000 is the ability to stitch larger monograms and intricate embroidery designs. These designs are stored on **Memory Cards** which slip into the right side of the machine. Two program cards come with the 8000—a monogram card that features block, small script, large script, and Old English lettering, and a decorative card that features twenty-five designs ranging from the zodiac to flowers and sports symbols. At press time there are four memory cards available with more to come (Fig. 1.6).

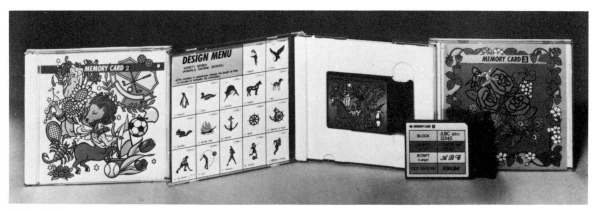

Fig. 1.6
Memory Craft 8000 memory cards.

Sew-How: *If you own an 8000, you will learn how to use the memory cards in your after-purchase lessons, so I will not explain how the system works, other than in a very general way. If you are interested in seeing the exciting decorative possibilities of the New Home Memory Craft 8000, visit your local New Home dealer.*

A memory card motif is stitched with up to five thread colors; the visual touch screen tells you what color to use for a particular part of a design. After one part of the design is complete, the machine automatically stops to tell you it is ready for you to change thread color and complete another part of the design.

The 7500 has a **visual sewing screen** which shows you what stitch or combination of stitches you have selected. It also reminds you to "Check feed dog," "Raise feed dog," or "Drop feed dog" for specific functions. When the **program check** key is pressed, the screen suggests one or two feet to use for each stitch. If you have programmed two or more stitches, the pattern combination can be seen on the visual sewing screen and checked by pushing the program check key. The beginning of a programmed pattern is also shown when the program check key is pressed. After programming a stitch combination, push the program check key until the red light flashes; then, to return to the beginning of the programmed combination, push the **pattern turn over** key (for more information on the pattern turn over key, see next page). To go to the end of the programmed combination, push the **M/memory** key to check for mistakes before stitching (see the control panel on model 7500 in Fig. 1.4). This is also helpful when you are matching stitch patterns or starting a programmed stitch after stopping in the middle of the design.

Sew-How: *Some New Home Memory Craft models have self-diagnostic checklists that appear on the screen so a service technician can check for function errors.*

For most sewers, the method for locking off stitches is to backstitch at the beginning and end of each seam. The factory method for locking off stitches is to prevent the fabric from feeding for a few stitches so the stitches lock on top of each other. New Home has this **lock-off** or **auto-lock stitch** as one of the computerized functions on the 6000, 7000, 7500, and 8000. Use this on fine fabrics at the end of a decorative stitch or programmed stitch combination.

If you press the lock-off stitch key while you are sewing, the needle takes six locking stitches in place and automatically stops at the end of the stitch pattern. Push this key before you begin sewing to make the machine stitch six stitches in place at the beginning of a stitch pattern and stop automatically.

A single stitch pattern can also be isolated. For instance, if you want to stitch a single diamond, select the stitch, then stop and tie off at the end of the pattern by pushing the lock-off key while the stitch is being sewn. Certain stitches on the 6000, 7000, 7500, and 8000 have a **memory lock** function that automatically locks off at the beginning and end of the stitch pattern. Memory lock stitches are described in the Encyclopedia of Stitches.

The **pattern elongater** key is used to elongate the satin stitch patterns up to five times their original size while maintaining the stitch density. See your *Instruction Book* for those stitches that can be elongated.

The **letter style selection** or **monogram** key is used to select block or script lettering in either uppercase or lowercase. Select a letter and then push the monogram key to scroll to the correct letter style and size. To spell a name or saying, select the letter, style, and size; then push the M/memory key.

Note: The first letter or number must be selected before you can use the monogram key.

Needle stop up or down enables you to keep your hands on your work rather than turning the flywheel by hand to stop the needle in the up or down position for pivoting, bringing the bobbin thread up, embroidery stitches, and long continuous seams.

The **clear button** is pushed to clear a programmed stitch. To clear a memorized program you must delete each stitch, one at a time, until the straight stitch pattern appears on the visual sewing screen. This feature enables you to edit before stitching when you are programming stitch combinations.

If your New Home sewing machine has the **pattern turn over** key, you can create a mirror image of a stitch, which is important when matching stitches or centering designs. The stitch pattern will be flipped over and underlined on the visual screen. When you press the pattern turn over key, letters and numbers are reduced to two-thirds their original size. This key also lets you return to the beginning of a programmed pattern without having to sew to the end of the stitch combination.

The **M/memory** key is used in programming stitch combinations. Select a stitch and press M/memory to have the machine "memorize" the stitch. The memory holds up to thirty-one patterns in a row—helpful when you are using letters and numbers, or for long stitch combinations. On the 7000 and 7500, the memory key can also be used to make a series of buttonholes that are identical in length. (See preceding page to learn about using the memory key with the program check function.) The memory key is also used to enter a stitch pattern into the memory before storing it (see **store** key below).

The **reverse sewing button** on the 7000 and 7500 has a number of functions. When using this feature with a straight stitch, you will sew continuously in reverse at the same stitch length you selected in the forward direction. When the "lock-a-matic" stitch is selected, it ends the stitch at the end of a seam or row of stitching (see page 147). The reverse sewing button also sets the length of the automatic bartack, and if you press it while sewing a stitch other than the straight stitch, it will immediately sew six stitches in place and stop automatically. This way if you have run out of bobbin thread while sewing a row of programmed stitches, you can stop sewing without having to complete the entire program.

The 8000 reverse sewing button enables you to backstitch at the end of a straight-stitched seam. It can also be pushed at the end of any other stitch to make the needle automatically take six stitches in place.

On the 7500, the **scroll** keys are pattern selection keys. Each scroll contains fourteen stitches; when a key is pushed, the stitch picture and number appear on the visual sewing screen (Fig. 1.7).

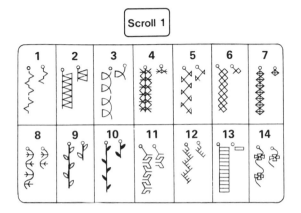

Fig. 1.7
Memory Craft 7500 scroll keys.

The **store** key enables you to store up to thirty-one patterns for immediate recall even if you want to select another stitch, sew awhile, and then return to the programmed stitch combination. Program the stitch combination, press the program check key, and then press the store key. Then you can use your machine for regular sewing. To recall the programmed stitch combination, push the store key. Note that up to thirty-one patterns can be stored in the memory; these patterns plus the thirty-one patterns stored in the "store" give you the possibility of storing a total of sixty-two patterns.

Note: When the 7500 is turned off, the stored program is erased.

Another helpful computerized function is the **beginning** key, available on the 8000. If you are sewing a series of programmed stitches and you stop sewing in the middle of the series, you can push this key to make the series start from the beginning.

Finally, there are a number of "character stitches" (see the Encyclopedia of Stitches) that can be reduced. For example, if you want to stitch a family of penguins, you can reduce the size of the figures by narrowing the stitch width or pressing the **size** key on the visual sewing screen.

THREADING

Upper Threading

Although every machine threads a little differently, each follows a similar threading procedure. From the spool, threading usually follows this order (Fig. 1.8). Note that there may be a thread guide or two between one or more of the following:

1. Slit
2. Thread guides
3. Check spring
4. Take-up lever
5. Thread guide
6. Needle clamp
7. Needle

Sew-How: *Sometimes inferior thread leaves a residue of extra fuzz between the discs of your upper tension, which may cause uneven tension on the thread as you sew. To clean this lint out, raise the presser foot and run the straight edge of a dollar bill up and down between the tensions discs in the upper tension. The paper in the bill has fibers in it so it won't rip, and the natural oils in it from handling help to clean and lubricate.*

Bobbin Winding and Threading

Bobbin winding varies from model to model, so check your *Instruction Book.*

Sew-How: *For a front- or side-loading bobbin, thread your bobbin so that when the thread is pulled, the bobbin turns clockwise. This prevents the bobbin thread from backlashing, which can cause uneven tension and thread breakage.*

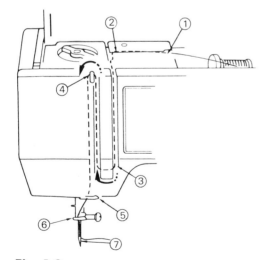

Fig. 1.8
Upper threading (see text).

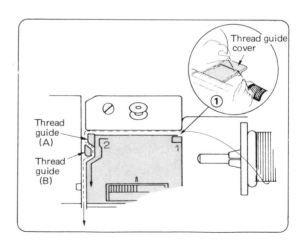

Hold the bobbin for a top-loading model so the thread runs counterclockwise over the top of the bobbin and the tail is to the left (Fig. 1.9). Then drop the bobbin in place, guiding the thread through the notches. This ensures that the bobbin is threaded properly.

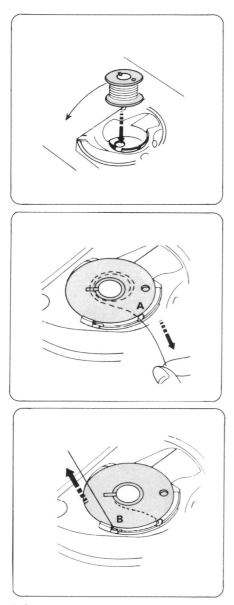

Fig. 1.9
For a top-loading model, place the bobbin in the bobbin holder with the thread running counterclockwise. Guide the thread into the notch A on the front side of the bobbin holder. Draw the thread to the left, sliding it between the tension spring blades. Continue to draw the thread lightly until the thread slips into notch B.

Sew-How: *To bring up the bobbin thread, place the top thread under the presser foot and hold it against the bed of the machine with the index finger of your left hand. Starting with the take-up lever at the highest position, turn the flywheel one complete turn by pushing the up/down key or by tapping the foot control one stitch so the top thread pulls up the bobbin thread loop. Rather than scraping over the feed dogs with a pair of scissors to free the bobbin thread, pull out a longer length of top thread and in both hands grasp a length about 5" (12.5cm) long; then pass the thread under the foot to free the bobbin thread.*

THREAD CONTROL (TENSION)

What do you think when you hear the word "tension"? A tension headache? I remember a sign in the home ec. lab that read "Don't Touch the Tension!"—my shoulders automatically tightened up every time I saw it. That's why I prefer to call thread tension "thread control." However, New Home has further defined thread control with the Memory Craft models.

Thread Tension versus Thread Control

Thread tension is the amount of resistance on the top and bobbin threads. If there were no thread tension, thread from the top and bobbin would reel out freely and result in a series of loops rather than stitches (you may have seen this in a machine that has been out of adjustment).

On the other hand, thread control, as defined by New Home, is a separate function and controls the amount of bobbin thread released for each stitch.

The best way to illustrate this is to look at the diamond stitch (7500, 65; 8000, 35). Only a small length of bobbin thread is necessary for the ends of the diamond, whereas longer lengths of thread are necessary to stitch the center of the diamond. To compensate, a bar under the needle plate pulls off longer lengths of thread when it is necessary, and the amount of thread pulled out for each stitch is programmed for each stitch. The advantage of this system is better stitch quality with less tunneling. Because of this, the bobbin tension on the top-loading Memory Craft models is preset at the factory and should not have to be adjusted.

If you have a removable front- or side-loading bobbin case, set your bobbin tension first, then adjust the upper tension to it. To set the bobbin tension:

1. Place the bobbin in the bobbin case. When you pull the thread, the bobbin should turn clockwise.

2. With the tiny screwdriver that came with your New Home, carefully loosen the screw on the side of the case closest to the thread, without removing it, so there is no drag on the thread. When you pull the thread, it should pull out easily.

Sew-How: *Loosen the tension screw over a box top so that if the screw falls out, it won't be lost.*

---

3. By quarter turns, tighten the screw until the thread supports the weight of the bobbin and bobbin case but there is still a little bit of slipping when you jerk on the thread (Fig. 1.10).

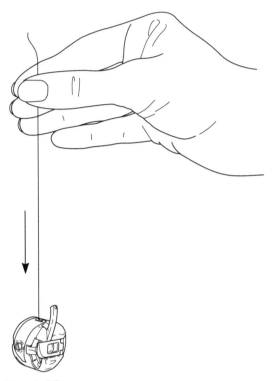

Fig. 1.10
For proper bobbin tension, tighten the tension screw until the thread supports the weight of the bobbin and bobbin case; then tighten the screw another quarter to half turn.

4. Tighten the screw *another* quarter to half a turn.

For balanced thread tension, the top thread and the bobbin thread should lock in the middle of the fabric. It's easier to check this if you use one color thread in the top and a different color in the bobbin. (Make sure they are the same weight and brand.) To test, set your straight stitch on a 2.5–3 length and sew on the bias, using a double thickness of medium-weight fabric. Pull on both ends of the stitch. Thread should break on both the top and the bobbin side of the stitch.

If the top thread breaks, loosen the upper tension. If the bobbin thread breaks, tighten the upper tension. Now stitch a 3 length, 3 width zigzag stitch. Turn the fabric over. Stitches should lock perfectly on one side of the stitch (Fig. 1.11).

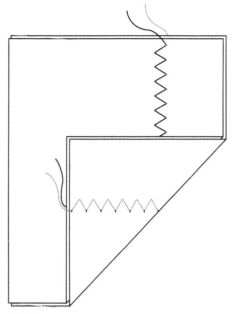

Fig. 1.11
Zigzag stitch should lock between the two layers of fabric.

Sew-How: *New Home sewing machines use both metal and transparent bobbins. Newer models come with the clear bobbins, which are recommended for use on all top-loading machines. Clear bobbins make it easier to check the thread supply and also make the machine run more quietly. Also, clear bobbins will not cause unnecessary wear on the bobbin case.*

PRESSURE

New Home machines have adjustable pressure which regulates the amount of force the presser foot exerts on the fabric. Newer models have three pressure settings. Use "3" for regular sewing, "2" for appliqué and cut work, and "1" for basting and sewing delicate fabrics (such as chiffon, batiste, lace, and organdy) and stretch fabrics (such as velour and stretch terry cloth).

NEEDLE SELECTION

The purpose of the needle is to poke a hole in the fabric big enough for the thread to pass through without fraying the fabric. Choose your thread to match the weight of fabric; the needle to match the size of the thread; and the point of the needle to match the type of fabric (see Table 1.1, Fabric, Needle, Thread, and Presser Foot Guide).

The best needle to use for any project is a new one. For the sewer, a new needle for every project is like the clean, sharp scalpel a surgeon uses for each operation. New needles prevent skipped stitches, snags, puckering, and unnecessary holes in your fabric.

Needles are sized by the American or European systems and are identified by numbers and letters. The best needles for your New Home are manufactured by Janome (the manufacturer of the New Home sewing machines) and are available through your New Home dealer. The number identifies the size; the letters identify the type of point. Tables 1.2 and 1.3 will help you in selecting your needles. Needle sizes and types are listed in the Machine Readiness Checklists for each project in Part II. In Table 1.3, the letters behind the numbers identify the needle point and describe its use.

Table 1.2 American and European Needle Sizes

American	European	Suggested Fabrics
8	60	silk organza, chiffon, sheers, fine silks
9	65	tissue faille, voile, georgette, blouse-weight silks
10	70	blouse and lightweight dress fabrics
11	75	American needles available in "universal" or "Blue Tip" point. Blue Tip is recommended for knit, interlock, Lycra swimwear, knit sheers, Ultrasuede, and other synthetic leathers and suedes. European needle available in "stretch" needle type only.
12	80	suit-weight silks, linens, and wool
14	90	denim, topstitching with topstitching thread, heavy duck cloth, real leather
16	100	use only if the size 90/14 breaks
18	110	use only if the size 100/16 breaks

Table 1.3 Needle Point Types

Classification	Point Type
15X1 or 705B	**Pierce-point:** a sharp needle used for sewing woven fabrics. Produces a very straight-looking straight stitch.
15X1SP or 130/705SUK	**Ballpoint:** a round-tipped needle designed for use on heavy knits and those with Lycra knitted into them. Not as widely available as the Universal. The ballpoint slips easily between the loops in a knit fabric.
15X1H or 130/705H	**Universal:** cross between a sharp and ballpoint tip; use on most knits and wovens. This needle is most widely available and sews beautifully on the majority of fabrics.
Blue Tip or 130/705HS	**Blue Tip** or **stretch** needle has a sharper point than a universal needle with a deeper scarf, which aids in stitch formation to prevent skipped stitches. Needle has a blue shank. Recommended for swim wear knits, synthetic suedes, and machine embroidery.
15X1DE or 130/705HJ	**Denim:** sharp point to penetrate closely woven fabrics easily without breaking the needle. Recommended on denim, corduroy, and upholstery fabric. Sometimes colored blue to avoid confusion with the other size 14/90 needles.
15X1ST or 130/705N	**Topstitching:** the eye and front groove of the needle is twice the size of a normal 11/75 or 14/90 needle to accommodate heavy topstitching thread. New Home's topstitching needle also has a pierce point to produce straight topstitching.
15X1LL or 130/705HLL or NTW	**Wedge:** large-eyed needle with a wedge point to penetrate leather. The point slices into leather rather than perforating it.
130/705H	**Wing:** has two flanges on either side of the needle shaft and is designed for hemstitching. The needle pokes a large hole while the stitch overcasts the hole open. This technique is used on French "hand-sewn" and heirloom projects.

SPECIAL NEEDLES

Twin Needles

Twin needles, also called double needles, have one shank and two needles fixed to a crossbar. They are sized by two numbers and a letter. For example, a 2.0/12(80)H means the needles are 2mm apart, are size 12/80, and have a universal point; a 4.0/90(14)H means the needles are 4mm apart, are size 14/90, and have a universal point.

Double Wing

A double wing needle has a wing needle on the left and a universal needle on the right and is designed for use with decorative hemstitches for heirloom sewing. Experiment with some of your stitches and put the samples in your notebook.

Triple Needles

Triple needles have one shank and three needles fixed to a crossbar so three top threads are sewing at once. Triple needles are used primarily with decorative stitches.

Sew-How: *Twin and triple needles stitch wider than single needles, and if the needle swings too wide, it surpasses the width of the needle hole. Therefore be sure to test the stitch width when using utility or decorative stitches to prevent needle breakage.*

RULES FOR THREAD SELECTION

When selecting thread, read the label and unwrap a little, then take a close look at it. It should have a smooth, even appearance.

Throughout this book, you will see a Machine Readiness Checklist for each technique. In each case, one of the following thread types if recommended·

- 100% cotton sewing
- all-purpose sewing
- 100% polyester
- cotton embroidery
- rayon embroidery
- acrylic embroidery
- nylon monofilament
- darning or basting

One hundred percent cotton sewing thread works well for most garment construction provided it is colorfast and mercerized. Mercerizing increases strength, luster, and affinity for dye, so it can also be used for embroidery, topstitching, and buttonholes. Cotton fibers are long and smooth, so you shouldn't experience tension problems. Cotton thread is not as strong as cotton-wrapped polyester, or 100% polyester; however, if used with the correct stitch for the fabric, cotton thread is strong enough for most projects. The only other disadvantage with cotton thread is that it is not as readily available as the others. Look for these brand names: D.M.C., Mettler Metrosene, Zwicky.

All-purpose cotton-wrapped polyester thread, referred to in the Machine Readiness Checklists as "all-purpose" thread, is also colorfast and mercerized and is recommended for garment construction. All-purpose thread has slightly less sheen than the 100% cotton thread. It is also stronger and stretches more than the all-cotton thread because of its polyester core, so it may require you to make some tension adjustments. All-purpose thread is widely available. Look for J.P. Coats (Dual Duty).

One hundred percent polyester thread was originally developed in the sixties and seventies to enable sewers to successfully sew knit fabrics with a straight stitch. At that time it was coarse and stretchy, so it was necessary to adjust both top and bobbin tension for acceptable results. Today, 100% polyester thread has improved considerably. The major brands are made with long staple fibers (at least 2″ [5cm]) and are softer, smoother, and easier to use than their predecessors. However, polyester thread does not have the sheen that 100% cotton, cotton/wrapped polyester, rayon, or acrylic threads have and is therefore not recommended for embroidery. Look for these brand names: Gutterman, Mettler Metrosene, Serelon, and Swisse.

Cotton embroidery thread is finer than cotton sewing thread, so it is *not* recommended for construction of seams. However, it is great for machine blind hemming and for machine embroidery. It is recommended for blind hemming because, when used with a fine needle and a loosened top tension, the stitches become almost invisible. Cotton embroidery thread is also colorfast, mercerized, and fills in a design smoothly and with less bulk than the all cotton sewing thread. Look for these brand names: D.M.C., Mettler Metrosene, Zwicky.

Acrylic embroidery thread is new on the home sewing market and was developed for embroidery use with the New Home Memory Craft 8000. It is a #50 weight static-free embroidery thread that has more shine than 100% cotton thread but less than rayon embroidery thread. It is available in twenty-four colors from your New Home dealer. Use this thread for intricate Memory Card embroidery patterns.

Rayon is not as strong a fiber as cotton or polyester, but it has a lot of shine. Therefore, **rayon embroidery thread** is not recommended for seam construction, but it is beautiful for machine embroidery. To prevent the thread from shredding and breaking, use a size 14/90 Blue Tip or stretch needle and a loosened top tension. Look for these brand names: Natesh, Paradise, Sulky.

Nylon monofilament thread looks like very fine fish line and blends with any color—helpful because you don't have to rethread your machine when using different color fabrics in the same project. It can also be used on the bobbin so that to change thread color you need only rethread the top. However, some kinds of nylon monofilament thread are wiry, won't hold a knot, and may irritate sensitive skin. See Sources of Supply for newer, softer forms.

Darning or basting thread is very fine and recommended for use on the bobbin when machine embroidering. It can be 100% cotton or 100% polyester and a lot can be wound on a bobbin. As with the nylon monofilament thread, use darning thread in the bobbin and simply change the top thread color for embroidery.

Buy your thread at the fabric store or from your sewing machine dealer, and stick with the major brands (see Sources of Supply). Buying five spools for a dollar is not a bargain when the thread breaks, fuzzes, and causes the fabric to pucker.

BASIC PRESSER FEET

Do you know where the accessories are that came with your New Home? Do you know what each item is for? The following information may refresh your memory (Fig. 1.12). Specific techniques and usage for these and other accessories are covered thoroughly in Chapter 9, Encyclopedia of Presser Feet. Consult Table 1.4 to see which presser feet should have come with your particular New Home model.

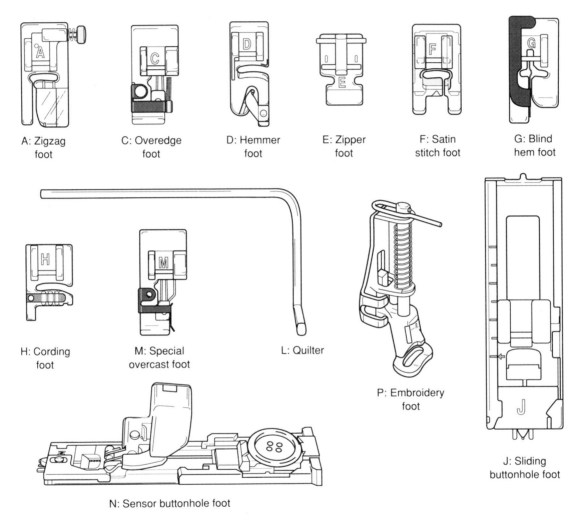

A: Zigzag foot

C: Overedge foot

D: Hemmer foot

E: Zipper foot

F: Satin stitch foot

G: Blind hem foot

H: Cording foot

M: Special overcast foot

L: Quilter

P: Embroidery foot

J: Sliding buttonhole foot

N: Sensor buttonhole foot

Fig. 1.12
Basic New Home feet: A, zigzag foot; C, overedge foot; D, hemmer foot; E, zipper foot; F, satin stitch foot; G, blind hem foot; H, cording foot; M, special overcast foot; L, quilter; P, embroidery foot; J, sliding buttonhole foot; N, sensor buttonhole foot. Note that standard feet on the Memory Craft 8000 include a slightly different-looking P embroidery foot and an R rather than an N sensor buttonhole foot.

Table 1.4 Presser Feet Included with Memory Craft

Foot	6000	7000	7500	8000
Zigzag foot	A	A	A	A
Buttonhole (transparent) foot	B	—*	—	—
Overedge foot	C	C	C	C
Hemmer foot	D	D	D	D
Zipper foot	E	E	E	E
Satin stitch foot	F	F	F	F
Blind-stitch hem foot	G	G	G	G
Cording foot	H	H	H	H
Sliding buttonhole foot	J	J	J	—
Buttonhole sensor foot	—	N	N	R
Craft foot	K	—	—	—
Quilter	L	L	L	L
Special overcast foot	M	M	M	M
Embroidery foot	P	P	P	P

* A dash (—) means that the foot is not included with purchase of the machine.

Note: Memory Craft 7000 has a new, narrower zipper foot that works better than the one included with the 6000, and a new, improved blind hem foot. However, owners of the 7000 should also purchase the 6000's blind hem foot because it is better for topstitching and applying braid.

The **A zigzag foot** is used for general straight and curved seams and for top-stitching on lightweight and heavy fabrics. The needle hole is oblong, and the underside is smooth and flat to keep the needle from pulling the fabric up and down with each stitch. Part of the toe is made with a transparent material for added visibility. The top front also has three lines struck in the left, center, and right to use as reference points for top-stitching, overcasting, and sewing close to a fabric edge.

Sew-How: To adjust the feed balancing dial, use the toe of the A foot or a nickel instead of a screw driver. It fits in the slot perfectly and will not strip the notch like a screw driver.

The **C overedge foot** is used for overcasting and seaming with the overlock, double overlock, and other overcasting stitches used on light- to medium-weight wovens and knits. Also use it for overcasting a raw edge on a single layer of fabric. The stitch forms over the bars and the brush tricks the needle into believing it is stitching over fabric when the needle passes through it. The combination of the bars and the brush on the foot releases more thread for each stitch, which prevents tunneling.

The **E zipper foot** has a center toe with a notch on either side. The notches provide support around three sides of the needle, while the flat underside holds the fabric and zipper firmly to prevent skipped stitches. To use the foot, move your needle to right or left needle position and sew next to the zipper coil.

Sew-How: To attach this foot properly, snap it on from the back so the back bar rests in the slot in the foot shank. Note that the foot appears to wobble when it is in the up position. It is designed this way because it makes contact with three feed dog runners to maintain the stitch quality even when sewing on uneven thicknesses.

The **F satin stitch foot** has a wide channel on the underside so it rides smoothly over decorative stitching. It is also transparent for added visibility and has a metal runner behind each toe to add stability where the fabric and feed dogs meet.

The **G blind hem foot** has a black blade centered in the foot which guides against the fold in the fabric while blind hemming. This way, the stitch forms over the blade, releasing the tension on the thread and ensuring an almost invisible blind hem. The underside is scored with ridges to prevent the fabric from shifting. Use the blind hem foot for edgestitching, too.

The **J sliding buttonhole foot** can make a buttonhole from $\frac{1}{4}''$ (6mm) to $1\frac{1}{4}''$ (3.2cm) and enables you to make all the buttonholes the same size without a lot of elaborate measuring. The prong on the front makes it easy to cord a buttonhole for extra strength.

The **N sensor buttonhole foot** comes standard with New Home models 7000 and 7500. The **R sensor buttonhole foot** comes with the 8000. Both are designed to measure and program one-step buttonholes precisely when stitching on uneven fabric thicknesses found on a front tab, cuff, or collar stand. Rather than counting the number of stitches in a buttonhole, the sensor buttonhole foot guides the fabric the exact length necessary for the button that rests in the back of the foot.

Sew-How: For a coat button or one that is thicker than normal, you will have to make a longer buttonhole. To do this simply pull back on the slide the button fits into.

The **P embroidery foot** is used when free-machine darning and embroidering. When the presser bar is down, the foot rests slightly off the fabric so you are free to move the fabric in any direction. When the needle is in the fabric, the foot drops onto the fabric while the stitch is made to ensure proper stitch formation. For free-machine embroidery or appliqué, guide the red mark on the right with the cut edge or outline.

Sew-How: The P foot in the 8000 is slightly different from the one that comes with the 7500, but it serves the same function.

The **L quilter** slides behind the foot shank and is tightened in position with a small screw. It rides over a row of stitching or next to an edge so that successive rows of stitching are evenly spaced.

CARE AND MAINTENANCE

Cleaning

Next to changing the needle with each project, cleaning the lint from the area under the feed dogs and the hook/race area is most important (Fig. 1.13). (The race is the area that houses the hook, bobbin, and bobbin case.)

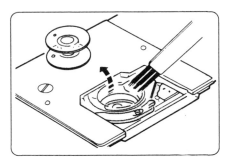

Fig. 1.13
To clean the New Home Memory Craft race, take out the bobbin, then brush out dust and lint.

1. Remove your bobbin, needle plate, bobbin case, presser foot, and needle.

2. Fluff your lint brush so each bristle can reach into a lint-infested area to pull the lint out. Dust the big chunks out of the race with the brush. Finish the job by blowing out the finer particles with canned air. (Do not use your breath, because the moisture in it may cause parts to rust.)

Did You Know? Because of environmental concerns, there has been some controversy about the use of canned air. A brand called TAC Air Blast does not hurt the ozone layer; it is available through mail order sources (see Sources of Supply).

Oiling

Newer top-loading New Home sewing machines do not require oiling in the workings of the machine because they have "oil-emitting" bearings. This means that when the machine is in use, the molecules in the part warm up and force the oil out to lubricate. When the machine is not in use, the oil returns to the part.

The only oiling spot in top-loading models is the wick centered under the bobbin case, and it is necessary to oil it only if the machine becomes noisy or the wick becomes a discolored gray or yellow. When you do need to oil the wick, use only *one* drop of oil.

Sew-How: If the noise is not eliminated by oiling, check to see if a part of a broken needle has become attached to the black magnetic ring that surrounds the wick under the bobbin case (if so, remove the needle part).

Older front- or side-loading models should be oiled in the hook/race area after every eight to twelve hours of sewing time or once a month to keep your machine running smoothly and quietly. Remember to use sewing machine oil because it is pure and fine and will not gum up your machine. See your *Instruction Book* for specific instructions for oiling your model.

Sew-How: After oiling your machine, plug it in and run it without the needle for a couple minutes until the oil has a chance to work. Then, put in a new needle and stitch on a scrap so any excess oil can come off on the scrap. Stitch until the fabric and stitches are dry.

Step Two:
ASSEMBLE YOUR TOOLS

Besides your New Home sewing machine, you will need a few tools and notions to measure, cut, mark, sew, and press your completed projects (Fig. 1.14). I refer to many of these throughout the book, so refresh your memory and check your sewing inventory. Besides the items below, there are hundreds of other notions to make sewing easier. See the Sources of Supply for mail-order companies or visit your local sewing store.

MEASURING TOOLS

Use a **tape measure** so pattern pieces are cut on grain and for other measurements as you lay out a pattern. Choose one that is made of paper or plastic-coated fabric, so it won't stretch with continued use. Most tapes are $\frac{5}{8}''$ (1.5mm) wide—the width of a standard seam allowance. It is also useful to have a different color on each side so you can easily tell if the tape is twisted.

Sew-How: *Wear your tape measure around your neck while sewing for ready reference.*

A **sewing gauge** has a sliding guide for measuring hem depth, button and buttonhole spacing, trim placement, and pleat width; ear length and eye spacing for toys and appliqués; and more. It is a must for anyone who mends or sews.

A **see-through cutting ruler** is thick enough to cut up against when you are using a rotary cutter. The O'Lipfa ruler is 24″ (61cm) long and $\frac{1}{8}''$ (3mm) thick and has a lip edge. This lip hangs off the edge of the cutting mat and is used like a T square. It is 5″ (12.5cm) wide and is marked every $\frac{1}{4}''$ (6mm) the length of the rule. Other see-through rulers have markings for length, width, and bias lines. Look for either type at your local fabric store or mail-order source.

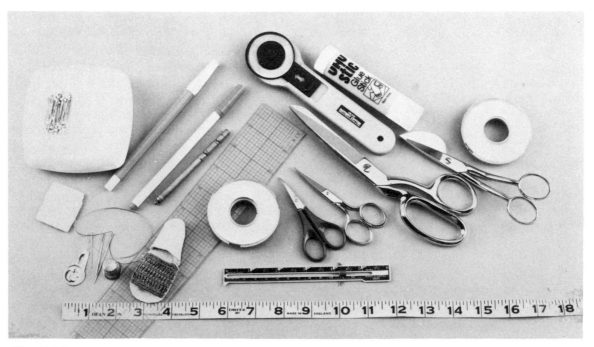

Fig. 1.14
Measuring, cutting, marking, and sewing tools.

CUTTING TOOLS

Shears have a thumb hole and an oblong hole for two or more fingers. They are designed for the best grip and extended usage, so you can cut for long periods of time without straining your hand. The bend provides a place to rest your index finger and allows you to cut without raising the fabric off the table.

Shear blades are made of hot-forged steel, stainless steel, or aluminum. Steel blades can be resharpened more often than their aluminum counterparts but are heavier to use.

Some shears are joined by a rivet; others, by a screw and nut. Generally, riveted shears cannot cut as heavy a fabric as can those joined by a screw and nut. Only those with a screw can be taken apart to be sharpened and adjusted for perfect cutting. When purchasing a pair of shears, test them by cutting through at least two thicknesses of medium-weight fabric. All scissors and shears should cut to the tip.

Scissors have a thumb and finger hole and are used for careful, accurate jobs such as trimming and clipping. There are specific scissors for specific jobs. For general-purpose sewing, use 5″ (12.5cm) scissors with one pointed and one round-tipped blade. This way you are less likely to snip a hole where it isn't wanted, or to push scissors through the fabric while pushing out a collar or pocket point. (Note that a collar point turner is recommended for pushing out collar or pocket points.)

A **rotary cutter and mat** are for the more serious home sewer. They are more expensive than shears, and you still need shears for cutting intricate designs and pattern pieces. However, the cutter cuts through multiple layers of fabric at one time—which is great for cutting quilt blocks, strips, and long, straight pattern pieces—but it must be used with a special mat to protect the layout surface.

Rather than sharpening the rotary cutter, you change the blade. If you're looking for a faster way of cutting, this is it.

HOLDING TOOLS

Pattern weights speed up the layout and cutting process. Rather than pinning the pattern pieces to the fabric, weights have pin-like tacks on the underside to hold the pattern tissue and fabric while cutting. If you are using a fabric that snags easily, use the weights with the smooth side down. Later on in this chapter you will make a paper or pattern weight.

Pins are necessary for sewing. If your pins are a collection scavenged from men's dress shirts or the floor of the home ec. room at school, buy some new ones. My favorites are fine, glass-headed quilting pins. They are extra long, and the glass heads won't melt if you iron over them. They are also easy to find when accidentally dropped on the floor or carpet.

A **pin cushion** or magnetic pin cushion is an ideal home for your pins. I use a wrist pin cushion while sewing. My magnetic pin cushion sits on the table and on the ironing board during layout, cutting, and pressing. This way, I have a place for my pins, no matter where I am in the construction process.

Tweezers are handy for grabbing too-short threads when you have to rip something out, removing tear-away stabilizer, and retrieving a needle or pin that accidentally falls into the workings of your machine. They also help you hold appliqué edges, threads, and tricky seam allowances and can be used to remove lint and broken threads from the race and bobbin area. My favorite tweezers are those that came with my serger. They have a sharp nose which is bent at a slight angle for easy use and visibility. If you don't have a serger, purchase a pair of tweezers through your local serger dealer.

MARKING TOOLS

Dressmaker's chalk or a sliver of soap marks well on dark fabrics but is sometimes difficult to remove. I like Clo-Chalk—disappearing dressmaker's chalk—because it marks well, comes with its own sharpener, and disappears in five days on its own or immediately when washed or ironed (see Sources of Supply). Use chalk to transfer pattern markings.

A **water-erasable marker** is like a felt-tipped marker for fabric. It marks well on light-colored fabrics and the marks erase with clear water.

Sew-How: *Use a water-erasable marker to transfer pattern markings by resting the tip on the pattern tissue. The ink bleeds through the tissue, the first layer of fabric, and then second layer of fabric, leaving an accurate mark.*

A **vanishing marker** is similar to a water-erasable marker except that the mark it makes disappears within 24 to 48 hours, depending on the humidity. You can mark darts and dots, transfer an appliqué pattern, or copy a monogram on the right side of the fabric— and if you make a mistake, the ink disappears, and no one is the wiser.

Tracing paper and a tracing wheel are used to mark large markings such as long darts or pleats. Place the tracing paper so the coated side is against the wrong side and between the two layers of fabric. Trace the dart by rolling the tracing wheel over the line to be marked. The resulting line is dotted. Some types of tracing paper are coated with air- and/or water-soluble ink (check with mail-order sources).

Transparent tape is another handy marking and basting tool. Stitch next to it for straight topstitching, to sew a straight dart, or to stitch in a zipper. Stick a button or appliqué in place before stitching. Just remember to hide your supply from your family, or it may disappear like the vanishing marker.

Sew-How: *I like the type of tape that has a cloudy appearance, because it is less sticky than the shiny tape and is easier to see on dark fabrics. Another type is called "removable" and is coated with the same adhesive as "sticky notes," so it should not change the nap of the fabric.*

SEWING TOOLS

"As ye sew, so must ye rip." A **seam ripper** is essential for fixing mistakes or "unsewing." The point picks the stitch out of the seam, while the blade cuts the thread. Like pins and needles, a ripper wears out occasionally, so replace it when it dulls. The best quality I've found is available through your local sewing machine dealer. Look for the little arrow etched on the blade.

Rather than tying off threads or backstitching, you can use a **liquid fabric sealant** (Fray Check or Stop Fraying) to prevent threads from fraying and coming unstitched.

Sew-How: Use sealant on the edge of ribbons, trims, and lace to prevent raveling.

A **glue stick** is a basting aid. Use it to stick a button, appliqué, lace, or trim in place before sewing.

As much as I like to stitch everything by machine, a **hand needle and thimble** are necessary in your sewing stash. Use a needle for pulling threads through to the wrong side of the fabric before tying them off and to sew on hooks, eyes, snaps, and other odds and ends. Use a thimble on the middle finger of your sewing hand to push the needle comfortably through the fabric.

Sew-How: There is nothing more annoying than hunting for a hand needle when you need one, so store your needle on one end of your wrist pin cushion away from the pins, or make yourself a needle case.

A **large-eye tapestry needle** is used to pull heavier threads and cord to the wrong side of the fabric before tying it off. Thread cord end from a corded buttonhole through the large eye of the needle, then pull cords between the facing and garment front to tie them off. Also tape a button to the fabric with a tapestry needle between the holes to create a shank when the button is stitched on by machine (see Fig. 8.17).

A **needle threader** is helpful not only for threading hand and machine needles but also for pulling threads, embroidery floss, and pearl cotton cord to the wrong side of the fabric so it can be tied off.

A **spring hoop** holds the fabric taut to minimize puckering for free-machine embroidery, free-machine quilting, and appliqué. It is also narrow enough to fit under the foot without removing the needle.

Waxed paper is used to make alterations, redraw a pattern, and to trace off patterns. Use an old, dry ballpoint pen, tracing wheel, or pencil to transfer the marks onto the waxed paper. Make a roll of waxed paper part of your sewing supplies. For a more permanent pattern, use a nonwoven product sometimes known as Do-Sew to trace or retrace pattern pieces.

PRESSING TOOLS

The art of pressing is essential to the art of sewing, so you need a few pressing tools (Fig. 1.15).

A **hand iron** is used to smooth yardage that has been preshrunk before cutting, to press seams and darts, and for countless other uses in the world of sewing.

Sew-How: *If your iron has a rough, uneven surface, clean it with hot iron cleaner, available through your local fabric store. After cleaning, put a piece of brown paper on your ironing board, then a piece of waxed paper over it. Run the warm iron over the waxed paper to restore the shine and smoothness to the soleplate.*

An **ironing board** is essential for pressing. A muslin cover works better for shaping and pressing a project than the heat-reflective type.

Sew-How: *If the pad under your ironing board cover is flattened, make another one, as Sara Bunje of San Mateo, California, did. She used the old pad as a pattern and cut a new pad from an army blanket.*

To prevent shine and overpressing, place a **press cloth** over the fabric before pressing or ironing on the right side of the fabric. Use a piece of 100% cotton unbleached muslin or a press cloth, available through your fabric store or mail-order source (see Sources of Supply).

Fig. 1.15
Pressing tools.

A **tailor's ham** is a curved, stuffed cushion used to press curved areas. A good ham has cotton drill cloth on one side and wool on the other. The cotton side is used to press cotton, cotton blends, and linens that require higher temperatures. The wool side is for wool, silk, and wool blends and, if used properly, will minimize shine.

A **seam roll** is a stuffed tubular cushion used to press seams open. When pressing over a seam roll, the seam allowance falls away from the seam line to prevent unsightly ridges from pressing through to the right side.

FABRIC STABILIZERS

Interfacing is used to stabilize areas in a garment that are likely to stretch out and wear—armholes, necklines, front tabs, plackets, cuffs, collars, and waistbands, to name a few. Fusible interfacing is applied with an iron or press to the fabric with heat, moisture, and pressure. Sew-in interfacing is usually hand- or machine-basted into place. To select the appropriate interfacing, refer to Table 1.5, Interfacing Selection Chart.

Paper-backed fusible web is a stabilizer and the adhesive used in appliquéing. With the adhesive side against the wrong side of the fashion fabric, iron with a dry iron. Draw the appliqué shape on the paper backing, cut out the shape, remove the paper, and the shape is ready to fuse to the base fabric. See Chapter 3 for specific application and use. There are many brands. Look for Trans-Web or Wonder-Under.

Plastic-coated freezer wrap, available at your local grocery store, is generally used to rewrap food for storage in the freezer. However, it can also be ironed to the wrong side of fabric to stabilize the fabric for embroidery, appliqué, or quilting, so you rarely need a hoop. Remove the wrap after stitching by peeling it off the back of the fabric. I refer to this as iron-on freezer wrap in the Machine Readiness Checklists throughout the book.

Tear-away stabilizer is used to stabilize fabric and to minimize puckering in machine embroidery and monogramming. Use it on top of or under the work and tear it away after stitching.

Water-soluble stabilizer is a plastic film that can be clamped in a hoop and placed on top of and together with the fabric. It can be drawn on and is removed by rinsing with warm water.

Table 1.5 Interfacing Selection Chart

Fabric Type	Interfacing "Hand"	Recommended Interfacing	Fusible or Sew-In	Other Information	Colors
Sheer to light-weight fabrics, such as chiffon, georgette, crepe de chine, charmeuse, voile, batiste, gauze, lace, silk broadcloth	Sheer	Self-fabric	S	Matches color and hand	—
		Organza	S	Available in many colors	—
		Pellon (#906F), Sheer weight	F	Light, crisp hand, nonwoven	Wht, bge, chrcl
		Bridal illusion, netting, or veiling	S	Adds crispness, won't show through	—
		Pellon sheer weight (#905)	S	Nonwoven, softer than 906F	Wht, bge
		Sheer D'Light Featherweight	F	Crosswise give; soft and drapable	Wht, chrcl
		Armo Sheer-Shape	S	Soft and drapable	Wht
		Sewin' Sheer	S	Sheer no-stretch tricot	Wht, blk
		So Sheer	F	Crosswise stretch, sheer tricot	Wht, blk, ivy
		Sew Shape Featherweight	S	Light, gentle support	Wht
Featherweight to midweight wovens, such as gingham, challis, tissue faille, jersey, polyester, silk crepe, broadcloth Knits: cotton and cotton blend interlocks, jersey, lightweight sweater knits	Soft	Pellon Sof-Shape (#880 F)	F	Nonwoven, all-bias	Wht, chrcl
		Dritz Soft 'N Silky	F	Warp-inserted knit	Wht
		Stacy Easy-Knit (#EK 130)	F	Nylon tricot knits with crosswise stretch and lengthwise stability. Use on knits and wovens.	Wht, bge, blk
		Dritz Knit Fuze	F		Wht, bge, blk
		Fusi-Knit	F		Wht, ivy, blk, gry
		Dritz Quick Knit	F		Wht, bge, blk, gry
		Armo Intra-Face Bias Featherweight	S	All-bias for knits and wovens	Wht
		Pellon (#910) Featherweight	S	Crosswise stretch, lengthwise stability	Wht
		Armo Press Soft	S	Soft shaping for lightweight wovens	Wht
		Form-Flex Woven	S	Soft shaping, gentle support	Wht
		Dritz Shape-Up Lightweight	S	Gentle control on lightweight knits and wovens	Wht
		Dritz Stretch 'N Shape	S		Wht
Other feather-weight to midweight wovens: shirtings, broad-cloth, oxford, muslin, seersucker, chambray, poplin, pincord, madras, lightweight linen (Heavier) knits: double knits, stretch terry, velour, regular-weight and heavy sweatshirt fleece	Firm	Armo PressFirm	S	Woven, permanent press	Wht, blk
		Pellon (#911FF) Featherweight	F	All bias; soft supple shaping for midweight knits and wovens.	Wht, gry
		Stacy Shape-Flex (#SF 134)	F	Woven	Wht
		Armo Uni-Stretch Lightweight	F	Crosswise give, stretch & recovery for knits and stretch-wovens.	Wht
		Sheer D'Light Lightweight	F		Wht, chrcl
		Fusi-Firm Lightweight	F		Wht, chrcl
		S.R.F.	F		Wht, chrcl
		Armo Intra-Face Bias Lightweight	S	All bias for midweight knits and wovens	Wht
	Crisp	Pellon Shapewell (#70)	S	100% cotton; crisp shaping for oxford cloth, poplin, calico and other light to medium-weight dress & blouse fabrics.	Wht
		Dritz Shape Maker Fusible	F		Wht, blk
		Dritz Classic Woven	F		Wht
		Pellon ShirTailor (#950F)	F	For shirt collars, cuffs and other details where firmness is desirable for a crisp tailored look.	Wht
		Armo Shirt-Shaper	F		Wht
		Dritz Shirt Maker	F		Wht
		Dritz Shirt Bond	F		Wht
		Armo Form-Flex Non-woven	F	Non-wovens for firm shaping in light to medium-weight fabrics	Wht
		Armo Intra-Face Lightweight	S		Wht
		Armo Intra-Face Medium Weight	S		Blk, wht
		HTC Intra-Face Durable Press	S	100% polyester for permanent press fabrics	Wht
Skirt, pants, or suiting fabrics, such as gabardine, chino, linen, linen blends, wool and wool-like crepe, duck, cotton and cotton blends, faille, velvet, velveteen	Soft	Armo Press Soft	S	Woven, permanent press	Wht, blk
		Pellon Sof-Shape (#880 F)	F	For tailoring loosely woven light- to midweight fabrics	Wht, chrcl
		Dritz Soft 'N Silky	F		Wht
		Fusi-Knit	F	Knit	Wht, ivy, blk, gry
		Stacy Easy-Knit (#EK-130)	F	Knit	Wht, bge, blk
		Whisper Weft	F	Lightweight weft insertion	Wht, bge, gry
		Stacy Shape-Flex (#SF-134)	F	100% cotton; use in lightweight wovens for soft shaping	Wht
		Pellon Easy-Shaper (#ES-114)	F	Soft supple controlled shaping for light and midweight knits and wovens	Wht, chrcl
		Dritz Shape-Up Lightweight	F		Wht, chrcl
		Sheer D'Light Medium Weight	F		Wht, chrcl
		Dritz Stretch 'N Shape	F		Wht, blk

Interfacing Selection Chart (cont.)

Fabric Type	Interfacing "Hand"	Recommended Interfacing	Fusible or Sew-In	Other Information	Colors
Other skirt, pants, or suiting fabrics: denim, poplin, flannel, wool, mohair, coating, corduroy	Crisp	Stacy Shape-Flex (#SF 134) Form-Flex All Purpose Dritz Classic Woven	F F F	100% cotton, use in light- to midweight wovens for crisp support	Wht, blk Wht, blk Wht
		Pellon Pel-Aire (#881) Form-Flex 50/50	F F	Poly/cotton blend for firm support	Chrcl Wht, natural
		Dritz Suitmaker Dritz Tailor Fuse	F F	Lengthwise and crosswise stability and bias give like a woven. Use in mid- to heavyweight tailoring projects.	Natural Wht, blk
		SRF Pellon Stretch-Ease (#921F)	F F	Stretch and recovery for midweight knits, wovens, and stretch wovens	Wht, chrcl Wht, chrcl
		Armo Uni-Stretch Suitweight Armo Fusi-Form Suitweight	F F	Use for collars, lapels and cuffs	Wht Wht, chrcl
		Pellon #930 Armo Press Firm HTC Intra-Face Heavyweight	S S S	Firm to very firm shaping of medium- to heavyweight knits and wovens.	Wht Wht Wht
		Sta-Form Durable Press Veri-Shape Durable Press Dritz Sew-In DuraPress Dritz Woven Form	S S S S	Crisp shaping in midweight wovens, stable knits.	Wht, blk Wht Wht Wht
		Formite II	S	Firm shaping for midweight and special occasion fabrics	Wht
Heavy, tailoring-weight wools and wool coating.	Tailored	Fusible Acro Armo Weft Pellon #931 TD Midweight (MVF) Dritz Shape Maker	F F F F	Washable hair canvas Weft insertion For firm support in midweight knits Weft insertion	Natural, blk, gry Wht, bge, blk, gry Wht Wht
		Dritz Shape-Up Suitweight Pellon Pel-Aire (#881F)	F F	Textured surfaces and heavier adhesive coating provides better adhesion to suit and coat-weight fabrics for tailoring.	Wht, chrcl Natural, gry
		Acro	S	Washable hair canvas for medium to heavy tailoring: 52% rayon/ 43% polyester/ 5% goathair	Natural
		Fino II	S	Hair canvas for fine couture tailoring: 35% wool/35% rayon/ 15% polyester/ 15% goathair	Natural
		P-26 Red Edge	S	Economy hair canvas: 57% cotton/ 32% rayon/ 11% goat hair	Natural
		Pellon Sewer's Choice (#90H)	S	Traditional hair canvas: 43% cotton/ 36% rayon/ 21% goat hair	Natural
Fur, fake fur, fleece	Stabilizing	Armo Press Firm Acro Pellon Sewer's Choice	S S S	Woven, permanent press Washable hair canvas Traditional hair canvas	Wht, blk Natural Natural
Waistbanding	Stabilizing	Armoflexxx Perfo-Fuse Pellon Waist Shaper	S F F	Woven, non-roll, in 4 widths Nonwoven, slotted for smooth edge 1-1/4" and 2" widths	Wht Wht, chrcl Wht
Paper-backed fusible web		Trans-Web Wonder-Under	F F	To make woven or knit fabrics fusible	Wht Wht

Pellon and Stacy are registered trademarks of The Pellon Company, a division of Freudenberg Nonwovens Limited Partnership. The Stacy products listed were purchased by Pellon when Stacy Industries went out of business. Armo is a registered trademark of Crown Textile Company; Handler Textile Corporation (HTC) sells Armo products to the home sewing market. Dritz has purchased J & R Textile Corporation.

Colors Legend:	White = Wht	Ivory = Ivy
	Black = Blk	Beige = Bge
	Grey = Gry	Charcoal = Chrcl

Step Three:
LEARN THE BASIC STITCHES

By now you have cleaned your New Home sewing machine. You have changed the needle. You have wound a bobbin, threaded it in the bobbin case, completed the upper threading, and balanced top and bobbin tensions. You have also assembled your tools, important notions, and supplies. Now let's look at some basic stitches and sew something.

STRAIGHT STITCH

New Sewer's Note: *If you have never operated a sewing machine before, you may want to practice sewing straight lines, pivoting corners, and sewing curves with an unthreaded machine, stitching on paper. (If you have done a similar exercise in the past, or simply need to brush up on your skills, advance to the next exercise.) If you use waxed paper, you can hang it up in a window, for pretty patterns of light. To practice, enlarge the designs in Fig. 1.16 to twice the original size at your local copy center. Trace the lines, rectangle, circle, and triangle on a piece of tracing paper. Press two sheets of waxed paper together with a moderately hot iron. This way the paper is stiff and easier to maneuver. Place waxed paper over the tracing paper so you see the stitching lines. Tape corners together with transparent tape. Note that the Memory Craft 8000 can sense when there is not any thread in the machine and will not sew. In this case, thread the machine to complete this warm-up exercise.*

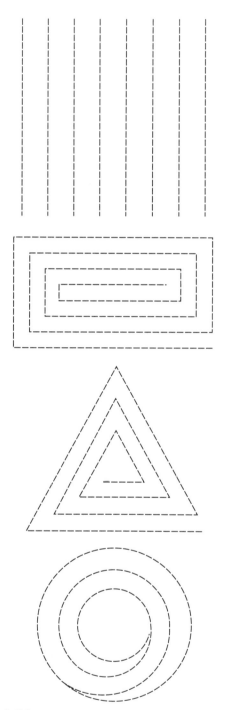

Fig. 1.16
Enlarge this pattern to twice the size at your local copy center. Then stitch lines, rectangle, circles, and triangle to practice sewing straight, pivoting, and sewing curves.

Warm-up Exercise

Supplies:

• waxed paper (optional)

• tracing paper

• water-erasable marker

1. Set the stitch length to 2.2, the most common stitch length used in sewing. Put the A zigzag foot on your machine. Place the edge of the paper under the foot and put the needle into the work. The needle is unthreaded (unless you are using the Memory Craft 8000—see New Sewer's Note on preceding page).

2. Lower the presser foot and start sewing.

3. To pivot a corner, turn the flywheel by hand or push the up/down key so the needle is in the waxed paper. Lift the presser foot, pivot, then lower the presser foot to continue.

4. To sew inside and outside curves, slow down and guide the fabric by using your fingers like the center point in a compass.

5. Remove the tracing paper. Press over the waxed paper again to flatten and set the holes. Put this sampler in your notebook, or hang it in a window. Now you're ready for the first exercise.

Exercise 1: Pressed Fabric Leaves

The best part of fall is its color. Whether or not it's fall in your neck of the woods, you can create colorful leaves any time of year while perfecting straight stitching, sewing inside and outside curves, and pivoting. This time, you will use thread and fabric.

Sew-How: Throughout this book you will see Machine Readiness Checklists with information on the settings and materials you need to ensure that each technique is successful. After the stitch name, you will see a number. This corresponds to the stitch number as it is shown on the New Home 7500 and 8000 (see Fig. 8.1). If you don't own one of these models, your stitches may not be identified this way. Therefore, photocopy Fig. 8.1 and post it so you can identify each stitch by what it looks like and compare it to what you have available for your New Home model.

Machine Readiness Checklist

Stitch:	straight (29, 7500; 1, 8000)
Length:	2–4
Width:	0
Foot:	A zigzag
Needle:	12/80 universal or 11/75 Blue Tip
Thread:	100% cotton or all-purpose one shade darker than fabrics
Feed dogs:	up
Fabric:	sheers (e.g., organdy, organza, batiste) in colors you like (I used light pink, blue, lavender, and peach.)
Accessories:	tear-away stabilizer or tracing paper, water-erasable marker, waxed paper, iron

1. Enlarge leaf patterns in Fig. 1.17 to twice their original size at your local copy center. Trace leaf patterns on tracing paper or tear-away stabilizer. Cut two of the small leaves and one oak leaf.

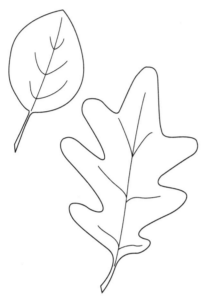

Fig. 1.17
Leaf pattern for Pressed Fabric Leaves exercise.

2. Layer two or three colors of sheer fabric, and pin them together so the stabilizer with the leaf pattern is on top.

3. Stitch around the leaf, including the veins, one complete time. Practice using a 2.2 stitch length on the curves and a stitch length of 3 or 4 on the veins.

4. Repeat sewing around the leaf three or more times, practicing curves and pivots and changing the stitch length.

5. Remove the stabilizer. Cut out the leaf and clip the threads close to the fabric.

6. Repeat for other small leaf and oak leaf.

Sew-How: For variation in color, trim away one or more underlayers from various sections of each leaf.

7. Arrange and sandwich leaves between two pieces of waxed paper.

8. Press over leaves and waxed paper with a moderately hot iron. Pressing means moving the iron in an up-and-down motion, lifting the iron off the paper, and then putting it down next to where you just pressed. After pressing, iron over the piece to eliminate wrinkles and creases. Ironing means sliding the iron back and forth with a long, smooth motion.

Hang your creation in a window to see the colors made by layering sheer fabrics.

Variations on Exercise

Layer two or three sheer fabrics and stitch geometric shapes, your initials, flower petals, or any other shape. Arrange shapes, add glitter, crayon shavings, and/or dried flowers, then press between waxed paper.

FORWARD CYCLE UTILITY STITCHES

On a mechanical machine, adding width to the straight stitch creates the zigzag stitch. On some New Home models you select the zigzag stitch by moving a dial or lever; on others, by touching a key or pad.

On a double layer of medium-weight fabric, stitch a sample for your notebook using the F satin stitch foot and zigzag stitch on a 1 length and 1 width. Stitch another row on a 2 length and a 2 width, the next row on a 3 length and 3 width, and so on.

Next stitch rows of zigzag stitches, keeping the stitch length on 0.5 and changing only the width. Start on a 1 width, then sew rows using a 2 through 7 width zigzag. This is called a satin stitch. It is used around appliqués, on napkin edges, in cut work, and in many other decorative ways (Fig. 1.18).

Fig. 1.18
Satin stitch sampler showing various stitch widths.

Sew-How: *If your fabric tunnels under the satin stitch, loosen the upper tension slightly. If tunneling continues, iron plastic-coated freezer wrap to the wrong side of the fabric.*

Finally, set the width on 4 and change only the stitch length. Start on a 1 length and work your way through to a 5 stitch length.

This exercise demonstrates the difference between width and length as it affects the zigzag stitch. You can also create designs by moving the width as you sew. However, it's almost impossible to stitch an even pattern with the unpracticed hand.

Forward cycle utility stitches are variations on the zigzag and are controlled by your machine. Examples are the multiple zigzag, blind hem, stretch blind hem, triangle, and diamond (Fig. 1.19). Once the stitch is selected, with the proper stitch width and length set, the machine stitches them automatically.

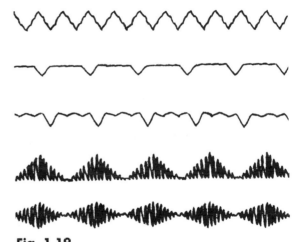

Fig. 1.19
Forward cycle stitches, top to bottom: multiple zigzag, blind hem, stretch blind hem, triangle, and diamond.

REVERSE CYCLE STITCHES

Other types of stitches available on New Home sewing machines are called reverse cycle stitches. While the needle zigzags from side to side, the feed dogs move the fabric forward and back, creating tracery patterns such as the overlock, double overlock, smocking, outline stretch, or patchwork (Fig. 1.20).

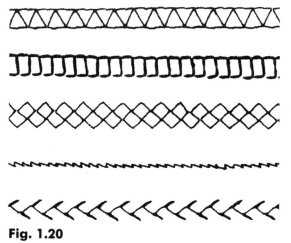

Fig. 1.20
Reverse cycle stitches, top to bottom: overlock, double overlock, smocking, outline stretch, and patchwork.

In Exercise 2 you will become familiar with what stitches are available on your New Home model, and you will practice upper threading and winding and threading a bobbin.

Exercise 2: Stitch Sampler

A good way to become familiar with the stitches on your machine is to make a sampler. In this exercise, your sampler will feature forward cycle and reverse cycle stitches. Then you'll turn it into a pin cushion.

Machine Readiness Checklist	
Stitch:	forward cycle; reverse cycle
Length:	forward cycle stitches: 0.5–2; reverse cycle stitches: varies
Width:	3–5
Foot:	F satin stitch
Needle:	11/75 Blue Tip
Thread:	100% cotton, all-purpose, or acrylic embroidery in color that contrasts with the fabric
Feed dogs:	up
Fabric:	striped cotton or cotton/poly blend with a white stripe (pillow ticking works well)
Accessories:	lightweight fusible interfacing, straight edge, vanishing marker, hand needle, polyester fiberfill (used to stuff toys), coffee mug, and rubber band.

1. Cut striped fabric 10″ × 5″ (25.5 × 12.5cm), so the stripes are going the short way. Fuse lightweight interfacing to wrong side of fabric.

Sew-How: *For the interfacing to bond permanently, use heat, moisture, and pressure. Place fabric wrong side up on ironing board. Cut interfacing a little smaller than fabric so it will not stick to the ironing board. Place interfacing fusible (rough) side down. Use the wool or cotton setting on your iron (check interfacing instructions on interleafing).*

With a very damp press cloth over the work, firmly press 10 to 20 seconds in one spot. Let the steam escape, then press again for a few seconds. Lift up the iron and press again, overlapping the iron on previously fused section. Repeat this bonding technique the length of your fabric until the interfacing has been applied (Fig. 1.21).

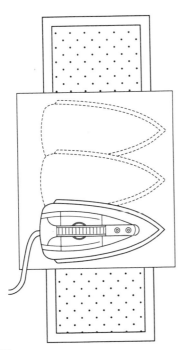

Fig. 1.21
To fuse interfacing, use a damp press cloth, then press for 10 to 20 seconds in one spot. Lift iron, then press, overlapping iron on previously fused section.

2. Decide which stitches you want on your sampler. With the New Home Memory Craft models there are an almost unlimited number to select from, so find your favorites.

3. Stitch a different forward cycle stitch on every other light stripe. Remember, for forward cycle stitches, the fabric feeds through the machine in one direction.

4. Stitch a different reverse cycle stitch on each of the remaining light stripes. For extra color, change the top thread and slightly loosen the top tension. (The bobbin thread shouldn't show.)

5. Place the sampler in your notebook or finish it as explained below.

FINISHING

Easiest Pin Cushion

1. Cut your sampler in half to make two 5″ (12.5cm) squares. Overcast the four edges of each piece with the multiple zigzag on a 1–1.5 length and a 5 stitch width. Guide the raw edge so the needle stitches just off the edge at the right. Put one sampler piece in your notebook.

2. Wrap the second half of your sampler around a small handful of fiberfill and put a rubber band around the bottom to keep the stuffing in place.

3. Stick the fabric-covered stuffing in a coffee mug, rubber-band-side down (Fig. 1.22). **Note:** If the stuffed sampler gets pushed down too far in the mug, pull it out and stuff it with more fiberfill. Set your pin cushion next to your machine, on the cutting table, or on the ironing board.

Fig. 1.22
Wrap the stitch sampler around some fiberfill and put a rubber band around the bottom. Set the stuffed sampler in a coffee mug and use as a pin cushion.

BUTTONHOLES

Contrary to popular opinion, buttonholes are not difficult. You don't have to avoid a pattern because it calls for them.

Each New Home model improves the method by which it makes buttonholes. If you are sewing on a new model, or the machine is new to you, take a few minutes to read your *Instruction Book* and see how truly easy it is. The next project is designed to help you practice.

Exercise 3: Buttonhole Sampler

Stitch your buttonhole sampler and put it in your notebook, or finish it by making a paperweight or pattern weight.

Sew-How: The New Home Memory Craft machines make a number of buttonhole styles. Use this exercise to practice the different styles, too.

Machine Readiness Checklist	
Stitch:	buttonhole (107, 108, 109, 7500; 12, 13, 14, 8000)
Length:	0.45–0.8
Width:	3.5–5
Foot:	J buttonhole or N or R sensor buttonhole
Needle:	12/80 universal or 11/75 Blue Tip
Thread:	all-purpose in four or five primary and secondary colors
Feed dogs:	up
Fabric:	white medium-weight cotton or cotton/poly blend, cut 6" (15cm) square
Accessories:	paper backed fusible web cut 6" (15cm) square, cardboard, small glass ashtray or paperweight globe (available at cross-stitch shops), craft glue, colorful buttons (optional), vanishing marker.

1. Wind bobbins for each thread color.

2. Fuse paper-backed fusible web on wrong side of fabric square.

3. On the right side of the fabric, stitch four or five different-sized buttonholes in each color all over your fabric square. (The fusible web paper acts as a stabilizer on the underside of the sampler.) Space buttonholes far enough apart so that your foot will not ride on another buttonhole. Place the sampler in your notebook or finish it as explained below.

FINISHING

Paper or Pattern Weight

1. Place the ashtray upside down on the right side of sampler, and trace its outline with the vanishing marker.

2. Cut out ashtray shape from the sampler.

3. Remove the fusible web paper from the wrong side of the sampler. Now it's ready to fuse to the cardboard.

4. Fuse the cut sampler to the cardboard using a dry iron on wool setting. After the cardboard cools, cut out the cardboard in the shape of the ashtray.

5. Place a few colorful buttons of varying sizes over the sampler (optional). They are loose, not sewn. Drop a few beads of craft glue on the rim of the ashtray and smooth it around. Lay the ashtray, upside down, over the sampler so the buttonholes can be seen through the glass (Fig. 1.23). Place a heavy book over your paper or pattern weight and let the glue dry for 24 hours.

Fig. 1.23
Buttonhole sampler paper or pattern weight.

TRANSFERABLE LEARNINGS

The information and techniques you have learned in this chapter have given you skills to sew other projects. You have learned:

• **Pressing versus ironing**—when you pressed your leaves between the waxed paper, you used both an up-and-down pressing motion and a side-to-side ironing motion. Pressing helps give a project a finished, professional look during construction. Ironing smooths out wrinkles after the project is complete.

• **Straight stitching**—necessary for sewing seams and topstitching. Standard stitch length is 2.2–2.5mm.

• **Inside and outside curves**—necessary for sewing any curve at a neckline, armhole, collar, pocket, or seam.

• **Pivoting**—necessary for turning any corner at a pocket, collar, or seam, or for topstitching.

• The **satin stitch** is used to appliqué, finish napkin edges and cut work, and for other decorative techniques.

• **Stitch length and stitch width** must be adjusted for forward cycle, reverse cycle, and decorative stitches if you have an older New Home model. Many of the newer models have a preset width and length that can be fine-tuned for specific needs.

• **Fusible interfacing** is used in many areas to add stability and increase wear. Proper bonding and application is important so interfacing stays put once a project is washed or cleaned.

• **Sewing in a straight line** is important. If you can sew a straight line by stitching accurately between stripes, you can seam or topstitch almost anything.

• **Buttonholes** are seen everywhere on clothing, crafts, and gifts. After practicing, you are ready to make buttonholes whenever a pattern calls for them.

• Use a **paper-backed fusible web** to bond appliqués so they don't shift when stitched. You will use this product and technique again for machine appliqué and for many other projects in this book.

Now that you have gotten to know your New Home sewing machine a little better, have learned what many sewing notions and tools are for, and have practiced some basic stitches, let's see how your skills can be used in the World of Sewing.

Part II walks you chapter by chapter through six categories. You will "Sew Fashion," "Sew Embellishments—Machine Appliqué and Embroider," "Sew for Your Home," "Sew a Quilt," "Sew Toys," and "Sew Gifts." Stitch through each in order, or skip to the one of most interest. Happy sewing!

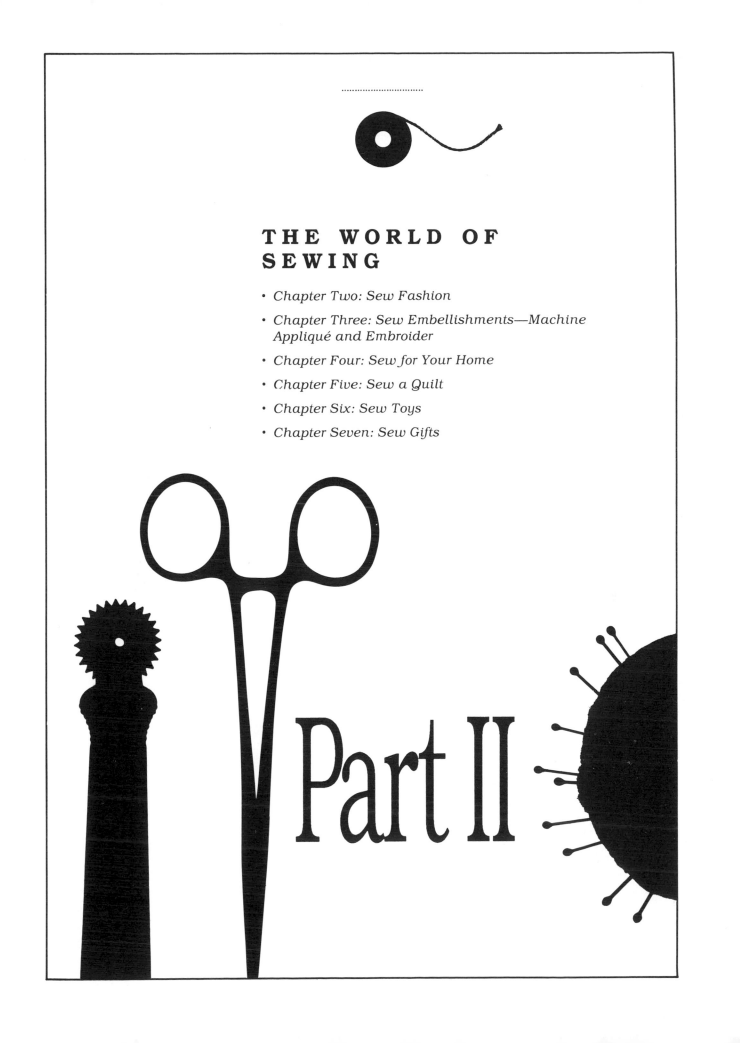

THE WORLD OF SEWING

Part II

PART II

THE WORLD OF SEWING

THIS PART OF THE BOOK explores six areas of sewing. Although you may know something about each area, you may not know the best way to complete a project using the stitches, presser feet, and features of your New Home sewing machine. Rather than making stitch samples, the objective here is to complete a project using all the tools available, so you can apply the techniques and shortcuts to any other project you attempt in the World of Sewing.

Each chapter has a series of steps. The first step helps you with fabric selection, layout, cutting, and marking—the all-important preliminaries. The next steps take you through each project and show you shortcuts and professional finishing techniques not usually covered in the pattern instructions. You also learn how to customize the basic project to your skill level, age, and gender.

At the end of each chapter you'll find **Transferable Learnings,** which is a review of what you've learned and a guide to how you can use the techniques in other areas of sewing.

If you have never sewn before, pay close attention to **New Sewer's Notes.** These tips will help you avoid common pitfalls so your experience is fun and the projects are successful.

ORGANIZE YOUR WORK SPACE

Before starting, let's organize some efficient work space for the three functions in sewing—cutting, sewing, and pressing.

Cutting Area

The cutting area can be as simple as a cardboard cutting board on a bed or dining room table, or as fancy as a cutting table designed especially for the area or room you sew in. Some people like to cut on the floor, but to save the carpet and your back, you may want to use a cutting table *at least* 29" (72.5cm) high and accessible from all four sides. If you are an experienced sewer and are setting up a permanent cutting table, the recommended optimum height for work done standing up is 36" (90cm).

On or near the cutting area, have a yardstick or straightedge of some kind and a tape measure. This way you can check grain lines, measure and mark strips and quilt blocks, check fabric width and length, plan your pattern layout—the list goes on—without hunting for measuring tools.

An extra station for pins is also helpful. I load my magnetic pin cushion with pins in case I use all those in my wrist pin cushion.

One of my best investments was a tall wastebasket. It's large enough to hold a lot of pattern and fabric scraps, I empty it less frequently, and it's close enough to the height of the table that I can brush scraps into it without dropping them all over the floor. My family also understands it's not for the disposal of food or unfinished drinks. (I never know when I'll have to dig through it for a scrap or something that fell into it by mistake.)

Sewing Area

Set your machine accessory box to the right of your machine so you don't have to hunt for a presser foot when you need it. A sewing caddy with marking tools, threads, extra scissors, and accessories is also helpful. If you don't have a caddy, empty checkbook boxes are a good substitute.

To me, a pattern is like toothpaste—once it's out of the envelope, it's almost impossible to put back. Tape a gallon-size resealable plastic bag on the table to the right of your machine for pattern storage. Keep the envelope, extra pattern pieces, and the pattern pieces that come off your fabric in this bag. Everything fits, and you can find your pattern pieces easily. (If you teach, have students put their names on all pattern pieces before cutting them apart. This way a student won't end up with another student's pattern piece.)

Sew-How: *Fold tissue pattern pieces so the name and number of each is on the outside. This way if you need to find a certain piece again, you don't have to fish around and unfold every one. It's also easier to get pattern pieces back in the envelope when they are folded this way.*

You'll need a place for pattern instructions. If your sewing machine faces a wall, you can tape pattern instructions to the wall or tack them to a bulletin board in front of you. Nancy Zieman, president of Nancy's Notions, Ltd., recommends taping an acetate sheet to the table and slipping the pattern instructions underneath. If you don't have an acetate sheet, try a dry cleaner bag instead.

Finally, have another wastebasket near your sewing machine for threads and fabric clippings.

Pressing Area

For your pressing area you'll need an ironing board, iron, tailor's ham, seam roll, and press cloth. Position your ironing board to one side of your machine and lower it so you can press while seated. This way you don't have to get up and down from your machine each time you press. Store the ham, seam roll, iron, and press cloth at the wide end of the board.

Sew-How: *If your press cloth is damp, store it in a resealable plastic bag pinned to the wide end of the ironing board.*

Are you ready to make something? The first project is a pair of woven, elastic-waist shorts. After completing them, you'll have the skills to make a pair of pants or culottes, a skirt, or a sweatshirt. Let's get started.

CHAPTER

2 SEW FASHION

Step One:
PLAN YOUR PROJECTS

A TRIP TO THE FABRIC STORE

Once you have mastered the skills needed to make a pair of woven shorts and a knit top, you can use those skills to make a pair of woven pants, a pair of culottes, or an elastic-waist skirt, as well as a knit shirt, sweatshirt, or knit dress. The style and fabric will be up to you. Before shopping for your fabric and pattern, however, take some measurements to determine your pattern size.

Dress in your underwear or a leotard. Tie a piece of elastic around your waist to find your natural waistline, and ask a friend or your spouse to take your measurements, filling in the chart on the following page (Table 2.1). When used to take circumference measurements, the measuring tape should be loose enough for you to get a finger between the tape and your body. Once you have taken measurements, determine your pattern category.

In the back of the pattern catalog you will find different figure types (Fig. 2.1). Find the one most like your figure or the figure of the person you are sewing for. Then look at the pattern you have chosen in the pattern catalog and find the size that most closely fits your measurements. Other information to help you find the right size is in the descriptive paragraph found on the catalog page or on the back of the pattern (Fig. 2.2). This often tells you if the garment is "fitted," "loose fitting," or "very loose fitting," which indicates how much ease is allowed in the pattern.

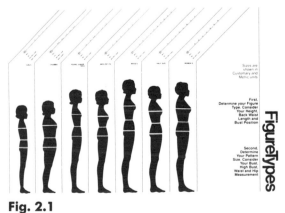

Fig. 2.1
Figure types found in the back of pattern catalogs (courtesy of the McCall Pattern Company).

Table 2.1	Measurement and Ease Chart			
WOMEN		**Your Measurement**	**Ease to be Added**	**Tissue Paper Measurement to Seam Line**
Bodice	High bust		3-5"	
	Bust		3-5"	
	Center front bodice length		1/2"	
	Length center back, neck to waist		3/4"	
	Back shoulder width		1/2"	
Sleeves	Upper arm circumference		2-3"	
	Arm length, shoulder to elbow		—	
	Arm length, shoulder to wrist		—	
	Wrist circumference		3/4"	
Skirt	Waistline		3/4"	
	High hip, 3" below waist		3/4"	
	Hips at fullest part, parallel to floor		2-3"	
	Waist to fullest part of hips		—	
	Thighs, parallel to floor		2-3"	
	Shirt length, waist to desired length		—	
Pants	Waistline		3/4"	
	Thigh circumference		2"+	
	Calf circumference		2"+	
	Inseam		—	
	Crotch depth (sitting)		1"	
	Crotch depth (standing)		1"	
MEN				
Upper body	Neck		1/2"	
	Chest		3-5"	
	Center front waist length		1/2"	
	Center back waist length		1/2"	
	Back width		1"	
	Shoulder width		—	
Sleeves	Shirt sleeve length		—	
	Upper arm circumference		2-3"	
	Arm length		—	
	Wrist circumference		3/4"	
Lower body	Waist		3/4"	
	Waist to fullest part of hips		—	
	Hips (seat)		1-2"	
	Thigh		1-2"	
	Trouser outseam (side length)		—	
	Trouser inseam		—	
	Waist to knee length		—	
	Crotch depth (sitting)		3/4"	
	Crotch depth (standing)		2-3"	

Note: Beginning sewers need take only the measurements found on the pattern envelope.

4044

MISSES', MENS' OR TEEN BOYS' CARDIGAN, TOP, PANTS AND SHORTS – CARDIGAN AND TOP FOR STRETCH KNITS ONLY: Cardigan has front button opening, patch pockets and long sleeves. Pullover top has short sleeves, patch pockets and top-stitching. Pull-on pants has elasticized waistline, side seam pockets with or without elastic at ankles. Shorts in two lengths has elasticized waistline.

SIZES	X-Small	Misses' or Men's/Teen Boys'				
		Small	Medium	Large	X-Large	
Bust/Chest	30½-31½	32½-34	36-38	40-42	44-46	Ins.
Hip	32½-33½	34½-36	38-40	42-44	46-48	"
Cardigan						
58/60" *	1⅝	1⅞	1⅞	2¼	2½	Yds.
Interfacing – 21" thru 25", ⅞ yd.						
Top						
58/60" *	1⅛	1⅛	1⅛	1¼	1⅜	Yds.
Interfacing – 21" thru 25", ⅜ yd.						
Pants						
44/45" ***	2⅜	2⅝	2⅝	2⅝	2¾	Yds.
58/60" ***	1½	1⅝	2¼	2¼	2⅜	"
Shorts (Longer Length)						
44/45" ***	1⅜	1⅜	1⅜	1⅜	1½	Yds.
58/60" ***	1	1	1	1¼	1½	"
Shorts (Shorter Length)						
44/45" ***	1⅛	1⅙	1⅛	1⅛	1¼	Yds.
58/60" ***	⅞	⅞	⅞	1⅛	1¼	"
FINISHED GARMENT MEASUREMENTS						
Back length from normal neckline						
Cardigan	27½	28	28½	29	29½	Ins.
Top	25	25½	26	26½	27	"
Measurement at bustline						
Cardigan	44	46½	50½	54½	58½	"
Top	40	42½	46½	50½	54½	"
Measurement at hipline						
Cardigan	43	45½	49½	53½	57½	"
Top	39	41½	45½	49½	53½	"
Pants, Shorts	38	40½	44½	48½	52½	"
Side length –						
Pants	41¾	42¼	42¾	43¼	43¾	"
Width, each leg –						
Pants	15¾	16¾	17¾	18¾	19¾	"

*With Nap   ***With or Without Nap – Use With Nap yardages and layouts for pile or one-way design fabrics. Additional fabric may be needed to match stripes.

SUGGESTED FABRICS: Top – Stretch Knits Only such as Cotton Knits • Jersey. **Cardigan and Pants** – Stretch Knits Only such as Sweatshirt Knits • Stretch Velour • Double Knits. **Pants and Shorts** – also Cotton • Cotton Blends • Cotton Twill • Chambray • Baby Cord • Poplin. **NOTE:** Not Suitable for Diagonals, Checks and Plaids.

NOTIONS: Thread; **Cardigan** – Five ¾" Buttons; **Pants or Shorts** – 3¾ Yds. of ⅜" Wide Elastic; **Pants** – also 1 Yd. of ⅜" Wide Elastic (Opt.).

Fig. 2.2
Descriptive paragraph and yardage information found on the back of pattern. Find the fabric width on back of pattern to determine how much fabric to buy (courtesy of the McCall Pattern Company).

Sew How: *Even a fitted garment has 2" (5cm) ease in its circumference. Loose fitting or very loose fitting garments usually have from 2" (5cm) to 8" (20.5cm) of ease and are subject to your interpretation of the words "loose" and "very loose." When in doubt, compare your measurements with the pattern tissue measured to the seam line. If there are darts, gathers, or ease, remember to subtract that amount to determine the finished circumference.*

FABRIC SELECTION

Which comes first, the pattern or the fabric? Judging from my personal stockpile, it must be the fabric. Besides, selecting the fabric is the part I like best—it's like eating dessert first.

For the shorts, choose a medium-weight woven fabric, such as poplin, weaver's (kettle) cloth, or duck. For easy care and comfort, choose fabric that is a cotton and polyester blend (see bolt end for fiber content, fabric width, and care instructions). A blend won't shrink or wrinkle as much as 100% cotton, and it's easy to sew. Have fun while you're in the store; look at and feel a lot of fabric. Then choose one without nap (see the New Sewer's Note below). If you need help, the salespeople will gladly show you different fabrics.

New Sewer's Note: *Plaids, stripes, one-way prints, and pile fabrics such as corduroy and velvet all have a nap. They must be laid out and cut so the pattern or design matches or so the pile or one-way design lies in one direction. This requires more yardage than fabrics without a nap. See the back of the pattern envelope for "with nap" and "without nap" yardage requirements.*

For the top, choose an all-cotton or cotton/polyester T-shirt knit to coordinate with your shorts fabric. Choose one that does not curl or run. To check for running and curling, pull the fabric across the grain at the cut end.

New Sewer's Note: *In a woven fabric, warp yarns are placed in the lengthwise direction on a loom. Filler or weft yarns are woven across the warp to create a piece of fabric. The lengthwise grain is parallel to the warp or lengthwise yarns; the crosswise grain is parallel to the weft or filler yarns.*

Grain lines indicate yarn direction; they are illustrated on the tissue pattern piece as a line with an arrowhead on either end. Most pattern pieces are laid out so the length of the pattern piece follows the lengthwise grain (Fig. 2.3). Lengthwise yarns are stronger than crosswise yarns, so the pattern piece is less likely to stretch out of shape or distort when laid out this way.

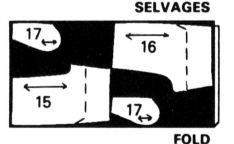

Fig. 2.3
Follow layout on the pattern guide sheet so pattern pieces are laid out on the straight of grain (courtesy of the McCall Pattern Company).

A knit fabric is made with a series of interconnecting loops. Although the fabric isn't stronger in the lengthwise direction, a knit is generally stable on the lengthwise grain and stretches across the grain.

PRESHRINKING

Care and washing instructions are written on the bolt end of most bolted fabrics. Stores should include care labels with your purchase (ask when you pay). If not, copy the information from the bolt end. It is important to preshrink washable fabrics, trims, and elastic before cutting so they won't shrink and so the colors won't run after the project is completed. Preshrinking also removes the sizing or finish put on some fabrics. Sizing gives fabric body, but it can cause skipped stitches if it is not washed out of the fabric before sewing.

Sew-How: As soon as you walk in your door from the fabric store, preshrink your washable fabric, elastic, interfacing, zippers, and trims in the manner in which you intend to care for the project after construction. For example, if your fabric is a dark blue print and is a cotton/polyester blend, preshrink in cold water and dry on the permanent press setting in your dryer. Read your notes from the bolt end for care instructions.

Note: *If the interfacing is fusible, immerse it in warm water, wring it out by hand, then dry it on the line.* ***Don't ever put fusible interfacing yardage in the dryer.***

When the fabric is dry, clip off a small square from a corner and tape or glue it to a piece of paper; list beside the sample its fiber content, cost, and where you bought it. Store the paper in your notebook.

How much fabric should you buy? You'll find out in the next section, which discusses selecting the pattern.

PATTERN SELECTION

For the shorts project, select a pattern recommended for woven fabrics that features elastic in a fold-over casing for the waistline and also a front or back patch pocket. For the top, select a pattern recommended for knits that features a crew neck, a raglan or set-in sleeve, and a straight hem (Fig. 2.4).

Fig. 2.4
Recommended patterns for woven shorts and knit top (courtesy of the McCall Pattern Company).

New Sewer's Note: *For the top, select a pattern marked "for knits only." You may find an ease chart printed on the pattern back to help you determine how stretchy a knit is and whether the pattern is appropriate for your fabric. For this project choose a knit in which, when the fabric is stretched across the grain, 4" (10cm) stretches to 5" (12.5cm) but not more than 8" (20.5cm). For the top, select a pattern with either a raglan sleeve, a set-in sleeve, or sleeve bands. You may find both top and shorts in one pattern; look in the pattern catalog under "coordinates" or "sportswear." If you are a new sewer, a pattern for a specific size rather than one that includes several sizes is easier to read and understand because there are fewer cutting lines to follow.*

Children and teens may enjoy using Kid-Sew or Kids Can Sew patterns or To Sew kits (see Sources of Supply). The instructions are well written and easy to understand. The styling is also simple and fashionable, so young people enjoy immediate success and are proud to wear and display their creations.

To buy the correct yardage, you need to know the width of the fabric. Fabric width is printed on the bolt end and is commonly 45" (1.1m) or 60" (1.5m). Read the back of the pattern for the correct width to determine how much fabric to buy. Also check the list of notions (see Fig. 2.2) and other supplies you'll need, to save another trip to the store later.

To make the shorts, you'll need elastic and thread. The easiest elastic to use has a knitted construction. When stretched, the holes open up and the elastic doesn't narrow. Knit elastic is comfortable to wear and doesn't stretch out, even when stitched through.

How much elastic should you buy? Enough to fit comfortably around your waist (or the waist of the person you're sewing for), with a little extra for experimenting. I usually buy enough at a time for the waistlines of two projects.

Select a thread color one shade darker than the fabric. If you are using a print, the thread color should match the background or the most dominant color (see Table 1.1, Fabrics, Needle, Thread, and Presser Foot Guide).

This knit top also requires ribbing. Ribbing is usually knitted in a tube and priced by the inch. See the pattern back for yardage requirements. Sometimes fabric stores do not place ribbing bolts in the same area as the regular knits, so you may need to ask for help locating the ribbing knits.

Sew-How: *If you can't find ribbing to match your knit fabric, you can often use the same knit fabric for bands. Cut and stitch as described on pages 65 and 66 for the knit ribbing neckband. If the fabric is a Jacquard knit, the right and wrong sides look different but obviously are made with the same color of yarn. For a contrasting band, use the wrong side of the fabric. This trick also works with stretch terry cloth and velour.*

Teaching yourself to sew means more than making just garments. You can sew alphabet blocks and a hobbyhorse (Chapter 6) and practice machine quilting on a wall quilt (Chapter 5).

Once you learn to construct a knit top and woven pull-on shorts (Chapter 2), you can embellish the pockets with flag designs (Chapter 3).

Make a fabric game board and pouch
(Chapter 7) and a Flag Tote Bag
(Chapter 3) for a family outing.

Master buttonholes, mitered corners, and professional edge finishes on the Envelope Placemats and matching "Lapkins" (Chapter 4).

Step Two:
WOVEN PULL-ON SHORTS

New Sewer's Note: *Before starting, remove and unfold the pattern instructions from the pattern envelope. On the instruction sheet you should find a list of common pattern symbols such as those shown in Fig. 2.5. To supplement and clarify the explanations given on your instruction sheet, I will explain what the symbols mean as we go along.*

LAYOUT AND CUTTING

If a garment is cut off-grain, perfect sewing technique and all the pressing in the world will not correct the mistake, so let's start off on the right foot.

1. Unfold the pattern tissue. Find the correct layout for the width of your fabric on the pattern instructions and circle it for easy reference. Your pattern instructions also list the pattern pieces needed for a particular view. They are identified by name and a number or letter (for example, Pants Back B). Cut the pattern tissue apart between the pieces. You can either cut on the black cutting lines or cut in the plain areas between the pieces. Put aside the pattern pieces you need. Put the rest in the pattern envelope. If you have selected a multi-sized pattern, trim away surrounding tissue to the proper size.

Sew-How: *Fold extra pattern pieces so the number and name of each is visible. This way, when you need a pattern piece again, you can find it easily. Since it's difficult to refold patterns small enough, you may want to store your pattern pieces in a larger envelope, pinning the original pattern envelope to the outside, or in a resealable plastic bag, as mentioned earlier.*

FOLD LINE: Lay and pin fold line directly on fabric fold. Never cut on fold line.

SEAM LINE: Broken line showing where to sew. Seam lines do not appear on multi-size patterns.

SEAM ALLOWANCE: Distance between sewing and cutting lines.

CUTTING LINE: Thickest black line around pattern tissue showing where to cut.

NOTCHES: Wedges cut outward, used to match one piece to another correctly.

CIRCLES: Also used for matching pattern pieces.

Fig. 2.5
Pattern symbols you need to know to read and understand a pattern (courtesy of the McCall Pattern Company).

2. If the fabric needs it, iron it flat; then, if appropriate for the layout, fold it in half the long way, right sides together, with the selvages even. If you need to straighten the grain, unfold your fabric and pull it on the bias to square it up (Fig. 2.6). (Note that some fabrics cannot be pulled straight. In that case, return the fabric to the store.) Then, if necessary, iron your pattern smooth with a hot, dry iron.

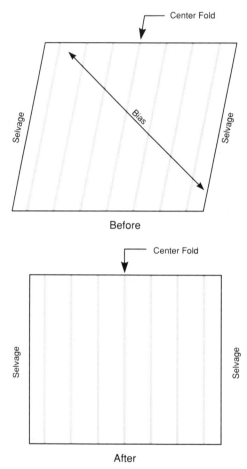

Before

After

Fig. 2.6
If the fabric is off grain, unfold it and pull on the bias to square it up.

New Sewer's Note: *Selvages are finished edges that run parallel to each other and with the lengthwise grain.*

Sew-How: *Even after preshrinking, the center crease may be difficult to press out on some fabrics. Either refold the fabric and lay out the pattern to avoid the crease or use a mixture of half white vinegar, half water on a press cloth to press out the crease. The vinegar/water mixture can also be used for setting creases in pants and pressed-in pleats.*

3. Follow the layout so the pattern pieces are laid out on the straight of grain (see Fig. 2.3). This means the grain line arrow on the pattern tissue runs parallel with the fold and/or selvage edge. When the distance from the printed grain line to one selvage is the same everywhere along the grain line, your layout is correct.

Sew-How: *Before pinning a pattern piece to the fabric, push a pin straight through one arrowhead of the grain line so the pattern piece pivots around the pin. This way you can pivot the pattern piece one way or the other so the grain line is parallel with the selvage edge or fold. Check that the grain line is parallel to the selvage or fold, measuring with your tape measure at both ends.*

4. Pin tissue pattern pieces to the fabric or use weights to hold pattern pieces in place. Cut fabric, following the black cutting line on the pattern tissue and using your shears or rotary cutter and mat.

Sew-How: *Notches on the cutting line are usually numbered and indicate where the pattern pieces match up to one another during construction. Single notches are usually found on front pattern pieces, double notches on back pattern pieces, and triple notches when front and back pieces are put together. Instead of cutting around every notch, cut across them. Then use the point of your shears and snip into the seam allowance ⅛" (3mm) to ¼" (6mm) at each notch (Fig. 2.7).*

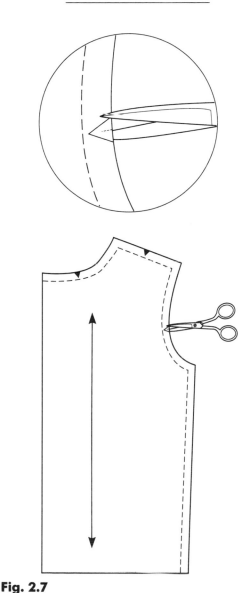

MARKING

The best time to mark your pattern is before removing the pattern tissue. An easy way to mark a light- to medium-colored fabric is with a water-erasable or a vanishing marker. If you plan to work on a project right away, use the vanishing marker; otherwise, use the water-erasable marker. Once the pattern piece is marked, repin the tissue to each piece so you know what it is when you get to it. For this project, we will mark the pocket position and the waistline casing line.

To mark, hold the point of the marker over the pattern tissue at a dot. Let the ink from the marker bleed through the tissue pattern piece, through one layer of fabric, then to the other layer of fabric. In a few seconds, both fabric layers are accurately marked.

Mark darker fabrics this way: From the pattern side, use a fine-head pin and push it through the dot. Turn the fabric over and push another pin through to the other side. Carefully pull pattern tissue off the fabric, then pull pattern pieces apart and mark pin placement with a soap sliver or disappearing dressmaker's chalk (see Sources of Supply).

If the fabric looks the same on both sides and the shapes of the pattern pieces are similar, identify the fabric pieces before removing the pattern tissue. To do this, label each pattern piece with masking tape on the wrong side of the fabric. The tape is easy to write on and won't melt if accidentally pressed over. **Note:** Before using masking tape, put tape on a scrap of your fabric to be sure it will not mark or damage the fabric when removed.

Fig. 2.7
Use the tips of your shears or scissors to snip a notch ⅛" (3mm)–¼" (6mm) at each notch on cutting line.

New Sewer's Note: *In addition to labeling the pattern pieces with masking tape, you may also want to indicate the top of each piece by drawing an arrow (Fig. 2.8).*

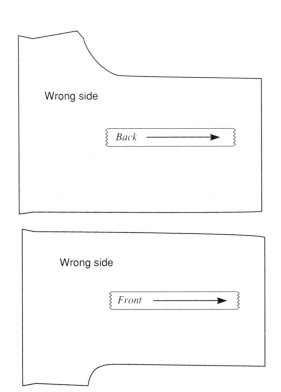

Wrong side

Back ────────►

Wrong side

Front ────────►

Fig. 2.8
On the wrong side of the fabric, label pattern pieces with masking tape. The arrow indicates the top of each piece.

Most of us who sew a lot don't follow the pattern instructions to the letter because we've learned easier, faster ways. I construct a project by using the New Home stitches and presser feet to best advantage, as well as shortcuts I've learned. The next few sections introduce you to some of the techniques and shortcuts used by experienced sewers.

PRESS-AS-YOU-SEW

Pressing each seam as you go is as important as using the proper sewing techniques. Throughout this project and the others in this book, you will be directed to press-as-you-sew.

The correct way to press a seam is first to press it flat and together to set or blend the stitches into the fabric. Then, from the wrong side, press seams open with steam over a seam roll, using an up-and-down *pressing* motion rather than a side-to-side *sliding* motion.

To prevent shine on the right side of the fabric, use a press cloth between the fabric and the iron. This is called top pressing.

SEAMS AND SEAM FINISHES FOR WOVEN FABRIC

Seam allowances on patterns are usually $\frac{5}{8}''$ (1.5cm). Depending on the project and the fabric, I generally use $\frac{5}{8}''$ (1.5cm) seam allowances on a woven fabric and $\frac{1}{4}''$ (6mm) seam allowances on a knit fabric. On the knit seam allowances, I usually trim to $\frac{1}{4}''$ (6mm) after stitching, which I'll explain later in the chapter.

To give the inside of the shorts a finished look and to prevent the fabric from raveling, overcast the raw edges using the multiple zigzag stitch (36, 7500; 18, 8000) (see Fig. 8.32). After finishing raw edges, steam-press edges flat on the right side.

New Sewer's Note: *Overcast the inseam, outseam, and crotch of the shorts. The waistline and hem edge will be evened and finished later.*

POCKETS

Here are two ways to put on patch pockets, using your New Home sewing machine to its fullest capability.

Machine Readiness Checklist	
Stitch:	straight (29, 7500; 1, 8000)
Length:	2.2–2.5
Width:	0
Foot:	A zigzag
Needle:	11/75 Blue Tip
Needle position:	left
Thread:	all-purpose
Tension:	normal (auto)

Patch Pocket (for New Sewers)

1. Fold down the pocket hem of the pattern tissue. Fold fabric right sides together perpendicular to the lengthwise grain; the entire pocket is cut on a double layer. Lay out and cut the pocket so the top is on the fold (Fig. 2.9).

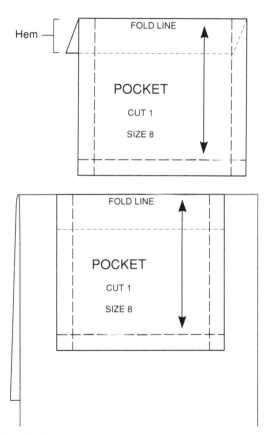

Fig. 2.9
Fold down pocket hem. Cut pocket on lengthwise grain and so top is on the fold.

2. With right sides together and the fold at the top, stitch around three sides of the pocket on the ⅝" (1.5cm) seam allowance, leaving a 1" (2.5cm) opening at the bottom.

Sew-How: *For sharp corners, take one stitch across the corner.*

3. Trim seam allowance and clip corners as shown (Fig. 2.10). Backstitch or tie off threads on either side of the opening on the bottom of the pocket. Turn pocket right side out. Gently push a point turner or the tip of blunt-nosed scissors into each corner of the pocket. Once the corners have been squared, top-press the pocket using a press cloth and steam.

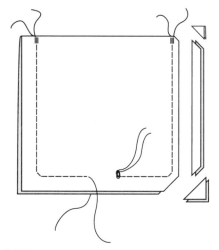

Fig. 2.10
Stitch pocket, leaving a 1" (2.5cm) opening at the bottom. For sharp corners, take one stitch across the corner. Trim seam allowance and clip corners.

4. Pin pocket on shorts front or back. Move the needle position to the right by touching the stitch width key to make a 5 width. On Memory Craft models with a 7mm width, you will be sewing $\frac{1}{4}$" (6mm) from the edge of the pocket. Align edge of pocket with the right edge of the A zigzag presser foot and topstitch with a 3 length straight stitch.

Sew-How: For other models, topstitch $\frac{1}{4}$" (6mm) from the edge by measuring the distance from the needle in the center position to the right edge of the foot. To do this, place the needle on the 1" (2.5cm) mark of your tape measure with the end to your right. Lower the foot. Does the right side of the foot rest on the $\frac{3}{4}$" (2cm) mark? If not, adjust the needle position as needed (see your Instruction Book.)

Curved Patch Pocket (for Intermediate and Advanced Sewers)

1. Cut the unlined pocket and light-weight fusible interfacing following the pattern instructions. Trim interfacing seam allowances to $\frac{1}{8}$" (3mm) and fuse interfacing to the wrong side of the pocket.

Sew-How: Use heat, moisture, and pressure to bond interfacing permanently to the fashion fabric. Heat the iron to a cotton or wool setting. Place the rough side of the interfacing against the wrong side of the pocket. Using a very damp press cloth over the pocket, press over the interfacing and press cloth with even pressure for about 10 seconds. Let the steam escape; then press again until the fabric is dry (see Fig. 1.21).

2. Overcast the pocket hem edge (see Fig. 8.32). With right sides together, stitch the sides of the pocket hem at the $\frac{5}{8}$" (1.5cm) seam line. Trim and clip the corner. Turn the hem right side out, and top-press the pocket using a press cloth.

3. Starting 1" (2.5cm) above each curve, easestitch "plus" $\frac{1}{4}$" (6mm) from the raw edge (See Fig. 8.5).

4. Place the pocket on the shorts back so there is a little slack, and topstitch $\frac{1}{4}$" (6mm) from the edge. The slack enables the wearer to put things in the pocket without putting stress on the stitches.

Sew-How: Put on the F satin stitch foot and set your machine on a 0.5 length, 2 width zigzag. Satin-stitch ¼" (6mm) at each corner for extra reinforcement (Fig. 2.11). Pull threads to the wrong side and tie them off. If you have a Memory Craft 7000, 7500, or 8000, use the automatic bartack (112, 7500; 10, 8000) instead.

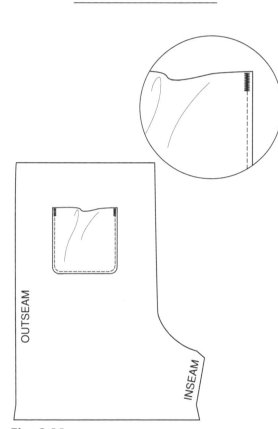

Fig. 2.11
Place pocket on shorts back so there is a little slack; then topstitch. Satin stitch ¼" (6mm) at each corner or use the automatic bartack.

CONSTRUCT ONE LEG AT A TIME

New Sewer's Note: To make the shorts fit, baste them together first (see Fig. 8.3).

You can construct a pair of shorts or pants in two ways. One way is to stitch the front of the pants and the back of the pants and then stitch the inside and outside leg seams. The other way is to construct each leg individually, then stitch the legs together at the crotch seam. For pull-on garments, the one-leg-at-a-time method is easier to alter and results in a better fit.

Machine Readiness Checklist	
Stitch:	straight (29, 7500; 1, 8000)
Length:	2.5–3
Width:	0
Foot:	A zigzag
Needle:	11/75 Blue Tip
Needle position:	left
Thread:	all-purpose
Feed dogs:	up
Tension:	normal (auto)

1. Find a front and back leg piece. Place and pin right sides together, matching notches so pins are perpendicular to the seam line. Stitch the inseam and outside seam at the ⅝" (1.5cm) seam line, removing pins before stitching over them. Repeat for other leg.

Sew-How: You may have been told your machine can sew over pins; however, this is not a good practice. When the needle hits a pin, the broken ends may fall into the workings of your machine or hit you in the face. It also dulls the needle or creates burrs, which may snag on your fabric.

Press seams flat and together; then press them open from the wrong side.

Sew-How: Sometimes a seam that is pressed open leaves a ridge on either side of the seamline. To prevent this, press seams open over a seam roll. This way the edges of the seam allowance fall away from the seam line and are not pressed against the wrong side of the fabric. Seam rolls are available at fabric stores.

---

2. Turn one leg right side out. Slip it inside the other leg, right sides together. Match notches; pin; and stitch the long front and back crotch seams at the $\frac{5}{8}''$ (1.5cm) seam line.

3. Press open the center front seam and center back seam from notches to waistline. Turn the shorts right side out, and try them on. Tie or pin a piece of elastic around the waist. Remember, the top of the shorts have a casing that folds down over elastic, so place the elastic where the finished waistline will be. Adjust gathers and check the fit.

Sew-How: If seams need to be adjusted, pin from the right side. If adjustments are made with the garment inside out, adjustments are made for the wrong side of the body (most of us are lopsided). After pinning, remove the garment and use a fabric marker to transfer pin marks on the wrong side by gently separating the fabric and marking where pin enters the fabric.

---

4. Once shorts fit, trim crotch seam, notch to notch, to $\frac{3}{8}''$ (1cm), and overcast the seam allowance with the multiple zigzag stitch (36, 7500; 18, 8000) on a 1 length, 4–5 width.

ELASTIC APPLICATION

Do you use a large safety pin or bodkin to pull elastic through a casing? Did either one hang up in the seam allowances or pull off the end before the elastic was all the way through the casing?

This one-step method takes about the same amount of time as pulling elastic through a casing, but it eliminates the frustration.

1. Cut elastic 3″ to 5″ (7.5cm to 12.5cm) shorter than waistline measurement so it is comfortable around your waist. Before cutting it to length, check that elastic fits over your hips. (You wouldn't want to get the elastic stitched in, then be unable to pull your pants up over your hips.) Join elastic into a circle by overlapping the ends. Stitch using the multiple zigzag stitch (36, 7500; 18, 8000) on a 1 length, 4–5 width. **Note:** Overlapping the join rather than seaming elastic ends eliminates bulk and evenly distributes stress on the stitches.

2. Overcast raw edge of fabric casing using the multiple zigzag (36, 7500; 18, 8000) (1 length and a 4–5 width), overcast (38, 7500; 5, 8000), or the double overedge (39, 7500; 22, 8000) on a 4–5 width. Fold down to the inside and press the casing the width of elastic plus $\frac{5}{8}''$ (1.5cm). Using a straight stitch, edge-stitch $\frac{1}{8}''$ (3mm) from the fold with the G adjustable blind hem foot (see Fig. 8.6).

3. Pin the elastic circle inside the casing, pinning under and parallel to the elastic (Fig. 2.12). Elastic should pull freely around the top of the shorts.

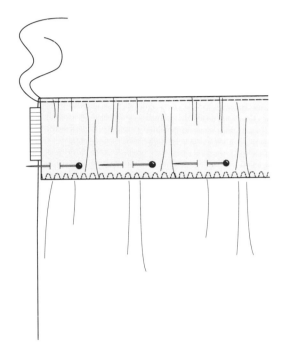

Fig. 2.12
Pin elastic in casing, under fold, pinning parallel to elastic. Elastic should pull freely around the top of shorts.

Machine Readiness Checklist	
Stitch:	straight (29, 7500; 1, 8000)
Length:	2.5–3
Width:	0
Foot:	A zigzag or E zipper
Needle:	11/75 Blue Tip
Needle position:	left
Thread:	all-purpose
Feed dogs:	up
Tension:	normal (auto)

4. With the wrong side up, place the casing under the foot so the needle does not stitch through the elastic. Smooth the fabric casing in front of and behind the needle so the elastic is relaxed and the fabric is flat.

Sew-How: Use a mark on your needle plate to guide the edgestitched fold. For example, if your elastic is 1" (2.5cm) wide, the line of stitching under the elastic should measure $1\frac{1}{4}$" (3cm) from the top of the casing fold so that the elastic moves freely within the casing. Therefore, guide the fold at the $1\frac{1}{4}$" (3cm) mark on the needle plate. If the elastic is too wide to guide by a mark in the needle plate, use the L quilter (see Fig. 9.23) or put a piece of masking tape on the bed of your machine. (Remove tape after stitching or it will become gummy.)

5. Stitch a short distance, stop with the needle in the fabric, raise the foot, and then pull the elastic toward you so the casing fabric in front of the foot is smoothed flat (Fig. 2.13). Stitch a short distance, then repeat. This way, the elastic is stitched flat and in one step—no more pins or bodkins.

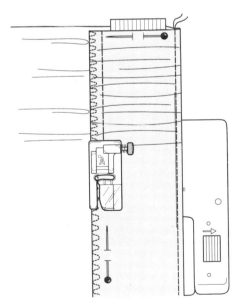

Fig. 2.13
Stitch a short distance, stop with the needle in the fabric, raise the foot, then pull elastic toward you so the casing is smoothed flat in front of the foot.

Sew-How: If you buy enough elastic for more than one waistline at a time, measure and mark the length of elastic needed for your shorts, leaving elastic in one long length. Pin and stitch elastic as described on previous page, leaving elastic flat all the way around the casing and leaving a 1" (2.5cm) opening. Pull elastic to length; then overlap, stitch, and cut elastic. This way elastic is applied flat and smooth. Stitch the opening closed.

6. Try on the shorts and adjust the fullness around the waist as desired. Then stitch-in-the-ditch at the center front, center back, and side seams through the casing and width of elastic, to prevent the elastic from rolling and to keep the fullness adjusted evenly (see Fig. 8.8).

HEMMING THE SHORTS

1. Measure and pin up leg hem to desired depth, but no deeper than 1¼" (3.2cm). Press hem without pressing over the pins.

2. Even up the raw hem edge, and overcast with the multiple zigzag stitch (36, 7500; 18, 8000) on a 1 length and a 4–5 width, or the decorative overlock (2, 7500; 58, 8000) (see Figs. 8.32, 8.44).

3. With pins perpendicular to the hem edge, blind hem each leg hem using the blind hem stitch (41, 7500; 6, 8000) and blind hem foot, pulling pins out before the machine gets to them (see Figs. 8.38 and 9.10).

Step Three:

KNIT TOP WITH RIBBING

Layout, cutting, and marking procedures are similar to the procedures used for the shorts. Let's review:

1. Lay out the top pattern so the center front and center back are cut on the fold. The lengthwise grain line will be parallel to the fold and the selvage or finished edge. When laid out this way, the stretch goes around the body, which is necessary for proper fit and ease (Fig. 2.14).

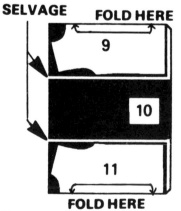

SELVAGE **FOLD HERE**

9

10

11

FOLD HERE

Fig. 2.14

Lay out top pattern so center front and center back are cut on the fold and with the most stretch around the body. (Courtesy of the McCall Pattern Company).

Sew-How: Sometimes the center fold on a knit cannot be pressed or washed out. In this case, refold the fabric on the straight of grain folding the selvages to the center. Remember, selvages must be the same distance the length of the fold.

2. Cut the pattern and fabric on the black cutting line using a pair of shears or a rotary cutter and mat.

Sew-How: Do not cut a knit (or any fabric) with pinking shears. The notched blades snag the fabric, and you lose the accurate edge to guide the seam line by.

3. Snip ⅛" (3mm) into the seam allowance to mark notches, as you did for the shorts.

4. Mark dots on pattern pieces with a vanishing or water-erasable marker.

5. Label pattern pieces with masking tape (optional). Note that sleeve pieces for a raglan-sleeve shirt look similar to back and front pieces. If you are a beginner, remember to label your pattern pieces to prevent confusion.

The following construction and stitching sequence makes the best use of your New Home sewing machine.

SEAMS AND SEAM FINISHES FOR KNIT FABRICS

A $\frac{5}{8}''$ (1.5cm) seam will not stay pressed open on most knits. Therefore, we will use $\frac{1}{4}''$ (6mm) seams and press them to one side. Rather than trimming the seam allowance to $\frac{1}{4}''$ (6mm) before stitching, however, leave the $\frac{5}{8}''$ (1.5cm) seam allowance to allow for fitting. In most cases, the seam also looks better when trimmed to $\frac{1}{4}''$ (6mm) after stitching. Exceptions are those areas where ribbing is applied at a neck edge or at a cuff and when making lingerie with nylon tricot. In these cases, it is generally easier to trim the seam allowance to $\frac{1}{4}''$ (6mm) and stitch.

Shoulder Seams

Because reverse cycle stitches are tough to rip out, speed-baste knit projects together to check fit (see Fig. 8.27). Here are two ways to stitch a $\frac{1}{4}''$ (6mm) seam, depending on the stitches available on your New Home. (If your pattern calls for $\frac{5}{8}''$ (1.5cm) seams, trim them to $\frac{1}{4}''$ (6mm) after stitching is complete.)

$\frac{1}{4}''$ (6mm) Seam, One-Step Method Using Reverse Cycle Stitches

Test for the appropriate stitch on a double layer of knit (for suggestions, see Figs. 8.45, 8.48, 8.53). Place test samples in your notebook. Identify the stitch and stitch setting on each sample.

Sew-How: When testing for the right stitch, remember this principle. If the fabric waves out of shape, lengthen the stitch. If the fabric puckers, shorten the stitch length. Remember that you can elongate the reverse cycle stitches on the Memory Craft models by adjusting the feed balance dial.

New Sewer's Note: If your shirt has raglan sleeves, pin each sleeve, right sides together, to front and back shirt pieces, matching notches. Double notches indicate the back of the shirt; single notches, the front of the shirt. You may find it helpful to lay the shirt on a large table to do this (Fig. 2.15).

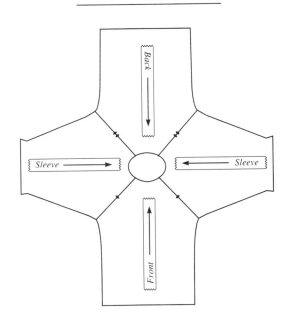

Fig. 2.15
Pin shirt, right sides together, matching notches. You may find it helpful to lay the shirt on a large table to do this.

Intermediate and Advanced Sewer's Note: To prevent cross-grain shoulder seams from stretching out of shape, place a double strand of elastic thread or a length of preshrunk twill tape under the foot. Sew across the grain without pulling the elastic thread or tape (see Fig. 8.48).

1. For all seams, pin right sides together so pins are perpendicular to the seam line. Guiding by the ⅝" (1.6cm) seam line, stitch the seam with the best reverse cycle stitch tested above, pulling pins out as you go.

2. Trim excess seam allowances up to the stitch. Press seam to one side.

Sew-How: *If seam is trimmed to ¼" (6mm) before seaming, guide fabric so the stitch falls over the raw edge on the right (see Fig. 8.45).*

¼" (6mm) Seam, Two-Step Method

If you don't have one of the reverse cycle stitches mentioned above, stitch ¼" (6mm) seams in two steps. If your pattern calls for ⅝" (1.5cm) seams, trim them to ¼" (6mm) after stitching is complete.

Machine Readiness Checklist	
Stitch:	tiny zigzag (35, 7500; 4, 8000) or outline stretch (33, 7500; 16, 8000)
Length:	1.5–2
Width:	1
Foot:	A zigzag
Needle:	11/75 Blue Tip
Needle position:	center
Thread:	all-purpose
Feed dogs:	up
Tension:	normal (auto)

1. For all seams, pin right sides together so pins are perpendicular to the seam line. Sew the tiny zigzag or outline stretch stitch guiding ⅝" (1.5cm) from the raw edge and removing pins before the needle reaches them.

2. Using the multiple zigzag (36, 7500; 18, 8000) on a 0.7–1 length and a 4–5 width, stitch to the immediate right of the tiny zigzag. Trim excess seam allowance up to the stitch (Fig. 2.16).

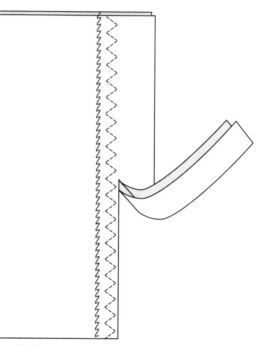

Fig. 2.16
Two-step ¼" (6mm) seam finish using the tiny zigzag or outline stretch and multiple zigzag stitch.

Set-in Sleeves and Side Seams

Set-in sleeves generally must be eased into each armhole (some sleeves more than others). The flatter the curve of a sleeve, the less fabric is eased into the armhole. If the knit you are working with will not stretch enough for the sleeve to fit into the armhole, use the method outlined below. This technique also works on woven fabrics.

1. Snip the notch at the top of the sleeve cap. Easestitch "plus" each sleeve from back notches to front notches, stitching ½" (1.3cm) from the raw edge (see Fig. 8.5).

2. Open the shirt flat and pin the sleeve into the armhole, right sides together, matching notches, and with the garment body on top. The snipped notch at the sleeve cap should match the shoulder seam of the top. Speed-baste the sleeve in place so the sleeve is down against the feed dogs. The action of the feed dogs helps ease in the fullness of the sleeve cap. After sleeve is basted so the seam is smooth and without tucks, final-stitch each sleeve using one of the two methods described above for a $\frac{1}{4}''$ (6mm) seam finish. Remove speed basting (see Fig. 8.27).

3. For the side seams, start at the bottom of the shirt and use a $\frac{1}{4}''$ (6mm) seam finish. Press side seams toward the front. At the break of the hem, twist the seam allowance and press the rest of the seam toward the back. This way, when the hem is turned up, there is less bulk at the seam and it is easier to stitch over without distorting the stitch.

NECK BAND

Neck band or ribbing patterns are often the wrong length for the openings. The following measuring and stitching techniques have never failed me. *Remember, cut bands with the most stretch around the body.*

1. To determine the proper band *length* for a crew neck or waistband, cut band two-thirds the circumference of the opening so the stretch goes around the body. To determine the proper band *width*, double the finished width and add $\frac{1}{2}''$ (1.3cm) (which allows for $\frac{1}{4}''$ [6mm] seam allowances). Therefore, a finished 1" (2.5cm) wide band starts out $2\frac{1}{2}''$ (6.4cm) wide because it is folded in half and stitched with a $\frac{1}{4}''$ (6mm) seam allowance.

2. Trim the neckline seam allowance to $\frac{1}{4}''$ (6mm). Pin the band into a circle so the narrow ends are right sides together. Stitch a $\frac{1}{4}''$ (6mm) seam using the tiny zigzag stitch (1.5 length, 1 width). Gently steam-press the seam open.

3. Fold the band in half the long way so the seam is on the inside of the band. If the ribbing is difficult to handle, speed-baste the raw edges together using the longest 4 width zigzag and a loosened upper tension. Gently steam-press the band without stretching it in the process.

4. Quarter and mark the bands with pins.

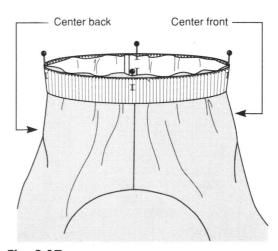

Fig. 2.17
Pin the band into the neckline opening at center front, center back, and shoulder seams.

Sew-How: For a V-neck or U-neck, quarter and mark the neckline in the shirt. The quarter marks will fall on the center front and center back and will be slightly forward of the shoulder seams.

5. With the band side up, stitch a ¼" (6mm) seam, using either method described above. **Note:** If you have a free-arm on your machine, slip the neckline around it and stitch.

Sew-How: To stretch the band to fit the opening, pull the band with your right hand while guiding the neckline with your left (Fig. 2.18).

HEMMING THE KNIT TOP

The fastest, easiest, and most professional-looking way to hem a knit is with twin needles. Two needles, positioned on a crossbar and shank, are threaded on the top. The bobbin thread shares itself between the two top threads, creating a zigzag stitch on the underside which, when stretched, will not break (see Fig. 8.10). The shirt shown in the color pages was hemmed with a size 4mm 11/75 stretch twin needle. This means the needles are 4mm (⅛") apart and the needles are a size 11/75 stretch.

To give a ready-to-wear look to the neckline ribbing, use your twin needle to top-stitch under the neckband through the seam allowance ⅛" (3mm) from seam line with a 3–4 length straight stitch.

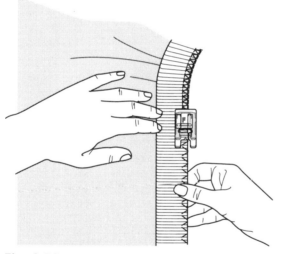

Fig. 2.18
Pull the band with your right hand while guiding the neckline with your left.

Step Four:

PROJECT VARIATIONS—INSTANT T-SHIRTS

For an "instant" coordinate to your shorts, purchase a ready-made T-shirt or sweatshirt and add custom touches such as buttons and bows. You can also add embellished pockets like the ones made in Chapter 3, Sew Embellishments.

Many households have a "button jar" or an odd collection of buttons that can be stitched to a T-shirt or sweatshirt. If you don't have such a collection, find interesting buttons at garage sales, flea markets, or in the bargain bin at your favorite discount or fabric store.

If this project is for a child, use a variety of buttons identifying a special interest—dinosaurs, hearts, or animal shapes, for instance—and bows or ribbons in the child's favorite color.

BUTTON SEWING WITH YOUR NEW HOME

The fastest and easiest way to stitch on a lot of buttons is by machine. **Note:** In this project, buttons sewn on the T-shirt or sweatshirt are for decoration only. They will never be buttoned through another layer of fabric; therefore, it's not necessary to create a shank between the fabric and button. See Figs. 8.17 and 9.30 for machine settings.

ATTACHING RIBBONS AND BOWS

Sandra Betzina, newspaper columnist and author of *Power Sewing*, said her daughter tied and stitched bows all over a ready-made T-shirt and was out the door wearing it in 45 minutes. Here's how she did it:

1. Preshrink a T-shirt and some ribbon. Mark bow or ribbon placement with a vanishing marker.

2. You can make bows using your spool pins. Put ribbon around spool pins, crossing ends in the front. This creates the loop ends of the bow. Holding the left end stationary, take the right end over the bow at the center and tie a knot (Fig. 2.19). Remove the bow from the spool pins. This way, all bows are the same size and are tied tightly enough that they won't come undone in the wash. **Note:** If your spool pins are too far apart to make small bows, ask someone to allow you to tie bows around their fingers instead.

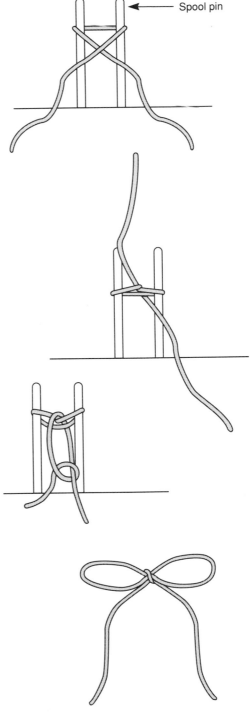

Spool pin

Fig. 2.19
Put ribbon around spool pins, crossing ends in the front. This creates the loop ends of the bow. Holding left end stationary, take the right end over the bow at the center and tie a knot.

3. Thread your machine with nylon monofilament thread so you don't have to rethread the machine and bobbin case for each color ribbon. Pin bows over the marks on the T-shirt.

4. Position the T-shirt under the presser foot so a bow is under the foot. Lower the foot, remove the pin, and tack across the knot in the bow (see Fig. 8.28 or 8.34). Repeat for other colors.

For a boy, add a fabric stripe, fabric paint, custom patches, or woven labels to a ready-made T-shirt or jacket. For adults, remove ribbing and hems from T-shirt. Then add a pocket, a knitted collar, and contrasting bands for the sleeves, neck, and waist.

TRANSFERABLE LEARNINGS

The information and techniques you have learned by making the woven shorts and knit top have given you the skills necessary to sew many other projects. You have learned how to:

• Read a pattern envelope and buy the correct type and amount of fabric and appropriate notions.

• Understand pattern layout and cutting:

Lengthwise grain is parallel to selvage or finished edge and/or fold.

Knits are laid out and cut with the most stretch around the body.

Patterns are cut on the black cutting line.

Notches are snip-marked using scissor tips for speed and accuracy.

• Mark pattern pieces:

Mark light-colored fabrics with vanishing or water-erasable marker.

Mark dark fabrics with soap sliver or disappearing dressmakers' chalk.

• Stitch and finish $\frac{5}{8}''$ (1.5cm) or $\frac{1}{4}''$ (6mm) seam allowances on knit and woven fabrics.

• Topstitch $\frac{1}{4}''$ (6mm) from a finished edge, adjusting the needle position and guiding the edge of the A zigzag foot by the finished edge of the fabric.

• Permanently bond a fusible interfacing to fashion fabric using heat, moisture, and pressure.

• Stitch elastic in a casing in one step. This technique can be used for elastic insertion at a waistline, wrist, or ankle.

• Use an up-and-down pressing motion to press seams open or to one side.

• Blind hem woven fabrics with the G blind hem stitch foot and blind hem stitch (41, 7500; 6, 8000); hem knits with twin needles.

• Easestitch "plus" set-in sleeves before they are stitched into the armhole; final-stitch sleeves into the armholes with the sleeve side against the feed dogs to ease in the fullness.

• Measure and cut knit bands to fit various parts of a garment.

You have learned a lot in this chapter about sewing woven and knit fabrics. I hope this approach encourages you to think through a project to make the best use of your tools, your accessories, and your New Home.

Next, you will "Sew Embellishments" and decorate a tote bag. The design used on the tote can also be translated to a pocket on the pair of shorts or T-shirt you just made (see color pages).

SEW EMBELLISHMENTS— MACHINE APPLIQUÉ AND EMBROIDER

ma·chine (me shen') *noun*, a structure consisting of a framework and various fixed and moving parts, for doing some kind of work; mechanism [a sewing machine]

ap·pli·qué (ap'le ka') *noun*, a decoration or trimming made of one material attached by sewing, gluing, etc. to another. *adj.*, applied as such a decoration. *verb* -quéd', -qué'ing, 1. to decorate with appliqué 2. to put on as appliqué

em·broi·der (im broi'der) *verb*, 1. to ornament (fabric) with a design in needlework 2. to make (a design, etc.) on fabric with needlework 3. to embellish (a story, etc.); add fanciful details to

This chapter will investigate machine appliqué and machine embroidery as ways to embellish a base fabric. We will appliqué a flag design to a base fabric that will be made into a tote bag. Then we will embellish a base fabric that can be put in your notebook or turned into a pocket to stitch to shorts, pants, or a skirt. Finally, we will freely embroider a label for the tote and embroider a pocket to add to a made-from-scratch or ready-to-wear T-shirt (see color pages). If the material here whets your appetite for machine embellishment, see the bibliography for more on machine appliqué and machine embroidery.

New Sewer's Note: *It takes practice to perfect your embroidery skills so you may want to practice the embroidery techniques on fabric squares to go in your notebook. If you find your practice squares acceptable, turn them into pockets to stitch to a T-shirt and shorts as instructed. If you aren't happy with your embroidery sample, and if you need more practice, either make a plain pocket, or stitch a purchased crest or woven label on the pocket in lieu of the embroidery.*

Step One:

PLAN YOUR PROJECT

The flag design teaches you how to turn corners, as well as how to use a variety of utility and decorative stitches on your New Home sewing machine. You will also have the opportunity to practice your free-hand embroidery skills.

In the Machine Readiness Checklists, note that each stitch is described by name and number for the New Home Memory Craft 7500 and 8000. Keep Fig. 8.1 and Table 8.1 in front of you while sewing for easy reference. But before you begin stitching your flag embroidery, you need to know about fabrics, threads, and other embroidery supplies (Fig. 3.1).

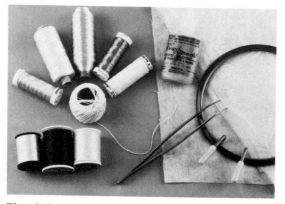

Fig. 3.1
Threads, fabrics, and other embroidery supplies.

FABRICS AND THREADS

All-natural fabrics are easiest to use for machine appliqué and machine embroidery because they are more forgiving than their synthetic counterparts. If puckering occurs, pressing usually removes the worst of it. Wool felt and woven fabrics are also easier to work with than knits because they don't distort in a hoop. Cut wool felt, all-cotton duck or kettle cloth, and organza into 9″ (23cm) practice squares. Use them as "doodle cloths" and for stitch testing, then put them in your notebook for future reference.

The best threads for machine appliqué and embroidery are **all-cotton, rayon,** or **acrylic embroidery thread.** All of these threads have a nice sheen and cause little or no tension problems. They are also generally finer than thread used for clothing construction. Look for brand names such as DMC, Janome, J. & P. Coats, Mettler Metrosene, Madeira, O.M.C., Star, Sulky, and Zwicky in your local sewing machine dealership or in better fabric stores.

Sew-How: If you have old thread that shreds, splits, or breaks when you are using it, put it in the refrigerator overnight. The moisture in the refrigerator is absorbed by the thread so that it regains its original tensile strength. If you don't have time to wait, accomplish the same thing by dribbling a line of Needle-Lube (a thread moisturizer) on the thread along the length of the spool (available through fabric stores and mail-order sources).

Other threads used for machine embroidery are **cotton darning thread** (sometimes called basting thread), **100% polyester bobbin thread** (available through New Home dealers only), and **nylon monofilament thread.** Because darning thread is very fine—a size 60, 70 or 120—it does not create bulk, even in heavily stitched areas, which makes it a good bobbin thread for embroidery. Since bobbin, darning, and basting thread is available only in white, it is necessary to loosen top thread tension so stitches lock under the fabric. This way, bobbin thread will not pull up to the surface and show. This method saves time because a single bobbin of darning thread can be used with a variety of colors. Also, because darning thread is so fine, a bobbin holds more of it than other threads.

Sew-How: Darning (basting) thread is too fine to use for clothing construction; however, when it's on the bobbin, it looks like any other white thread. To prevent confusion, mark bobbins wound with darning thread with fingernail polish.

Nylon monofilament thread is transparent and has many of the same advantages as cotton darning thread: you can get a lot on a bobbin, and you don't need to wind and thread new bobbins when changing the top thread color. However, some brands are stiff and wiry and won't hold a knot. The best type I've used is called "Invisible Wonder Nylon Thread." It's as fine as hair (.0004mm fine), breaks like regular sewing thread, and is available through mail-order sources and some sewing machine dealers.

OTHER EMBROIDERY SUPPLIES

To ensure a smooth finish, you need a way to stabilize the fabric so the embroidery does not pucker while you are stitching. This can be accomplished by using an embroidery hoop; by backing the fabric with a stabilizer such as iron-on freezer wrap, tear-away, or fusible interfacing; or by using a combination of the above.

The easiest type of embroidery hoop to use for machine embroidery is a **spring hoop.** It's narrow enough to fit under the presser foot and needle, and it's easy to move when your work is in the machine. Spring hoops are available in 3" (7.5cm), 5⅜" (13.5cm), and 7" (18cm) sizes. I use the 5⅜" (13.5cm) the most because it is easy to move under the needle without knocking into the inside of the machine. Purchase a spring hoop through your local sewing machine dealer or favorite mail-order source.

Plastic-coated freezer wrap or **freezer paper,** used as an iron-on stabilizer, helps prevent skipped stitches and puckering. It is also easily removed after stitching and is available at your local grocery store. Iron the shiny side to the underside of your fabric.

Tear-Away and **Stitch-n-Tear** are other fabric stabilizers. These do not iron on and are easily removed after stitching.

Fusible interfacing supports a limp fabric and can stabilize a knit fabric when the interfacing is fused to the back. This makes pucker-free embroidering on a knit possible.

Other supplies you will see listed in this chapter are:

• **Paper-backed fusible web**—fusible web on one side, paper on the other; makes any fabric fusible without "gunking up" the iron (see page 73). Popular and widely available brands are called Wonder-Under and Trans Web.

• **Water-erasable** and **vanishing markers**—marks are removed with clear water or disappear after 24 to 48 hours.

• **Liquid seam sealant**—put a drop on thread ends so they don't have to be tied off or to prevent a knot from coming untied. Popular brands are Dritz Fray Check and Aleene's Stop Fraying.

Step Two:
FLAG TOTE

We tote our possessions to school, to the beach, to class—and back. We tote things on vacation and tote notes to a lecture. We tote things home from the mall so we can tote the same things elsewhere. So why not make something large and attractive to do the toting? The finished dimensions of this tote are 14″ × 17½″ × 5″ (35.5cm × 44.5cm × 12.5cm).

The embroideries will be done with the feed dogs up. This means that your New Home sewing machine will move the fabric under the presser foot while the needle moves from side to side creating a satin or other decorative stitch.

After embroidering the flag pockets for the tote, you will freely embroider a label or name tag to stitch to the inside of the tote. For this step the feed dogs are lowered; the fabric is stretched in a hoop, then moved manually under the needle.

In addition to the embroidery supplies mentioned above, to make the tote you will need:

Supplies

• ½ yd. (45cm) paper-backed fusible web

• two 6″ × 22″ (15cm × 55cm) strips of white canvas or duck cloth

• four 22″ × 1″ (55cm × 2.5cm) strips of yellow knit or 1″ grosgrain ribbon

• 22″ × 37″ (55cm × 92.5cm) white canvas or duck cloth

• red woven fabric cut 2¾″ × 8″ (6.9cm × 20cm)

• royal blue knit fabric cut 1½″ × 16″ (3.8cm × 40cm)

• royal blue knit fabric cut 2½″ × 4″ (6.3cm × 10cm)

• water soluble stabilizer

• tear-away stabilizer

• disappearing dressmaker's chalk

• rotary cutter, mat, and see-through ruler to cut everything square

• heavy cardboard cut to fit the bottom of the bag

• twin needle

• 48″ (1.2m) of 1″ (2.5cm) webbing (belting) cut in half for handles.

Sew-How: *If you can't find matching webbing (see color pages), paint webbing to match with acrylic paint. Also, I could not find white canvas in November when I made this tote, so I made it out of cotton twill. To make it sturdy, I fused fusible fleece to a lining fabric and lined the tote. Cut the lining and fusible fleece 22″ × 35″ (55cm × 87.5cm), and fuse fleece to the wrong side of the lining (following the instructions on the fleece interleafing). Stitch the side seams and box the bottom of the tote and lining separately as instructed. Place lining in tote, wrong sides together, then turn tote hem as instructed, enclosing the top of the fused lining in the hem. Position handles and label and stitch hem as instructed.*

TRACE, TRANSFER, AND PREPARE THE FLAG POCKETS

1. At your local copy center enlarge the design in Fig. 3.2 to four times the size shown. Trace the enlarged flag design on a piece of tracing paper.

2. Fuse paper-backed fusible web to the backs of the red woven fabric and the blue knit fabrics. If you are using yellow knit strips instead of grosgrain ribbon, fuse paper-backed fusible web to them as well.

Sew-How: To use paper-backed fusible web, cut fusible web the desired size and place the textured side against the wrong side of the fashion fabric. Press for 3–5 seconds with a hot, dry iron. Let the fabric cool. Carefully peel off the release paper. Position this new fusible fabric, fusible side down, on the item to be embellished (shapes can be drawn or traced directly on the paper backing before cutting). Cover work with a dry press cloth and, with the iron on the "wool" setting, press with steam for about 10 seconds. Do not glide the iron back and forth; just press in one spot, then lift the iron and press again, overlapping iron on previously fused areas until all the fabric is fused. Always test on a scrap first.

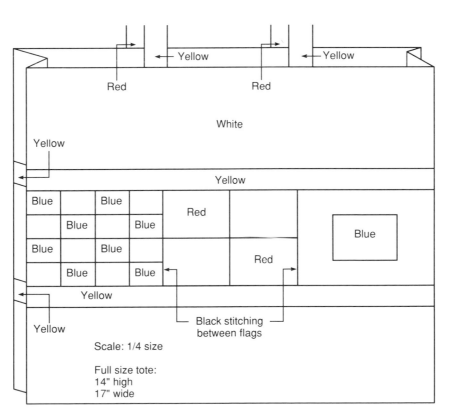

Fig. 3.2
Flag tote bag design.

3. Cut four red rectangles $2\frac{3}{4}'' \times 2''$ (6.9cm × 5cm). Cut sixteen blue rectangles $1\frac{1}{2}'' \times 1''$ (3.8cm × 2.5cm). Cut two blue rectangles $2\frac{1}{2}'' \times 2''$ (6.3cm × 5cm). These appliqués are used to create two flag pockets.

POSITION AND STITCH THE FLAG APPLIQUÉS

1. Fold canvas or duck cloth pockets in half lengthwise and press a center crease. Remove the release paper on the red rectangles and position them on either side of the center crease as shown in Fig. 3.3. Next to the red rectangles, fuse the blue rectangles as shown. Center and fuse the larger blue rectangle to create the third flag.

2. Satin stitch the red flags.

Machine Readiness Checklist	
Stitch:	zigzag (35, 7500; 4, 8000)
Length:	0.4–0.5
Width:	7
Foot:	F satin stitch
Needle:	14/90 stretch
Thread:	top, rayon or acrylic embroidery; bobbin, darning (basting)
Feed dogs:	up
Tension:	top, loosened slightly; bobbin, normal

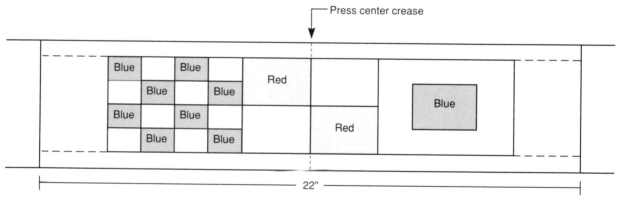

Fig. 3.3
Position and fuse red rectangles for the center flag first. Position and fuse the blue rectangles for the checkerboard flag. Position and fuse the large rectangle for the remaining flag.

Center the F satin stitch foot down the center of the red flag (over the center crease in the pocket) and sew a row of vertical satin stitches. Half of the stitch is formed on the red fabric, and the other half is formed on the white pocket strip. Turn your work 90 degrees and repeat satin stitching across the pocket, starting and stopping at the end of the flag (Fig. 3.4). Lock off stitches at the beginning and end of each row of stitching; pull threads to the back and clip them off.

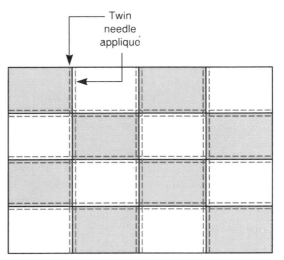

Fig. 3.5

Starting in the upper left corner, center twin needles over the blue rectangle and sew the length of the appliqués, vertically and then horizontally.

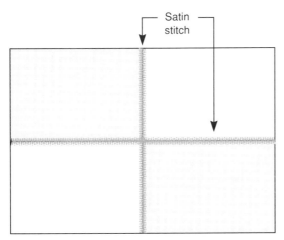

Fig. 3.4

Center the F satin stitch foot down the center of the red rectangle and sew a row of vertical satin stitches. Turn work 90 degrees and repeat satin stitching across the pocket, starting and stopping at the end of the appliqué.

3. With a twin needle in place, rethread your machine with royal blue rayon or acrylic embroidery thread (see your *Instruction Book* for threading instructions). Starting in the upper left corner, center the needles over the blue rectangle and sew the length of the appliqués on the second flag, stitching vertically and then horizontally (Fig. 3.5).

4. For the last flag, select a closed decorative satin stitch. I used the triangle (58, 7500; 31, 8000), but experiment to see which one you like the best.

Sew-How: It is a little tricky turning the corners so you are not in the middle of the motif, so practice on a scrap first to see how many triangles fit lengthwise and widthwise on the rectangle.

Machine Readiness Checklist	
Stitch:	closed triangle (58, 7500; 31, 8000)
Length:	0.4–0.6
Width:	7
Foot:	F satin stitch
Needle:	14/90 stretch
Thread:	top, blue rayon or acrylic embroidery; bobbin, darning (basting)
Feed dogs:	up
Tension:	top, loosened slightly; bobbin, normal
Accessories:	tear-away stabilizer or iron-on freezer wrap

Place stabilizer on the wrong side of the pocket strip under the larger blue rectangle. Guiding the fabric so the straight edge of the stitch falls on the straight side of the rectangle, stitch around all four sides of the rectangle (Fig. 3.6).

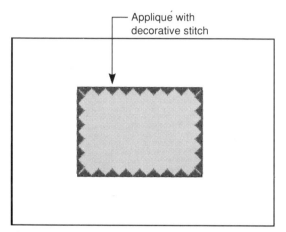

Fig. 3.6
Using a decorative stitch, guide the flag so the straight edge of the stitch falls on the straight side of the rectangle.

5. Satin stitch between each flag.

Machine Readiness Checklist	
Stitch:	zigzag (35, 7500; 4, 8000)
Length:	0.4–0.6
Width:	4–6
Foot:	F satin stitch
Needle:	14/90 stretch
Thread:	top and bobbin, black rayon or acrylic embroidery
Tension:	top, loosened slightly; bobbin, normal

Starting at the top, stitch a row of satin stitches between each flag, centering the appliqués under the foot (Fig. 3.7).

6. Remove the release paper from the back of the yellow stripes and position the stripes on the top and bottom edges of the pocket (see Fig. 3.7). (If you are using ribbon to make the stripes, pin them to the pocket as shown.) Rethread the top with yellow thread. Topstitch both edges of the top stripe and the top edge of the bottom stripe to the pocket strip using the (outline) stretch stitch (33, 7500; 16, 8000) on a 2.5 length and 1.5–2 width, and the F satin stitch foot. Or topstitch with a straight stitch.

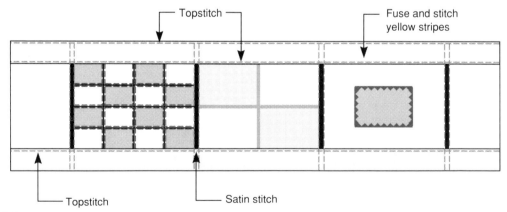

Fig. 3.7
Starting at the top, stitch a row of satin stitches between each flag.

7. Position decorated pocket strips 6″ (15cm) from the narrow ends of the tote and topstitch the bottom edge of the pocket to the tote bag using the (outline) stretch stitch (33, 7500; 16, 8000) or straight stitch (Fig. 3.8).

8. Rethread the top and bobbin with yellow rayon or acrylic embroidery thread. To create three pockets, topstitch the pocket in place with the triple-strength stitch (32, 7500; 15, 8000) or saddle stitch (34, 7500; 17, 8000), guiding the stitching along the edge of the black satin stitching (see Fig. 3.7).

EMBROIDER THE LABEL

To create your own label you may want to stitch your initials or your name or design something unique. To do this you can use the decorative stitches at your fingertips and combine them with a block or tapered monogram. If you have the Memory Craft 8000, you can make your label or stitch your monogram using one of the nautical Memory Card designs (see *Instruction Book*). If you don't have the Memory Craft 8000 or if you want to design your own label, try the following warm-up exercises and perfect tapering a satin stitch and free-machine embroidery.

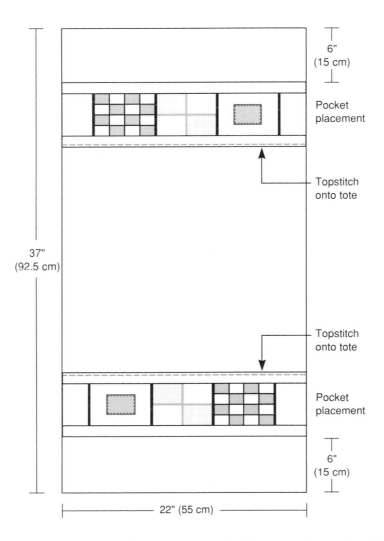

Fig. 3.8
Position decorated pocket strips 6″ (12.5cm) from the narrow ends of the tote and topstitch the bottom edge of the pocket.

Warm-Up Exercise: Tapered Satin Stitch

One of the features I like best about my New Home sewing machine is how much control I have in tapering any stitch. To get a better understanding of tapering, try the following exercise on a 9″ (23cm) practice square backed with freezer wrap and put your stitch sample in your notebook.

Machine Readiness Checklist

Stitch:	zigzag (35, 7500; 4, 8000)
Length:	0.4–0.5
Width:	0–7–0
Foot:	F satin stitch
Needle:	11/75 Blue Tip
Needle position:	center
Thread:	all-purpose or 100% cotton, rayon, or acrylic embroidery
Feed dogs:	up
Tension:	top, loosened slightly; bobbin, normal

On your practice square, satin-stitch while you touch the stitch width key from 0 to 7 and back. Once you gain some confidence, run the machine at the fastest speed. You should find that tapered satin stitch shapes are smoother and more uniform when you run the machine quickly and touch the width key slowly.

Warm-Up Exercise: Sewing Machine Spaghetti

Another way to embroider is freely by machine, which means moving the fabric freely under the moving needle as if you were moving a piece of paper under a stationary pen or pencil. If you have never tried this technique, try the following warm-up exercise on a 9″ (23cm) practice square.

Machine Readiness Checklist

Stitch:	straight (29, 7500; 1, 8000); zigzag (35, 7500; 4, 8000)
Length:	0
Width:	2, 3, 4, 5, 6, 7
Foot:	P embroidery
Needle:	14/90 stretch
Thread:	top, dark-colored rayon or acrylic embroidery; bobbin, darning (basting)
Feed dogs:	down
Tension:	top, loosened slightly; bobbin, normal
Fabric:	9″ (23cm) square of light-colored woven cotton
Accessories:	tear-away stabilizer, spring hoop, vanishing marker

1. Place a practice square in the spring hoop, and pull it taut. Then place the piece of tear-away stabilizer under the fabric. The stabilizer prevents the fabric from puckering.

Sew-How: When fabric is stretched in a hoop for free-machine embroidery, it looks upside down as compared to hand embroidery because the flat side must be against the bed of the machine. The fabric should be taut enough that, when you tap it with your finger, it sounds like a drum beat.

2. Set your width at 2. Pull the bobbin thread to the surface of the fabric, take a couple of locking stitches, clip threads off at the fabric, and run the machine at a moderate-to-fast speed while moving the fabric smoothly to the left, then to the right. The faster you run the machine and the slower you move your work, the closer together the zigzag stitches become. Practice moving the fabric smoothly from side to side, creating a spaghetti-like row of stitching (Fig. 3.9). Do not sharply pivot the hoop at a curve; you want the stitches to taper as you change direction. (The resulting stitches look as if the line was created by a calligrapher's pen.) Try this exercise with varying zigzag widths until you are comfortable with the process. Then practice writing your name or initials. Remove tear-away stabilizer after stitching. When you have perfected your name or initials, you are ready to embroider your label.

Fig. 3.9
Practice moving the fabric smoothly from side to side, creating a spaghetti-like row of stitching.

Sew-How: To cross the letter "t" or dot the letter "i", extend the stem of the last letter and bring it around as shown in Fig. 3.10.

Fig. 3.10
To cross the letter "t" or dot the letter "i," extend the stem of the last letter.

3. To make the label, set your machine as follows:

Machine Readiness Checklist	
Stitch:	zigzag (35, 7500; 4, 8000)
Length:	0
Width:	2–6
Foot:	P embroidery
Needle:	14/90 stretch
Thread:	top, black rayon or acrylic embroidery; bobbin, black darning; Thread Fuse
Feed dogs:	down
Tension:	top, loosened slightly; bobbin, normal
Fabric:	$\frac{1}{4}$ yd. (23cm) of $1\frac{1}{2}$" (3.8cm) wide white grosgrain ribbon
Accessories:	vanishing marker, water-soluble stabilizer, spring hoop

Baste ribbon on a double layer of water-soluble stabilizer using Thread Fuse as the top thread.

Sew-How: Thread Fuse is a water-soluble basting thread. Use it to baste the stabilizer to the ribbon; then when the stabilizer is rinsed out, the thread is too, and so there is no need to rip out basting stitches.

Stretch ribbon in the spring hoop so the stabilizer is underneath. Draw your initials, name, or design on the ribbon, and freely embroider as you did on your practice squares. Remove the ribbon and wash away the stabilizer. Cut the label beyond the lettering or design so you can fold ¼″ (6mm) hems at the raw edges. The label will be stitched into the tote at the center back.

Sew-How: If you have the Memory Craft 8000, use one of the Memory Card designs to create a label.

FINISH THE TOTE

Machine Readiness Checklist	
Stitch:	overcast (38, 7500; 5, 8000)
Length:	2–3
Width:	5
Foot:	C overedge
Needle:	14/90 jeans
Needle position:	center
Thread:	white all-purpose
Feed dogs:	up
Tension:	normal (auto)

1. To make the body of the tote, fold the bag in half, right sides together, and stitch a ¼″ (6mm) seam allowance guiding the raw edge by the ½″ (1.3cm) line in the needle plate (Fig. 3.11). Trim away excess seam allowance and press it to one side (see Fig. 8.46).

Fig. 3.11
Fold bag in half and seam edges together using the overcast stitch. Position webbing handles and your label, then stitch around the top of the bag, catching the handles and label in the stitching.

2. To finish the top of the bag, fold a double hem. To do this, fold down the top edge 1″ (2.5cm) toward the inside of the tote and press. Fold the hem down again and press.

3. Draw a line 1½″ (3.8cm) from each end of webbing handle. Make an arch with one length of webbing and position it on the front 6½″ (16.3cm) from either edge of the tote. The lines on each end of the webbing should be even with the top of the bag. Pin handle in place. Repeat for the back of the bag (see Fig. 3.11).

4. Position your embroidered label between the webbing handles on the back of the bag.

5. Topstitch around the top of the bag, guiding ⅛″ (3mm) from the fold.

6. Remove the C overedge foot and replace it with the A zigzag foot. Place the L quilter so the second row of stitching guides slightly less than 1″ (2.5cm) from the fold, catching the bottom edge of the hem and top edge of the label in the stitching (see Fig. 3.11).

7. To box the bottom corners of the bag, at the side seams measure up from the bottom fold 2½″ (6.4cm) and mark a dot in the seam allowance with the dressmaker's chalk. Fold one side seam so it lies along the bottom fold in the fabric (Fig. 3.12). Draw a line on either side of the dot in the side seam, perpendicular to the side seam, and straight-stitch along this line. Repeat for the other side.

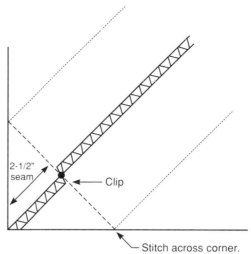

2-1/2″ seam

← Clip

Stitch across corner.

Fig. 3.12
Fold one side seam so it lies along the bottom fold in the fabric.

8. Turn the tote inside out and push the triangles against the bottom of the bag.

9. Cut a piece of cardboard to fit snugly into the bottom of the bag to give it shape, to hold the triangles against the bottom, and to add stability at the base.

Step Three:

PROJECT VARIATIONS—POCKET AND T-SHIRT EMBELLISHMENT

POCKET EMBELLISHMENT

Embellish a pocket to stitch to the back of the shorts you made in Chapter 2, or to give an old pair of shorts, pants, a shirt, or a skirt a new look. You can do these project variations using supplies used to make the tote, plus some sheer organdy (or organza) and a vanishing marker.

Embroidered Flag Pocket

You can make a flag pocket embellishment using the stitches on your New Home sewing machine.

1. Cut a woven pocket as described in Chapter 2 (see Fig. 2.9). Press the fold at the top of the pocket. Iron freezer wrap to the wrong side of the pocket under where the flags will be embroidered so the freezer wrap extends beyond the design.

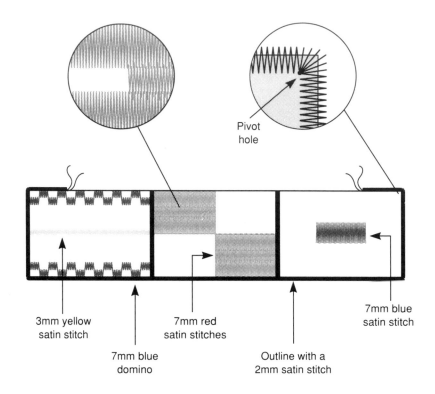

Pivot hole

3mm yellow satin stitch

7mm blue domino

7mm red satin stitches

Outline with a 2mm satin stitch

7mm blue satin stitch

Fig. 3.13

Flag embroidery pattern. Each red rectangle is made with three rows of 7mm satin stitching; stitch the top and bottom rows first, then fill in the middle, as shown in the inset at left. To turn a corner when stitching between the three flags, lift the presser foot, pivot the fabric slightly, and stitch again so the stitches fan out from the same pivot hole around the corner (see inset at right).

2. Using the vanishing marker, draw a line to mark the pocket fold and another line parallel to and 1″ (2.5cm) below the first. This is where the flags will be embroidered (Fig. 3.13). Using Fig. 3.13 as a guide, mark flag placement with the vanishing marker.

3. To create the flags (see color pages), set your machine as follows:

Machine Readiness Checklist	
Stitch:	domino (69, 7500; 42, 8000); satin stitch (35, 7500; 4, 8000)
Length:	0.4–0.6
Width:	varies
Foot:	F satin stitch
Needle:	14/90 stretch
Thread:	top: royal blue, red, yellow, and black rayon or acrylic embroidery; bobbin: darning (basting)
Feed dogs:	up
Tension:	top: loosened slightly; bobbin, normal
Accessories:	iron-on freezer wrap

Top-thread your machine with blue thread and stitch the dominoes on the top and bottom edges of the left flag on a 7mm width. Then sew a 7mm satin stitch in the center block of the third flag.

4. Top-thread with red thread and stitch the center flag. Each red rectangle is made with three rows of 7mm satin stitches. Sew along the top and bottom of each rectangle; then fill in the middle with 7mm satin stitches (see inset at left in Fig. 3.13).

Sew-How: *To eliminate hand tying, touch the reverse/lock-off key at the end of each row of stitching.*

---

5. Top-thread with yellow thread and stitch a 3mm satin stitch in the center of the first flag (see Fig. 3.13).

6. Top-thread with black thread and stitch between the three flags with a 2 width satin stitch. Then stitch around the flag embroidery with a 2 width satin stitch, fanning stitches around a pivot hole at each corner (see inset at right in Fig. 3.13). Remove freezer wrap.

7. Press embroidery, face side down, on a clean white terry cloth towel. Press it from the wrong side to set the piece. The stitches nestle into the soft terry cloth, while the fabric between the stitches presses flat.

8. Finish and place pocket on a T-shirt; topstitch it in place as described in Figs. 2.10 and 2.11.

Checkerboard Pocket

This easy pocket variation adds interest to any pocket. Try this color-blocking technique, or use different textures in each square. If you have a Memory Craft 8000, decorate two squares with Memory Card embroidery designs or monogramming.

1. Cut two red and two white squares using the pattern in Fig. 3.14. Cut one white square using the pattern in Fig. 3.16.

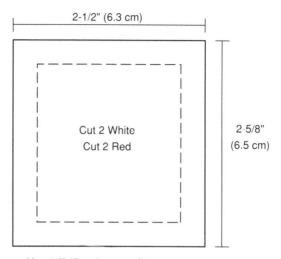

Use 1/4" (6mm) seam allowances.
Pattern is full size.

Fig. 3.14
Checkerboard pocket pattern.

2. Using a $\frac{1}{4}''$ (6mm) seam allowance, straight-stitch one small white and one small red square, right sides together, along one longer ($2\frac{5}{8}''$ [6.5cm]) edge. Repeat for the other small red and white squares. Press seams open.

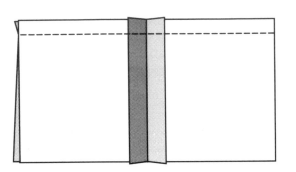

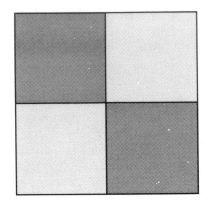

Fig. 3.15

Stitch four squares together using ¼" (6mm) seam allowances, alternating colors to create the checkerboard.

3. Now stitch the four squares together along the long edges alternating the colors to create a checkerboard effect (Fig. 3.15).

4. Press a strip of paper-backed fusible web across the *wrong* side of the large

pocket under where the buttonhole will be made. Using the J sliding buttonhole foot or the N or R buttonhole sensor, make a large buttonhole in the center of the large white pocket (see Fig. 3.16). Cut the buttonhole open (see Fig. 8.59).

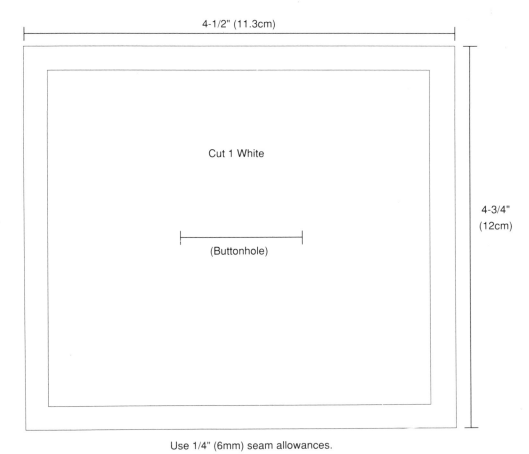

4-1/2" (11.3cm)

Cut 1 White

(Buttonhole)

4-3/4" (12cm)

Use 1/4" (6mm) seam allowances.

Fig. 3.16

White pocket facing pattern.

5. Place the checkerboard pocket and large white pocket pieces right sides together, and stitch a $\frac{1}{4}''$ (6mm) seam around all four sides of the pocket (Fig. 3.17).

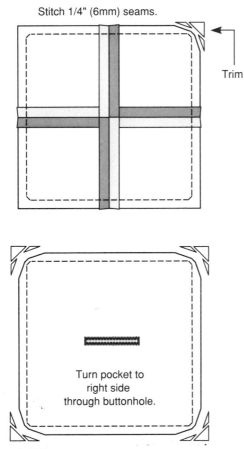

Stitch 1/4" (6mm) seams.

Trim

Turn pocket to right side through buttonhole.

Fig. 3.17
Place checkerboard pocket and large white pocket pieces right sides together, and stitch around all four sides. Turn pocket through the buttonhole and press it.

Sew-How: *To make square pocket corners, remember to take one stitch across each corner of the pocket.*

6. Remove the release paper from the back of the buttonhole. Turn the pocket through the buttonhole. Using a point turner, push out the corners. Press the pocket so the buttonhole is centered in the seam line of the checkerboard pocket.

Because you have used fusible web under the buttonhole, it will be fused shut. Top-press this pocket.

New Sewer's Note: *To top-press, place the pocket on the ironing board with the right side up. Cover the pocket with a press cloth and press the pocket with steam.*

7. Place the pocket where desired and topstitch it in place (Fig. 3.18) (see Figs. 2.11, 9.10, and 9.17). If you don't want to put this pocket on the shorts you made or a T-shirt, put it in your notebook with your other samples.

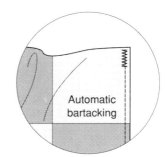

Automatic bartacking

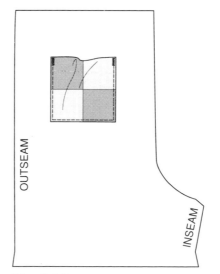

OUTSEAM

INSEAM

Fig. 3.18
Place the pocket and topstitch it in place leaving a little slack at the opening. Use the (automatic) bartack to reinforce the pocket corners.

TRANSFERABLE LEARNINGS

The information and techniques you have learned by embellishing the tote bag pocket and pockets for the shorts and T-shirt and by constructing the tote bag give you the skills necessary to sew many other projects. You have learned how to:

• Fuse and use paper-backed fusible web. Besides using it for appliqué, you can cut it into small pieces or strips and use it to fuse-tack facings or to press up a hem.

• Use a spring hoop; and use iron-on freezer wrap, tear-away stabilizer, or water-soluble stabilizer under your work when using decorative stitches and when free-machine embroidering to eliminate skipped stitches and puckering.

• Loosen the top thread tension when embroidering so stitches lock on the underside of the fabric. This also applies for satin-stitching an edge and for free-machine monogramming.

• Use a satin-stitch or satin stitch variation around woven appliqués. Use a twin needle to topstitch over knit appliqués; you can also use a twin needle to make pintucks and to topstitch knit hems.

• Satin-stitch around the corner of an appliqué, fanning stitches out from the pivot point.

• Turn a pocket right side out through a buttonhole. Buttonholes are used on many projects in the World of Sewing.

• Move the fabric under the needle as you would move a piece of paper under a stationary pen or pencil for free-machine embroidery. Use this technique for free-hand monogramming and fill-in, free-machine quilting, and other free-machine techniques (see bibliography for *Know Your Sewing Machine* book series by Jackie Dodson, Chilton Book Company).

• Press embroidery and appliqué right side down on a lofty terry cloth towel so stitches bury themselves in the loft and the fabric between the stitches can be pressed flat.

• Topstitch a pocket close to and even from the edge using your G or G adjustable blind hem foot. This technique is used to topstitch collars, cuffs, front tabs, yokes, and other parts of a garment.

Next, we will "Sew for Your Home." Besides the personal gratification it offers, sewing for your home is a great way to stretch your decorating budget and give a new look to an old room—in this case, your kitchen or dining area. We will make placemats and matching "lapkins" while practicing edge finishes, buttonholes, and topstitching at the same time.

4 SEW FOR YOUR HOME

Step One:
PLAN YOUR PROJECT

Although a lot of us sew for the pleasure of it rather than to save money, one of the best places to economize is by sewing for your home. A lot of projects for the home involve straight sewing, so the challenge is finding fabrics that work effectively with your color scheme.

Unlike a piece of clothing, which you can hang in the back of your closet if you don't like it, a project you stitch for your home requires careful planning because you may have to live with your decision until you can afford to change it. For that reason, many people consult an interior designer. However, if you keep some basic principles of color in mind, you can acquire confidence and train your eye well enough to do the planning and designing yourself.

COLOR SELECTION

Color has either a blue or yellow base. If you have had your personal colors done, you may know that so-called winter and summer colors are cool, blue-based colors. Spring and autumn colors are warm, yellow-based colors. Color for your home works the same way.

When selecting colors for your home, work with the large surface areas first—for example, the floors and counter tops. Once colors for these areas have been chosen, everything else is planned around them. If you are not going to change the floor covering or counter tops, then take a closer look at what you have.

Is it bright and clear, or grayed earth tones? To determine if your colors have a cool or warm base, take carpet swatches with you when you go shopping and compare them with other fabrics and colors in natural light. If you have to, take fabric and carpet swatches outside in the shade for a better look. The shade best duplicates a room in natural light. When you put a fabric next to your carpet, does the fabric look dirty? If so, chances are one of them is a cool blue-base and the other a warm yellow-base—neither one enhancing the other. After some comparison, you should begin to see the difference between blue-based and yellow-based colors.

Another principle of color selection is to work with an odd number of colors in one room—three or five colors are more interesting than two or four. For example, if you've chosen three colors, two dominate and the third is used sparingly in a room as an accent. You could have a white carpet, a black bedspread, and black-and-white draperies, and use red as an accent color in a pillow or flower arrangement. If a bathroom or sitting room adjoins, the accent color (in this case red) can dominate with black or white. The third color becomes the accent.

Once you have trained your eye, you'll begin to notice what works well and what doesn't. If you have to study something for a while or aren't sure your choices complement each other, they probably don't.

Now, let's start with something small and spruce up your dining area with a new table setting. In this chapter we'll make four placemats and matching "lapkins." A lapkin is a napkin that has slots to hold the silverware; it unrolls to be used on your lap.

FABRICS, THREADS, AND OTHER SUPPLIES

Once you have decided on the color scheme, select the fabric you will use. A woven cotton or cotton blend is your best bet for easy care and trouble-free sewing. Poplin, kettle cloth, and lightweight duck are good choices. If you choose to make a contrasting appliqué, as we did here (see color pages), be sure the fiber contents of both fabrics are similar. As always, preshrink the fabric before cutting (see page 51 for preshrinking instructions).

Threads used in this project are:

- cotton, rayon, or acrylic embroidery thread in the appliqué color
- white or black darning or basting thread wound on a bobbin
- nylon monofilament thread wound on a bobbin
- size #5 pearl cotton in the contrasting appliqué color
- all-purpose sewing thread in the prominent color of the placemat

You also need some paper-backed fusible web for the appliqué, a straightedge (preferably a see-through cutting ruler), a vanishing marker, and, for easy cutting, a rotary cutter and mat.

Step Two:
ENVELOPE PLACEMATS

The placemat looks like the back of an envelope with a button closure (see color pages). Each mat has a contrasting appliqué and a topstitched flap with a buttonhole for a machine-stitched button. The corners of each mat are mitered, then satin-stitched with a narrow border.

The techniques used in this project apply to many aspects of sewing, and, because you will stitch each technique four times (by making four placemats and four lapkins), you will master each one.

Supplies:

- 1½ yds. (1.4m) paper-backed fusible web
- 3 yds. (2.8m) of 45" (1.1m) white poplin, weaver's (kettle) cloth, or lightweight duck
- ¾ yd. (68.5cm) fabric contrasting poplin
- four ½"–⅝" (1.3cm–1.6cm) buttons (two- or four-hole)
- black cotton, rayon, or acrylic embroidery thread
- transparent tape (optional)

Yardage requirements are for four place-mats and four lapkins; instructions below are written for one placemat and one lapkin.

CUT

1. Cut one piece of white poplin 16" × 12" (40.5cm × 30.5cm). This we'll call the base mat. Cut another piece of white poplin 18" × 14" (45.5cm × 35.5cm). This we'll call the back mat. Note that the lengthwise grain is parallel to the short sides of each mat piece.

2. Cut two pieces of white poplin 10" × 12" (25.5cm × 30.5cm). **Note:** Lengthwise grain is parallel to the 12" (30.5cm) side. In the upper left corner, mark the lengthwise grain on all poplin pieces using the vanishing or water-erasable marker.

3. Cut one piece of the contrasting appliqué fabric 10" × 12" (25.5cm × 30.5cm) long. Mark lengthwise grain in upper right corner with a marker.

Sew-How: If contrasting fabric is dark, mark grain line on a piece of transparent tape and stick tape in the upper right corner.

---

4. Cut one piece of paper-backed fusible web 10" × 12" (25.5cm × 30.5cm) and fuse it to the back of the contrasting 10" × 12" (25.5 cm × 30.5cm) fabric.

Sew-How: See instructions for use of paper-backed fusible web in Chapter 3, page 73.

---

5. Mark a dot along the edge of the longer side 6" (15cm) down from the top of all three 10" × 12" (25.5cm × 30.5cm) fabric pieces. Cut a triangle from each piece as shown in Fig. 4.1. On the contrasting triangle, trim angled edges ¼" (6mm).

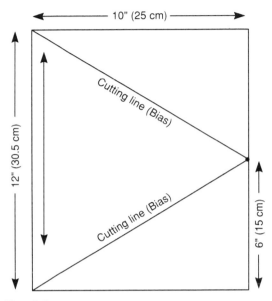

Fig. 4.1
Mark a dot 6" (15cm) down from the top and cut a triangle. On the contrasting fabric, trim bias-cut edges ¼" (6mm).

Sew-How: This triangle has two bias-cut edges and one edge cut on the lengthwise grain. Notice the bias-cut edge hardly ravels compared to the edge cut on the lengthwise grain. Because of this, the bias-cut edge of the appliqué is finished differently than other raw edges are finished.

APPLIQUÉ

1. Remove the paper backing. Center contrasting triangle on the 16″ × 12″ (40.5cm × 30.5cm) poplin so the lengthwise grain of the appliqué and the lengthwise grain of the base mat are in the same direction (Fig. 4.2). Fuse the contrasting triangle to the base mat.

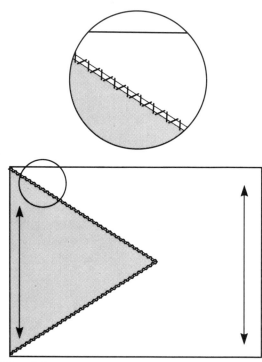

Fig. 4.2
Center triangle so the lengthwise grain of the appliqué is positioned on the lengthwise grain of the base mat.

2. Appliqué the contrasting triangle to the base mat.

Machine Readiness Checklist	
Stitch:	zigzag (35, 7500; 4, 8000)
Length:	2
Width:	2.5
Foot:	H cording or one-groove cording
Needle:	14/90 stretch
Needle position:	center
Thread:	top, rayon embroidery to match contrasting fabric; bobbin, darning thread
Feed dogs:	up
Tension:	top, loosened slightly; bobbin, normal
Accessories:	double strand of #5 pearl cotton

Place a double strand of pearl cotton under the center clip in the H cording or one-groove cording foot. Place the bias-cut edge of the triangle appliqué under the foot so the pearl cotton is stitched on the edge of it. Sew. The needle will stitch over the cord, attaching it to the fabric. This technique is called couching (see Figs. 8.20, 9.18, 9.19, 9.20, 9.21). At the corner, stop with the needle on the inside of the corner, lift the presser foot, pivot the work, and pull the pearl cotton under the foot so it will follow the other edge of the appliqué. Lower the presser foot, and couch over the pearl cotton along the other edge of the appliqué.

MAKE THE TRIANGLE FLAP

1. Place two poplin triangles right sides together; then, using the A zigzag foot, straight-stitch (30, 7500; 2, 8000) at a 2.5–3 length a ¼″ (6mm) seam on the two bias-cut edges. Shorten the stitch length and take one or two stitches across the corner (Fig. 4.3). This ensures a sharp corner when the flap is turned and pressed.

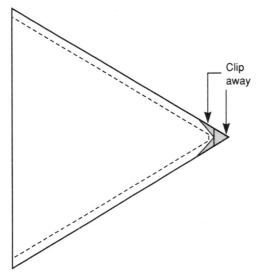

Fig. 4.3
Shorten the stitch length and take one or two stitches across the corner.

Sew-How: *Use this technique on collar points, cuffs, or when lining a square-cornered pocket.*

---

2. Clip away the fabric at the corner as shown in Fig. 4.3, and turn the flap right side out. Using a point turner or the rounded end of a pair of scissors, gently push the corner out to a nice point without pushing the points through the fabric.

3. For a straight, crisp edge, pin the flap around the edge so the seam line is on the edge of the flap. Press the flap *without* pressing over the pins.

4. Using a straightedge and a vanishing marker, draw a line to mark the center of the flap. Measure ⅝″ (1.5cm) in from the point and draw a line perpendicular to the center line. The buttonhole starts where the lines intersect (Fig. 4.4).

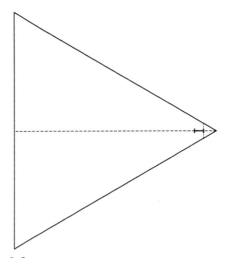

Fig. 4.4
Start the buttonhole where the lines intersect.

5. Set your machine for a bartack buttonhole (107, 7500; 12, 8000) and stitch a sample buttonhole on a double layer of scrap poplin to determine what size is needed for your button.

Sew-How: To determine what size buttonhole you need for a particular button, cut a narrow strip of paper about $2\frac{1}{2}$ times longer than your button is in diameter. Fold the paper strip in half and slip the button into it as shown in Fig. 4.5, snugging one edge of the button in the fold of the strip. Hold the paper firmly and crease it at the opposite edge of the fold with your fingernail. Remove the button and flatten the paper strip. The length of the buttonhole needed is the distance from the fold to the fingernail crease in the strip of paper (Fig. 4.6).

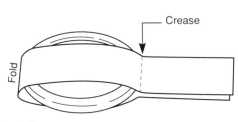

Fig. 4.5
Snug one edge of the button into the folded paper strip.

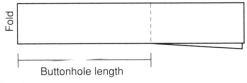

Fig. 4.6
The length of the buttonhole needed for this button is the distance from the fold to the fingernail crease in the paper strip.

6. Make the buttonhole starting at the mark $\frac{5}{8}''$ (1.5cm) from the point of the flap. Cut the buttonhole open (see Figs. 8.57, 8.58, 8.59, 8.60).

7. Pin poplin triangle flap on base mat and mark the button placement. To do this, find the middle of the buttonhole and push a pin straight through the buttonhole and base mat. Using a fabric marker, put a dot on the base mat where the pin enters the fabric. Remove the pin.

8. Remove the flap and machine-stitch the button in place (see Figs. 8.17, 8.18, 9.30, 9.31).

9. Button flap over button and pin flap on base mat for topstitching. Topstitch flap in place.

Machine Readiness Checklist	
Stitch:	straight (29, 7500; 1, 8000)
Length:	3.5–4
Width:	0
Foot:	A zigzag or G or G adjustable blind hem
Needle:	14/90 stretch
Needle position:	left
Thread:	two all-purpose threads through the same needle in a thread color to match appliqué
Feed dogs:	up
Tension:	normal (auto)

Topstitch around the flap, guiding $\frac{1}{4}''$ (6mm) from the edge. Note that sewing in left needle position allows you to avoid hitting the button. Two threads through the same needle gives the topstitch a bolder appearance (see Fig. 8.9).

Sew-How: Heavier topstitching threads are available in a rainbow of colors at your local fabric store. Most are 100% polyester and must be used with a heavy needle. Although a size 14/90 needle is usually large enough, there is a special topstitching needle with an elongated eye designed to accommodate the heavier thread. See Table 1.1.

ATTACH BASE MAT TO BACK MAT

So that we don't need to stitch on a separate border, which is tricky and cumbersome, the back mat is cut larger than the base mat so it can be folded over the base mat to create the border. The corners are mitered, and then the border is top-stitched all the way around both to finish the border and to frame the placemat.

1. Center the base mat on the back mat, wrong sides together. Fold the edges of the back mat over the base mat to create a 1″ (2.5cm) border. Use an iron and steam to crease a border all the way around on the right side. Remove the base mat.

2. To miter a corner, press one border edge toward the right side. Fold a triangle at the corner the depth of the border (Fig. 4.7).

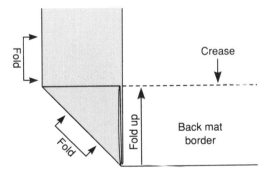

Fig. 4.7
Fold a triangle at the corner the depth of the border.

3. Fold edge perpendicular to the border over the triangle made in Step 2. Crease and press (Fig. 4.8).

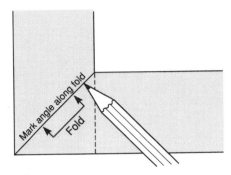

Fig. 4.8
Fold edge perpendicular to the border over the triangle. Crease and press. Mark the angle of the miter on the border, and along the side of the fold.

4. With a water-erasable or vanishing marker, mark the angle of the miter on the border, following the angle folded in Step 2. Also mark a line along the long side of the folded triangle.

5. Unfold the corner. When connected, your lines make a large triangle in the corner which becomes the stitching line (Fig. 4.9).

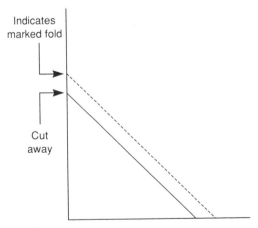

Fig. 4.9
Unfold the corner. The line makes a large triangle which becomes the stitching line.

6. Place right sides together, and straight-stitch on the line marked in Step 5. Trim the seam allowance to ¼" (6mm) and finger-press the seam open. Turn mitered corner to the right side, push out the corner with a point turner, and press corner with an iron and steam.

Sew-How: *For a sharp point at the corner of each miter, clip excess seam allowance at the corner close to the stitching line as you did at the point of the flap.*

FINISH THE ENVELOPE PLACEMAT

1. Slip the base mat into the back mat, snugly fitting the corners of the base mat into the mitered corners of the back mat. If the base mat ripples a little or does not lie flat, remove it from the back mat and slightly trim around the outside edge.

2. Using one or two strands of pearl cotton, couch the cord around the edge of the border as you did for the appliqué, guiding ⅛" (3mm) from the raw border edge.

3. Using cotton, rayon, or acrylic embroidery thread on the top and darning or basting thread on the bobbin, stitch over the cord with a 3 width satin stitch to create a narrow border (see Fig. 8.25). The cording gives the stitch a higher, rounded appearance.

4. Steam-press the envelope mat with the right side against the ironing board.

Step Three:

PROJECT VARIATION—ENVELOPE ''LAPKINS''

The lapkin is also appliquéd like the placemats. The edge is finished with a corded satin stitch to emulate a serged rolled hem.

1. Cut a 16" (40.5cm) square out of white poplin.

2. Cut a 9½" (24cm) square out of contrasting fabric and of paper-backed fusible web.

3. Fuse the web on the wrong side of the contrasting fabric square. Cut the square in half diagonally so you have two triangles.

4. Remove paper backing and fuse contrasting triangles on opposite corners of the poplin square (Fig. 4.10).

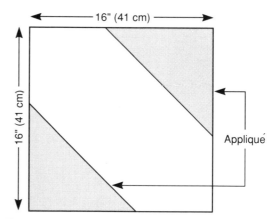

Fig. 4.10
Fuse contrasting triangles on opposite corners of the poplin square.

5. Appliqué the triangles (on the bias edges only) as described above for the contrasting appliqué on the placemat, using monofilament thread on the bobbin. This way the bobbin thread will not show when the lapkin is loaded with silverware and rolled up next to the placemat.

6. Cord the edge of the lapkin.

Machine Readiness Checklist	
Stitch:	zigzag (35, 7500; 4, 8000)
Length:	2
Width:	1.5–2
Foot:	H cording or one-groove cording
Needle:	14/90 stretch
Needle position:	center
Thread:	top, cotton, rayon, or acrylic embroidery to match contrasting fabric; bobbin, darning or basting
Feed dogs:	up
Tension:	top, loosened slightly; bobbin, normal
Tension:	top, loosened slightly; bobbin, normal
Accessories:	#5 pearl cotton

Place a strand of pearl cotton in the center clip in the foot and couch over it, guiding ¼" (6mm) from the raw edge. When you come to the corner, leave the needle on the inside corner, lift the presser foot, and pivot the work, pulling the cord so it will follow the second edge of the lapkin. Lower the foot and continue sewing. This gives the corner a slight curve.

7. Trim the excess fabric up to the stitching, being careful not to cut the stitches (Fig. 4.11). Using the F satin stitch foot satin-stitch around the outside edge of the lapkin with a 4–5 width satin stitch (see Fig. 8.25). Guide the fabric halfway under the foot so the needle stitches just over the cord on the left and swings off the raw edge on the right. Satin-stitch around the lapkin. Pull threads to the back and tie them off.

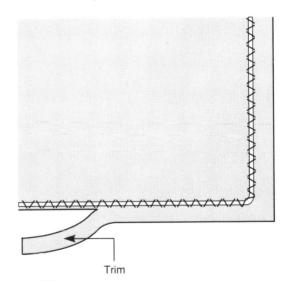

Trim

Fig. 4.11
Trim excess fabric up to the corded stitching, being careful not to cut the stitches.

Sew-How: *For a professional-looking satin-stitch corner, stop with the needle on the inside, lift the presser foot, pivot the fabric slightly, lower the foot, and then take a stitch over the cord and back, stopping with the needle on the inside corner in the same pivot hole as before. Continue so the stitches fan out to form the corner (Fig. 4.12). You may find it easier to release the foot pressure to "2" when stitching around the corner.*

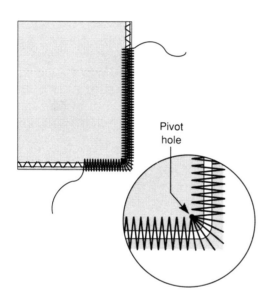

Fig. 4.12
To turn a corner with a satin stitch, stop with the needle at the inside corner. Lift presser foot and pivot fabric slightly. Lower foot, stitch, and pivot from the same pivot hole so stitches fan out around the corner.

8. Stitch the silverware slots. Fold the lapkin in half to make a triangle so the appliquéd corners are at the top and appliqués are on the inside. On the bottom of the triangle, measure 9″ (23cm) in from the left corner and mark a dot. Mark three more dots along the fold to the right, spacing them 1½″ (3.8cm) apart. Fold down top appliquéd corner, creasing it 6″ (15cm) above the first fold. Unfold corner, and draw a straight line on the crease using a vanishing marker.

9. Draw four lines perpendicular to the bottom fold, up to the line drawn on the crease, as shown in Fig. 4.13.

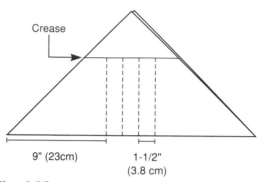

Fig. 4.13
Draw four lines perpendicular to the bottom fold, up to the line drawn on the crease. Straight-stitch over the lines to create the slots for the silverware to slip into.

10. Using all-purpose sewing thread to match the poplin, run four rows of straight-stitching from the fold to the line marked in Step 9, backstitching at the top and bottom of each row. Fold the appliquéd corner down and press. Slide a knife, fork, and spoon in each slot. Then roll up the lapkin and put it beside the placemat so the appliquéd corner shows (see color pages).

Lapkins can be made from scratch or from purchased fabric napkins to match your favorite table setting. For a formal occasion, make them out of linen; for backyard picnics and barbecues, use print bandanas. Play with different color schemes to learn how colors interact.

TRANSFERABLE LEARNINGS

The information and techniques you have learned by making this table setting have given you skills necessary to sew other projects. You have learned to:

• Build a color scheme in a room around the large surface areas, such as counter tops and floors.

• Identify the difference between blue-based and yellow-based colors.

• Use an odd number of colors in a room for interest.

• Identify the differences between a piece of fabric cut on the bias and one cut on the straight of grain.

• Stitch, clip, turn, and topstitch a facing to create the flap on the placemat. These techniques are used when sewing a collar or cuff or when lining a pocket.

• Make a machine-stitched buttonhole to fit a button. Use this technique on other projects.

• Sew a button on by machine. Now you can sew buttons on to stay.

• Topstitch using two threads through the seam needle to give a bolder look to any area you want to topstitch.

• Miter corners. This technique is handy for creating a fabric border on a quilt, mitering a corner with ribbon or trim, and mitering a placket on a sleeve or kick pleat.

• Couch a strand or two of pearl cotton to a base fabric. Use this method to provide a decorative topstitch or to edge appliqués.

• Cord a satin-stitched edge. This edge finish can be used to edge placemats, appliqués, or cut work, or to narrow-hem the edge of chiffon.

• Turn a satin-stitched corner so the stitches fan out from a pivot point. This technique is used to go around the corner of an appliqué and to turn a corner with a satin stitch.

Are you ready to try some machine-quilting techniques by making a small wall hanging? In Chapter 5, you'll try enough to find out whether you like machine quilting. If so, you can make a larger lap blanket or a full-sized quilt.

5 SEW A QUILT

What is a quilt? Robbie and Tony Fanning define it in *The Complete Book of Machine Quilting* (Chilton, 1980) as "a sandwich of three distinct layers: a *top*, some *filler* (usually called batting, regardless of the material used), and a *backing* (sometimes called a lining). The top is secured to the backing through the filler with thread to keep the three layers from shifting around."

Some quilts are stitched entirely by hand; others, entirely by machine; and still others are a combination of both. As much as I would like to try hand quilting, like many people these days, I don't have the time to perfect it—so let's quilt with our New Home.

The small quilt wall hanging we'll make in this chapter is designed to help you explore and practice the following machine-quilting techniques:

- free-machine quilting
- piecing and $\frac{1}{4}''$ seam allowances
- quilt-as-you-go
- stitch-in-the-ditch quilting
- adding borders
- straight-stitch quilting
- machine tying

As you gain experience in each of these techniques, you can decide whether you want to tackle bigger and more complex quilting projects on your New Home sewing machine.

Step One:
PLAN YOUR PROJECT

FABRIC SELECTION

To me, the most exciting part of making a quilt is selecting the fabric. However, it's also the most confusing. I used primary colors in this quilt project, as in the other projects in this book. Primary colors work well together, and I can use the fabric scraps from the other projects in my quilt. After all, isn't that what many quilts used to be—a collection of fabric scraps from "Susie's dress," "Johnny's shirt," and "Grandma's wedding dress"?

The best fabrics for quilting are light- to medium-weight woven cottons or cotton/polyester blends. Many fabric stores have a special section devoted to quilting fabrics and supplies. Before leaving the fabric store be sure to choose a batting.

Sew-How: For larger, more complex quilts, read Speed-Cut Quilts—1200 Speed-Cut Quilt Blocks *and* The Quilter's Guide to Rotary Cutting *by Donna Poster (Chilton, 1989, 1991). In the first book Donna not only presents principles of good color selection—talking about hue, value, and intensity of color—but also illustrates 400 quilt blocks in three sizes. She has devised an ingenious plan for selecting the yardage for each part of the block, lattice strips, and borders— what a time-saver! In the second book she shows how to cut any shape with your rotary cutter.*

Batting

Bonded polyester batting is the easiest batting to work with for machine quilting. It keeps its loft, is easy to handle, washes well, holds up well over years of use, and doesn't have to be quilted as closely as cotton batting. It also comes in a variety of sizes and weights. Use lighter weight batting for clothing and table coverings; use medium- to heavy-weight batting for quilts.

Preshrinking

Preshrink your fabric the way you intend to care for your quilt after construction. Wash light and dark fabrics separately to prevent dark colors from running on light-colored fabrics. Trim off all selvage edges *after* washing. It is not necessary to preshrink bonded polyester batting.

Sew-How: To cut down on raveling and tangling, snip a ¼" triangle off each of the four corners of your fabric before washing.*

NEEDLES, THREADS, BOBBINS, AND PRESSER FEET

Needles

As for any new project, for a quilting project your machine must be lint-free and outfitted with a new needle. For piecing, an 11/75 Blue Tip needle is recommended. For machine quilting, use a needle with a larger eye so the thread will not shred, wear, or break when you stitch through the quilt sandwich. A 14/90 universal or stretch needle works well. A curved hand needle is also helpful for hand basting the quilt sandwich (optional).

Threads

The rule of thumb for almost all sewing projects is to select a thread made of the same fiber or blend of fibers as the fabric. Because it's easier to repair stitches than to repair shredded fabric after the quilt has been washed a few times, use a thread that is less strong than the fabric. Therefore, if the top and backing are 100% cotton, use 100% cotton thread. If fabrics are a cotton/poly blend, a cotton-wrapped polyester (all-purpose) thread works well. If your fabric is lightweight, use a machine-embroidery thread to piece the top so the fabric won't pucker. When free-machine quilting, use a lighter-weight cotton machine-embroidery thread if possible. Choose colors to blend with the predominant colors of the top and backing fabrics.

Extra Bobbins

Before starting a quilting project, decide on the colors you'll be using and wind bobbins of each. This saves time and encourages more testing and experimentation because you don't have to take time to wind a bobbin.

Presser Feet

The presser feet used the most in machine quilting are described below:

• The P embroidery foot is used for free-machine quilting. It provides support around the needle and promotes better stitch formation when you stitch freely through the quilt sandwich (see Fig. 9.27).

• The A zigzag foot is for precise $\frac{1}{4}''$ seams (see Figs. 9.4, 9.5).

Sew-How: *There is a low-shank foot perfect for $\frac{1}{4}''$ seams called "the Little Foot" available through mail-order sources. Use it on New Home machines with a low shank.*

• The walking foot is for straight quilting and quilt-as-you-go techniques. It prevents the quilt sandwich from shifting and minimizes puckering (see Fig. 9.44).

OTHER MACHINE-QUILTING SUPPLIES

Machine quilters find the following items helpful (each is described in Chapter 1, under Step Two: Assemble Your Tools):

• Rotary cutter and mat—if you become a serious machine quilter, purchase the largest cutter and mat available.

• See-through cutting ruler—for accuracy, use one marked off every $\frac{1}{4}''$ and use the same ruler throughout a quilting project.

• Glass-head quilting pins—they're extra long and sharp and pin easily through the quilt sandwich. I love to use them for most other sewing, too.

• Nickel-plated safety pins, $1''$ long, to baste your quilt together. Nickel-plated pins will not rust, even if they remain in the quilt for some time.

• Water-erasable marking pen or disappearing dressmaker's chalk.

• $8''$ spring or screw-type embroidery hoop—necessary for free-machine quilting.

Step Two:

QUILTED WALL HANGING

This wall hanging is constructed from the center out. Let's preview how we'll make it together. First, the center medallion, or focal point, is free-machine quilted. Look for light- to medium-weight fabric with an allover print of big shapes, or a print panel. I used a child's print for my project. Note that yardage requirements and the size of the pieced border are based on a $10''$ center medallion square (see color pages).

Sew-How: *If you can't find a medallion print you like, create your own. Find an allover print and cut out shapes to appliqué to a solid-color background fabric.*

After the center medallion has been quilted, a pieced border is constructed. The most important principle to practice with machine quilting is accuracy—accuracy in measuring, cutting, and sewing.

Sew-How: *Notice that there are no metric conversions in this chapter. Machine quilting requires such precision and accuracy that I couldn't convert inches to centimeters closely enough to guarantee that each piece would fit.*

Next, the backing is attached. A lattice border and the pieced border are added in separate steps to frame the medallion. Each is attached to the batting and backing so that you can learn the quilt-as-you-go and stitch-in-the-ditch quilting techniques.

The last border is created by bringing the backing over the front. Corners are mitered; edges are turned under, then topstitched. This last "frame," created by the backing, is straight-stitch machine-quilted or "channel quilted" for depth and dimension.

Got the picture? Let's begin.

Supplies:

• 10″ square light- to medium-weight allover print or print panel for center medallion

• $\frac{1}{8}$ yd. each of black, white, and yellow solid-colored fabric and red mini-print cotton fabric (or colors to match your center medallion fabric)

• $\frac{5}{8}$ yd. blue print cotton fabric

• $\frac{5}{8}$ yd. medium-weight bonded batting

• three $\frac{3}{4}$″ plastic drapery rings

• curved hand needle, masking tape (optional), or nickel-plated safety pins

---

Sew-How: Before starting on your finished project, practice each technique on a scrap until you are comfortable with it. Put stitch samples in your notebook.

FREE-MACHINE QUILT THE MEDALLION

1. Because you're using bonded batting, you don't need a fabric backing to quilt the center medallion to. Lay batting on a large flat table and cut it into a 20″ square. Center and pin medallion on batting. Baste in place around four sides using the walking foot (see Fig. 9.44) and a 4–5 length straight stitch.

Machine Readiness Checklist	
Stitch:	straight (29 or 30, 7500; 1 or 2, 8000)
Length:	0
Width:	0
Foot:	P embroidery
Needle:	11/75 Blue Tip or 14/90 stretch
Thread:	cotton embroidery thread in predominant color of print background
Feed dogs:	down
Pressure:	1
Tension:	normal (auto)
Fabric:	center medallion print, batting
Accessories:	8″ spring or screw-type embroidery hoop, extension table (accessory box) to cover the free-arm

2. Put outer hoop of embroidery hoop on a flat surface. Place medallion, basted to the batting, over the hoop with the right side up. Loosen the screw on the inner hoop, or pinch the handles together on the spring hoop. Press in the inner hoop so the fabric is taut. Tighten the screw or release the handles on the inner hoop. Place project under the needle by tipping the hoop if necessary. Put presser bar lever down to engage the upper thread tension. Turn the flywheel one stitch or touch the needle up/down key, and then pull bobbin thread through the surface of the fabric. Take a few up-and-down locking stitches before cutting the threads off at the fabric.

Sew-How: To clip threads clean at the fabric use a small pair of curved-blade scissors. These may have come with your New Home; if not, they are available through mail-order sources. The blades are curved so they won't accidentally snip into the fabric while you are clipping off threads.

---

3. Begin stitching at medium speed while moving the fabric freely under the needle following the outline of the print medallion. Slowly stitch around each shape. If shapes are not connected, stitch around to where you started, take a few locking stitches by pushing the reverse/lock-off key, lift the presser foot to release the upper tension, and move the fabric to the next shape. Put the presser foot down, take a few locking stitches, then proceed as described above for all shapes (Fig. 5.1). Clip connecting threads and pull them to the wrong side.

Fig. 5.1
With project under the needle and darning foot, lower the presser bar lever, turn the flywheel one stitch or touch the needle up/down key, and pull the bobbin thread to the surface of the fabric. Lock a few stitches, and clip threads off at the fabric. Then free-machine quilt around shapes on your medallion.

ADD THE BACKING

Cut backing fabric 23″ square. Lay the backing, *wrong* side up, on a large, flat surface. Center the quilted medallion, right side up, on the backing so the lengthwise grain is parallel to the sides. Starting from the center and working out, baste the quilt sandwich together with safety pins, pinning safety pins every 3″–4″ through all layers across the medallion.

Sew-How: It is difficult to close the pins when the quilt is on the table. Therefore, simply pin into the quilt sandwich as if with a straight pin. Then pick up the quilt to close the safety pins. After each pin, straighten the backing by pulling on all four sides to avoid pinning in wrinkles.

Sew-How: For this small project, you may want to hand baste using a long running stitch. To do this, tape the backing, wrong side up, to a table top, smoothing out all the wrinkles. Center quilted medallion, right side up, over the backing. Using a curved needle and thread of a contrasting color, hand baste a row of 1″ basting stitches to the backing. Stitch a center row, then successive rows about 1½″ apart on either side, working from the center out (Fig. 5.2).

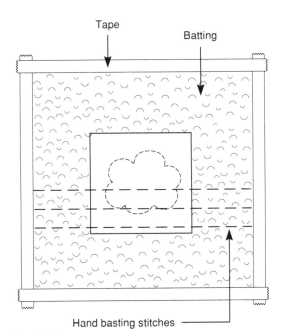

Tape

Batting

Hand basting stitches

Fig. 5.2
Hand baste quilted medallion to backing with a curved hand needle, making 1″ basting stitches and working from the center out.

PIECE A BORDER

1. Using the rotary cutter, mat, and see-through cutting ruler, cut two each 2″ × 12″ strips of black, white, yellow, red print, and blue print so the 12″ length is cut across the grain.

2. Cut one 3″ square each of black, yellow, red print, and blue print.

Machine Readiness Checklist	
Stitch:	straight (30, 7500; 2, 8000)
Length:	2.2–2.5
Width:	varies: 5 for Memory Craft models; de-center needle so the right edge of the foot is ¼″ from the needle
Foot:	A zigzag
Needle:	11/75 Blue tip or 10/70 universal
Thread:	all-purpose
Feed dogs:	up
Pressure:	normal
Tension:	normal (auto)
Needle position:	variable
Fabric:	a couple of strips cut as described in Step 1 above for practice stitching
Accessories:	sewing gauge, iron, and ironing board

3. Using two of your test strips, place right sides together and stitch an exact ¼″ seam. Check it for accuracy against the ¼″ mark on your seam gauge.

Sew-How: If there is not a clear-cut place on your presser foot or needle plate to guide for ¼″ seams, move your needle position slightly to the right or left as needed (see your Instruction Book to find out how to adjust your needle position). Accuracy is important. If you're off only $\frac{1}{16}$″, the overall difference measures ½″ ($\frac{1}{16}$″ multiplied by eight cut edges), which can throw off piecing and overall finished quilt dimensions.

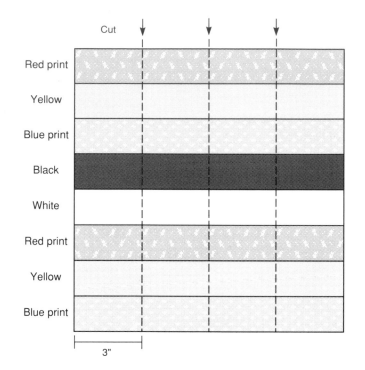

Cut

Red print

Yellow

Blue print

Black

White

Red print

Yellow

Blue print

3"

Fig. 5.3
Cut pieced border into four 3″ widths.

4. To make a pieced border, pin and stitch strips together in the order shown in Fig. 5.3, piecing with perfect ¼″ seams.

5. From the wrong side, press seam allowances flat and together to set the stitches. Then press the seams to one side toward the darker color. Cut pieced border into four 3″ widths (Fig. 5.3).

6. On one of the pieced border strips, stitch the yellow square so it is above the red print strip using a ¼″ seam allowance. On the other end of that strip, stitch the black square to the blue print strip.

7. On another pieced border strip, stitch the red print square to the blue print strip. On the other end of that strip, stitch the blue print square to the red print strip (Fig. 5.4). Press seams to one side toward the darker color and set these pieced border strips aside.

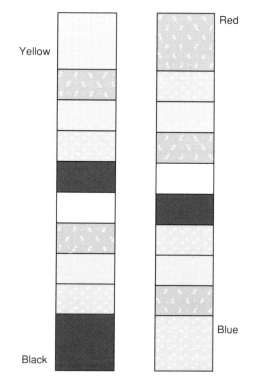

Yellow

Black

Red

Blue

Fig. 5.4
On one strip stitch yellow square next to red print, and stitch black square next to blue print. On another strip stitch red print square next to blue print, and stitch blue print square next to red print.

ADD LATTICE BORDER AND QUILT-AS-YOU-SEW

You will be using the walking foot to complete the rest of this quilt.

1. Cut two black border strips $1\frac{1}{2}'' \times 10''$. Cut two more black border strips $1\frac{1}{2}'' \times 12''$.

Machine Readiness Checklist	
Stitch:	straight (30, 7500; 2, 8000)
Length:	3–3.5
Width:	varies
Foot:	walking
Needle:	11/75 Blue Tip or 14/90 stretch
Thread:	top, all-purpose, to match border strips; bobbin, all-purpose, to match backing fabric
Feed dogs:	up
Tension:	normal (auto)

2. Remove any safety pins that may be in the way and pin short black border pieces, centering them on either side of quilted medallion. Stitch a $\frac{1}{4}''$ seam allowance starting and stopping at the ends of each border piece. Lock threads by pushing the reverse/lock-off key or by putting the stitch length to 0 and taking three to four stitches in one place; or pull threads to the front and tie them off. Press side border pieces so the seam allowance is to the inside (Fig. 5.5).

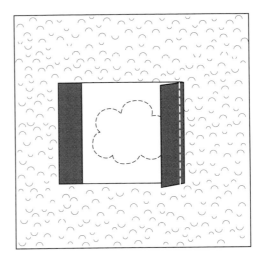

Fig. 5.5
Press side border pieces so the seam allowance is to the inside.

Sew-How: To tie a secure knot, give yourself thread tails at least 7'' long. Hold threads together in your left hand and form a loop (Fig. 5.6). Bring the

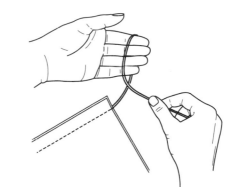

Fig. 5.6
Form a loop.

thread end around and through the loop (Fig. 5.7). Holding the loop in your left hand, work the loop down to the base and hold it in place with your left thumb (Fig. 5.8). Pull the thread taut with your right hand so the loop forms a knot at the base of the fabric.

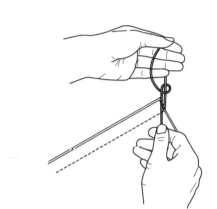

Fig. 5.7
Bring thread end around and through loop.

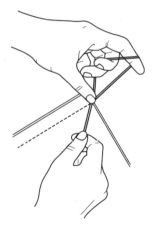

Fig. 5.8
Work loop down to the base of the stitch with your thumb.

3. Place longer border pieces across the top and bottom of the quilted medallion, right sides together, so ends are even with side border pieces. Pin and stitch, using $\frac{1}{4}''$ seams, starting and stopping $\frac{1}{4}''$ from the end of each strip. Pull threads to the back side and leave them free. Press longer border pieces so seam allowance is to the inside (Fig. 5.9).

Fig. 5.9
Press longer border pieces so seam allowances are to the inside.

ADD PIECED BORDERS AND QUILT-AS-YOU-GO

The pieced border is stitched in the same sequence as the frame border described above—the sides first, then the top and bottom strips. If you have pin-basted, remove safety pins that may get in the way of stitching.

1. Center short pieced borders (made previously) on each side, aligning cut edges, right sides together, against the frame border. Position the red print at the top for the shorter right pieced strip. Position the blue print at the top for the shorter left pieced strip (see color pages). This way contrasting fabric will be on either side of the squares in each corner.

2. Pin and stitch a ¼″ seam. Pull threads to the right side and tie them off as before. Press the seam flat. Repeat for the other side.

3. Place the longer pieced border strips so the red square is in the upper left corner, the yellow square is in the upper right, the black square is in the lower right corner, and the blue square is in the lower left (see color pages). Pin top and bottom strips so the square, piecing, and frame border match perfectly in each corner (Fig. 5.10, inset). Stitch a ¼″ seam. Pull threads to the right side of your work and tie them off.

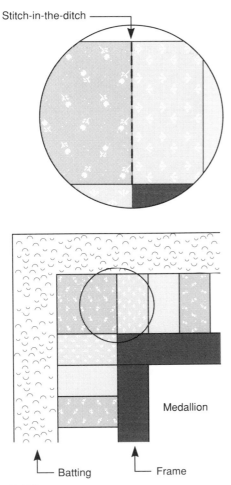

Stitch-in-the-ditch

Medallion

Batting   Frame

Fig. 5.10
Pin top and bottom strips so the square, piecing, and frame border match perfectly in each corner, as shown in the inset. Stitch-in-the-ditch on one side of the square in each corner.

Sew-How: Although sewing over pins is not generally recommended, you must stitch precisely when matching pieced sections. Therefore, slow down and carefully stitch over pins when quilting by machine. Remove pins afterward.

4. Press pieced border so seam allowance is to the inside. Stitch-in-the-ditch on one side of each corner square so the squares have been quilted around the two inside edges as shown in Fig. 5.10 (see also Figs. 8.8 and 9.44).

FINISH BACKING AND LAST BORDER

Instead of adding another border, the backing is brought over the front, encasing the batting and covering the raw edge of the pieced border.

You have handled your quilt a lot during its construction, so you may have to square up the batting and backing. Measure and trim where necessary so batting and backing are square.

1. Press a ½″ hem to the wrong side all the way around the backing square.

Sew-How: Instead of measuring, pinning, and pressing a narrow hem, take your sewing gauge to the ironing board and move the guide the desired distance required for the hem. Fold the edge over the end of the gauge so the raw edge is even with the guide, and press (Fig. 5.11). Continue down the length of the edge, folding and pressing as you go.

For longer hems, use this same pressing technique with a metal Dritz Ezy-Hem gauge, available in sewing stores.

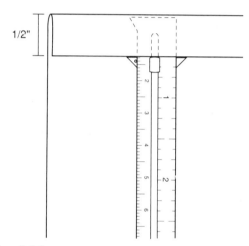

1/2"

Fig. 5.11
Fold fabric edge over end of gauge so raw edge is even with the guide. Press.

2. Miter each corner as described in Chapter 4 (Figs. 4.7, 4.8, 4.9). Note that once the stitching line is established, the miter in your quilt is made by stitching through the $\frac{1}{2}$" pressed hem made in Step 1 above.

3. Trim a $\frac{1}{2}$" square out of each corner of the batting to reduce bulk. Turn batting under $\frac{1}{2}$" all the way around. This extra loft gives a fuller look to the outside edge of the border.

4. Turn miter right side out. Pin backing so the hem edge covers the raw edges of the pieced border. Stitch $\frac{1}{16}$" inside the folded edge (Fig. 5.12).

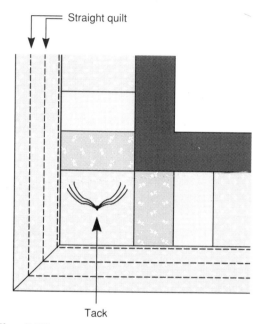

Straight quilt

Tack

Fig. 5.12
Using the walking foot, straight quilt two rows inside the backing border, $\frac{5}{8}$" apart.

Sew-How: For precise stitching, guide the folded edge by the inside of the presser foot. Then move the needle position so stitching is $\frac{1}{16}$" from the fold.

STRAIGHT-STITCH QUILTING

1. Using the walking foot, and top and bobbin thread to match the backing, straight-stitch quilt $\frac{5}{8}$" inside the backing border. Quilt another row, $\frac{5}{8}$" next to the first (see Fig. 5.12). Either guide the stitching by a line on your needle plate or put masking tape on the needle plate to use as a guide.

2. Turn your quilt over. You should see a square quilted in each corner and two concentric squares quilted in the middle around the medallion. Look at the threads you have not tied off yet. Are they even with the outside concentric square? If not, loosen a couple of stitches so the rows meet. Then tie off free threads. You should do three rows of straight quilting around the edge of the quilt to create a border.

3. Hand stitch plastic drapery rings on the top back of the wall hanging.

TIE A QUILT

Another option to the quilt-as-you-go or stitch-in-the-ditch quilting you did at the squares in each corner is to tie the quilt together. Use the multiple zigzag (36, 7500; 18, 8000) and tack a triple strand of a 3″–4″ length of pearl cotton in the center of the strand, through the quilt sandwich (see Fig. 8.34). Lock and tie off the stitches; then tie the pearl cotton into a square knot. Clip ends to $\frac{1}{2}$″. You could also use the F satin stitch foot and tie using a single decorative stitch such as the heart (118, 7500; 111, 8000).

TRANSFERABLE LEARNINGS

The information and techniques you have learned and practiced by constructing the quilted wall hanging have given you skills necessary to sew other projects. You have learned how to:

• Preshrink woven fabrics by snipping a triangle off each corner to cut down on raveling. This is helpful when preshrinking any woven fabric.

• Measure, mark, and cut accurately— necessary for tailoring and more complicated quilting projects.

• Move the fabric freely under a stitching needle. The movement and technique for free-machine quilting are similar to those used for free-machine embroidery.

• Use a larger-eyed needle when stitching through quilt sandwich or other heavy fabric so thread won't shred or break.

• Quilt using the stitch-in-the-ditch technique. The same technique is used to tack down facings and waistbands.

• Quilt with a straight stitch (30, 7500; 2, 8000) to create a textured border. This technique is done with the walking foot to stitch yardage that is cut for jacket linings, tote bag linings, and so on. Using a lighter-weight batting and the F satin stitch foot and L quilter you can straight-stitch quilt table coverings and other lighter-weight projects.

• Create a border for a quilt or any wall hanging by turning the backing over the front and mitering the corners.

• Adjust your needle position, rather than moving the fabric, for precise seam allowances and topstitching.

• Press a narrow hem using your seam gauge and iron, which saves a lot of hand pinning.

• Tie a quilt using the multiple zigzag (36, 7500; 18, 8000). This technique is also a way to tack down facings, small appliqués, and embroideries.

In the next chapter, "Sew Toys," we'll make stuffed fabric blocks and a stuffed hobbyhorse, whimsical projects that can help you discover what fun it is to use the fringe foot and a rug fork you can make yourself.

SEW TOYS

Step One:
PLAN YOUR PROJECTS

Fabric lends itself beautifully to making toys. It's pliable, washable, and, when stuffed, irresistibly cuddly. In this chapter, new sewers start by making fabric blocks. The principles learned here will be helpful in making other stuffed fabric structures, so don't skip this section because you don't currently have a little person in your life. Instead, decorate the blocks and make them smaller for Christmas ornaments, or make them much larger and use canvas or Naugahyde for a hassock or a beanbag chair.

The hobbyhorse is made of both straight and curved shapes, so you'll clip and notch seam allowances to make smooth, continuous curves. You'll also use the fringe foot to make eyelashes and use a rug fork to make the mane—these accessories help you to add texture and dimension to projects.

FABRIC AND THREAD

The fabrics and supplies used in both projects are easy to work with: woven cotton/polyester blends, felt, and polyester fiberfill.

Make both projects washable by preshrinking the fabric in the same way you plan to take care of the finished project. Although you may come across wool felt, for this project look for washable polyester felt, available in a rainbow of colors at your local fabric or craft store. Make the mane of the hobbyhorse out of a washable nylon or cotton yarn.

Because both the blocks and the hobbyhorse are constructed of several colors of fabric, use nylon monofilament thread, top and bobbin, unless directed otherwise. This way you don't have to rethread with each fabric color change.

Step Two:
JUMBO FABRIC BLOCKS

The following instructions are for making three fabric blocks at a time.

Supplies:

- $\frac{1}{4}$ yd. (23cm) each of woven cotton/polyester in a red print and green print and in blue, black, white, and yellow solids

- 2 black polyester felt squares

- $\frac{1}{2}$ bag of polyester fiberfill (save remainder for hobbyhorse)

- nylon monofilament thread

- red, blue, green, white, and yellow all-purpose, rayon, 100% cotton, or acrylic embroidery thread

- 5″ wide (12.5cm) strip of paper-backed fusible web (if you are making the game board later in this book, buy a yard [meter])

- rotary cutter, mat, and see-through ruler

- tracing paper and vanishing marker

- iron-on freezer wrap

- print motif fabric to cut appliqués from (e.g., trucks, airplanes, flowers, etc.)

- woven fusible interfacing

- blunt-nosed scissors, point turner, or wooden spoon

DECORATE THE SQUARES

1. Cut three 6″ (15cm) squares each in white, black, blue, and yellow solids and in green print and red print.

2. At your local copy center, enlarge the letters to twice the size shown in Fig. 6.1. Using the tracing paper and marker, trace letters from the photocopy to make your pattern.

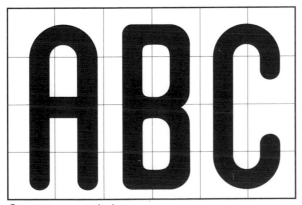

One square = one inch.
Pattern is 1/2 size.

Fig. 6.1

Trace letters to make the pattern for the fabric blocks.
Pattern is half-size.

3. Fuse paper-backed fusible web on the wrong side of the black felt squares and the appliqué fabric, following manufacturer's instructions.

4. Cut out three each of the letters from the black felt and remove the paper backing.

- Center and fuse the letter A to two red squares and one yellow square.

- Center and fuse the letter B to two blue squares and one green square.

- Center and fuse the letter C to two green squares and one yellow square.

- Center and fuse the appliqués cut from printed fabric to the three white squares.

5. Stitch black felt letters to the squares.

Machine Readiness Checklist	
Stitch:	straight (29 or 30, 7500; 1 or 2, 8000)
Length:	2.2–2.5
Width:	0; varies
Foot:	A zigzag, G or G adjustable blind hem
Needle:	11/75 Blue Tip
Needle Position:	varies
Thread:	nylon monofilament
Feed dogs:	up
Tension:	normal (auto)

Straight-stitch around each letter guiding $\frac{1}{8}$″ (3mm) from the cut edge.

Sew-How: *If you use the G or G adjustable blind hem foot, guide the edge of the letter along the inside right edge of the guide. You may have to decenter the needle slightly to stitch $\frac{1}{8}$″ (3mm) from the edge (see your* Instruction Book *and see Figs. 9.10 and 9.17).*

Backstitch or touch the reverse/lock-off key to lockstitch at the beginning and end of each letter. Press each lettered square with the right side down using a hot iron and steam.

6. Stitch around the appliqué with a 2 width satin stitch (see Fig. 8.25).

7. Iron freezer wrap to the wrong side of each decorated square. Fuse woven interfacing to the wrong side of each undecorated square. Stack the decorated squares and set them to one side of your machine. Set the undecorated squares aside.

Machine Readiness Checklist

Stitch:	zigzag (35, 7500; 4, 8000)
Length:	0.3–0.5
Width:	2
Foot:	F satin stitch
Thread:	top: red, blue, yellow, green, and white rayon, 100% cotton, or acrylic embroidery; bobbin: darning, basting, or nylon monofilament
Tension:	top, loosened slightly; bobbin, normal

---

8. Top thread your machine with red thread. With the right side up, stitch a row of satin stitches, guiding $\frac{1}{2}''$ (1.3cm) from the raw edge of one side of each square.

9. Using yellow thread on one side, blue thread on one side, and green thread on one side of each square, rethread and satin-stitch $\frac{1}{2}''$ (1.3mm) from the raw edge (Fig. 6.2).

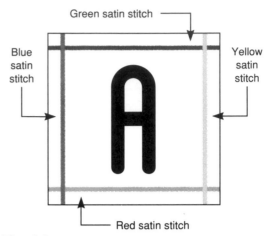

Fig. 6.2

With red thread, stitch a row of satin stitches, guiding $\frac{1}{2}''$ (1.3cm) from the raw edge on one side of each square. Rethread and repeat for the other three sides, using yellow thread on one side, blue thread on one side, and green thread on one side.

Sew-How: *On those sides where the thread color matches the fabric, satin-stitch with white thread.*

Sew-How: *To satin-stitch each square quickly, butt one square up to the next, and satin-stitch one side, stitching one color at a time. When stitched, the squares resemble a kite tail. Clip threads between the squares to separate them then restack for the next satin-stitched color (see Fig. 8.32).*

ASSEMBLE JUMBO BLOCKS

1. Separate squares so each block is made of one appliqué square, three letter squares (A, B, and C), and two plain squares. Remove the freezer wrap from the decorated squares. Using the vanishing marker, mark dots $\frac{1}{4}''$ (6mm) from each corner on each square.

2. With right sides together, pin lettered A, B, and C squares next to each other. Then pin appliquéd square next to the letter C square as shown. Straight-stitch squares together using exact ¼″ (6mm) seam allowances starting and stopping seams at each dot (Fig. 6.3). Press seams flat and together; then press seams open. Press ¼″ (6mm) seam allowances on the two short ends of the row of stitched squares.

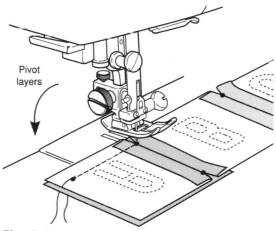

Fig. 6.4
Align the bottom of A square to one side of plain bottom square, and stitch a ¼″ (6mm) seam, starting and stopping at the dots in the corner.

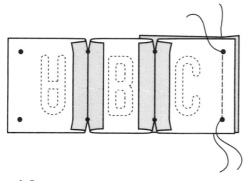

Fig. 6.3
Mark a dot ¼″ (6mm) from the corner in each square. Pin A, B, C, and appliquéd squares together, and stitch ¼″ (6mm) seams, starting and stopping at the dots in each corner.

4. Lift the presser foot and pivot work 90 degrees. Align the bottom of the B square with the corresponding side of the bottom square. Lower the presser foot and stitch the bottom of the B square to the second side of the plain square, stopping with the needle in the dot at the corner (Fig. 6.5). Repeat for the other two sides of the bottom square to create the block.

Sew-How: *To save time hand tying threads at the beginning and end of each seam, start and stop each seam by touching the reverse/lock-off key. (This feature is not on all New Homes, so check your Instruction Book or call your dealer and ask about it.)*

---

3. With right sides together, align the bottom of the A square to one side of the plain bottom square, matching dots. Place the block under the A zigzag foot so the plain square that makes the bottom of the block is against the feed dogs. Starting at the dot and ¼″ (6mm) from the corner, sew the first side, stopping with your needle in the fabric at the dot in the opposite corner (Fig. 6.4).

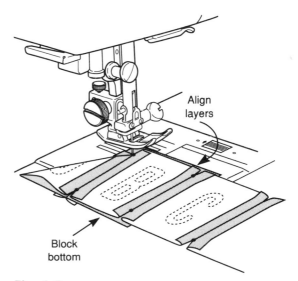

Fig. 6.5
Pivot both layers 90 degrees, and align the bottom of B square with the corresponding side of bottom square. Stitch to the next dot. Repeat for the other two sides.

5. Repeat Step 3 to stitch the top square to the block (Fig. 6.6). Clip the corners of the top and bottom squares.

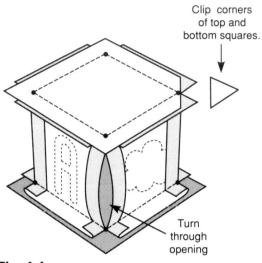

Clip corners of top and bottom squares.

Turn through opening

Fig. 6.6
Stitch the top plain square as shown to create the rest of the block.

6. Turn the block right side out, through the opening. Using a pair of blunt-nosed scissors or a point turner, gently push out each corner of the block so it's sharp and square.

7. Using a handful of fiberfill, begin stuffing the block until it is comfortably full. Use scissor points, a wooden spoon handle, or a point turner to push fiberfill into each corner.

8. Turn the seam allowance of the opening toward the inside of the block, and pin the opening shut.

9. Decenter your needle to the far left (29, 7500; 1, 8000) (see your *Instruction Book*), and straight-stitch the opening closed guiding ⅛″ (3mm) from the edge. Tie off thread ends.

Aren't the blocks cute? And they're so easy to make. Now, are you ready for something more challenging? Then let's make the hobbyhorse.

Step Three:
HOBBYHORSE

Supplies:

• ½ yd. (45cm) red cotton print

• ⅛ yd. (11.5cm) blue-and-white cotton print

• 1 black polyester felt scrap for eyes and nostrils

• 1 white polyester felt scrap for eyes

• one-oz. (28g) ball of cotton or nylon yarn for mane

• two 1″ (2.5cm) red or blue buttons for the bridle

• nylon monofilament thread

• black cotton, rayon, or acrylic embroidery thread

• all-purpose thread to coordinate with other fabrics (optional)

• paper-backed fusible web

• ½ bag of polyester fiberfill (remainder of that used for Jumbo Fabric Blocks)

• graph paper (1″ [2.5cm] square preferred), tracing paper, pencil

• French curve (optional)

• 2 yd. (183cm) blue 1″ (2.5cm) grosgrain ribbon for bridle and reins

• size #3 pearl cotton

• hand needle

• 1 broom handle

• heavy wire coat hanger

• adding-machine tape

• liquid seam sealant (e.g., Fray Check or Stop Fraying)

• dressmaker's chalk

MAKE THE PATTERN

1. If you have access to a photocopy machine, enlarge the pattern two times the size shown in Figs. 6.7, 6.8, and 6.9. Note that the gusset must be joined at the arrows as shown.

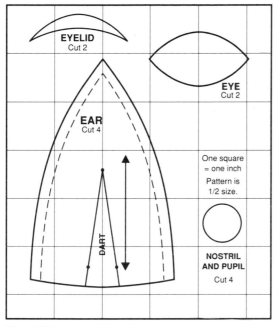

Fig. 6.7
Hobbyhorse pattern ear and eye pieces. Pattern is half-size.

2. Use the French curve, moving and pivoting it between the dots marked, to approximate the curves. Note that each pattern piece includes the seam allowance. The ear pattern uses $\frac{1}{4}''$ (6mm) seam allowances; other pattern pieces have $\frac{5}{8}''$ (1.6cm) seam allowances.

3. On each pattern piece, mark the grain line, dots, and ear and eye placement; then label each piece and mark how many of each one to cut.

MAKE THE HORSE

1. Fuse a piece of paper-backed fusible web to the underside of the black and white felt pieces. Cut out eye pieces and nostrils. Remove the paper backing from the black pupils. Center and fuse the pupils to the white eye pieces. Remove paper from eyelids. Align outside curve and fuse.

2. Lay out and cut the horse pattern pieces, following the grain lines marked on each piece. Cut gusset and ear pieces from blue-and-white print. Cut face pieces from red print.

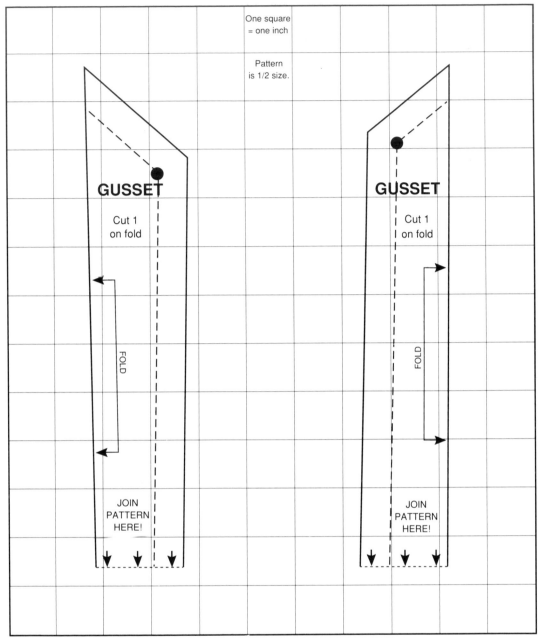

Join two pieces to form one pattern

Fig. 6.8
Hobbyhorse pattern gusset piece. Pattern is half-size.

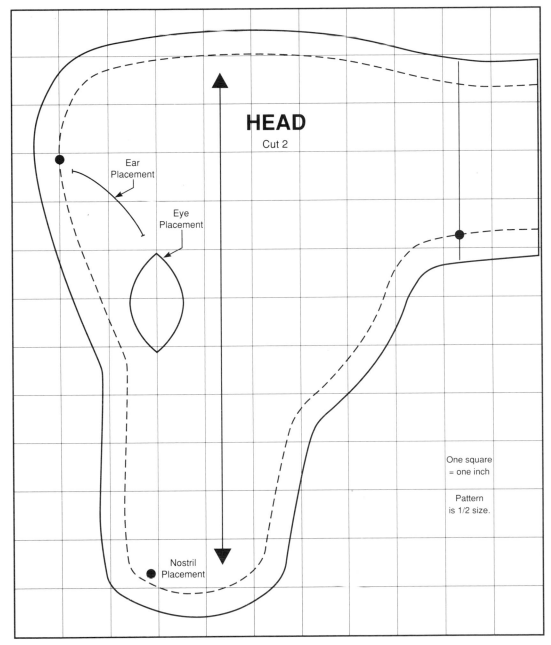

HEAD

Cut 2

Ear
Placement

Eye
Placement

Nostril
Placement

One square
= one inch

Pattern
is 1/2 size.

Fig. 6.9
Hobbyhorse pattern head piece. Pattern is half-size.

3. Mark darts on ear pieces by pushing pins straight through the dots as shown; then mark with chalk (Fig. 6.10).

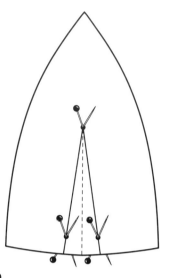

Fig. 6.10
Mark darts on ear pieces by pushing pins straight through the dots on both pattern pieces.

Ears

Machine Readiness Checklist	
Stitch:	straight (29 or 30, 7500; 1 or 2, 8000)
Length:	2.2–2.5
Width:	0
Foot:	A zigzag
Needle:	11/75 Blue Tip
Thread:	all-purpose to match fabric or nylon monofilament
Feed dogs:	up
Tension:	normal (auto)

1. Fold and stitch darts; then press dart to one side over a pressing ham.

New Sewer's Note: *A dart makes a curved shape out of a flat piece of fabric. Start stitching a dart at the wide end, stitching to the point. Do not backstitch at the point because you may end up with a pouch that will not press out. Tie off threads at the point of the dart.*

2. Place two ear pieces right sides together and sew a $\frac{1}{4}''$ (6mm) seam with a 2 length straight stitch, leaving the straight side open. Clip across the point at the top, close to the stitching line (Fig. 6.11). Press ear flat. Repeat for other ear.

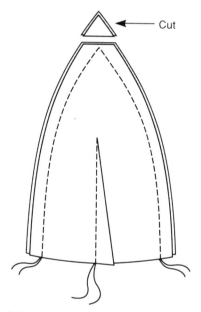

Fig. 6.11
Place two ear pieces right sides together and sew a $\frac{1}{4}''$ (6mm) seam with a 2 length straight stitch. Clip across the point and press seams flat and together.

3. Trim seam allowance to $\frac{1}{8}''$ (3mm). Turn ears right side out. Gently push point out with the blunt end of scissors or with a point turner. Turn under the raw edge $\frac{1}{4}''$ (6mm) at the base of each ear and press.

4. Stuff a little fiberfill in each ear, pushing it to the points with blunt-nosed scissors or point turner. Do not overstuff.

5. Turn under raw edge ¼" (6mm) and pin.

Head

1. Remove paper from eye piece and fuse the eye to the head as marked.

Machine Readiness Checklist	
Stitch:	straight (29 or 30, 7500; 1 or 2, 8000); zigzag (35, 7500; 4, 8000)
Length:	2.2–2.5
Width:	0; 4
Foot:	F satin stitch; fringe
Thread:	nylon monofilament; black cotton, rayon, or acrylic embroidery
Feed dogs:	up
Tension:	top, loosened slightly; bobbin, normal

With the nylon monofilament thread, topstitch ⅛" (3mm) from the cut edge, first on the white eye piece and then on pupil.

2. Rethread top and bobbin with black thread. Using the fringe foot, stitch the eyelashes on each eye guiding the middle of the foot where eyelid and white pieces overlap (see Fig. 9.33).

Sew-How: *At press time, there was not a fringe foot that fit the Memory Craft 8000 because it has a high shank. Check with your New Home dealer to see if this foot is now available in a snap-on version, or check with mail-order sources for a generic snap-on fringe foot.*

3. Position and pin ears on each side of the head. Whipstitch ears to head pieces.

New Sewer's Note: *A whipstitch is an overhand stitch done with a hand needle and thread to join two edges tightly. To do this stitch, thread a needle and tie or sew a knot. Insert the needle at right angles and close to the folded edge, picking up a few threads from the ear and head fabrics. Stitches should be close together and slightly angled so ears are stitched securely to the head piece (Fig. 6.12).*

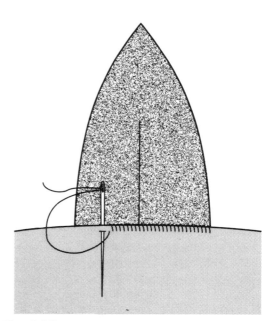

Fig. 6.12
Whipstitch ears to head piece by inserting the hand needle at right angles and close to the folded edge, picking up a few threads from the ear and head fabrics. Stitch close together and at a slight angle so ears are stitched securely to the head.

4. Clip ½" (1.3cm) into gusset and head piece seam allowance where it turns a corner.

New Sewer's Note: A clip is a short, ½" (1.3cm) cut in a ⅝" (1.5cm) seam allowance. When stitching a straight piece to a curved or angled piece of fabric, clipping allows a curve or corner to open and lie flat so the fabric pieces fit together easily. For an inside, concave curve, the straight piece is clipped when joined to an outside curve. Use your scissor tips to clip so you don't cut too far into the seam allowance. Don't cut too much; you can always cut more, but you can never cut less.

Starting at the dot on the wide end of the gusset, place right sides together, pinning one head piece to one side of the gusset, following down and around the head piece to the dot at the neck.

5. Straight-stitch on the ⅝" (1.5cm) seam allowance, stitching from the dot at the top of the head and stopping at the dot at the neck. Repeat pinning, clipping, and stitching procedure for the other side of the head piece. Seams should come together at the point of each gusset. Clip seam allowance at each curve as shown (Fig. 6.13). Turn right side out.

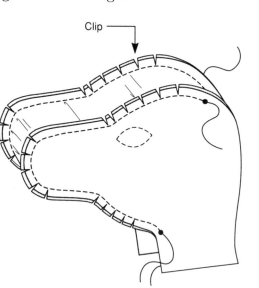

Fig. 6.13
Clip ½" (1.3cm) into gusset seam allowance each time it turns a corner. Also clip into the seam allowance at each curve as shown so the fabric smoothly follows the curve of the seam.

6. Place nostrils at the end of the nose and fuse in place. Zigzag tack in the center of each nostril (see Fig. 8.28). It may be easier to stitch this with the head turned inside out.

Make the Fringe Fork

Jackie Dodson, author of *Twenty Easy Machine-Made Rugs* (Chilton, 1990), makes various sizes of fringe forks out of heavy wire coat hangers. She says, "Fringe forks come in various sizes. Buy them or make your own. To make a fringe fork, first decide how high you want the fringe. Will you stitch one side? Then make the fork the size of the fringe plus ¼" (6mm) to allow for the thickness of the fork and stitches. If you plan to stitch down the center of the fringe fork, double the height of the fringe plus ¼" (6mm). For example, for fringe 1" (2.5cm) high, make the fringe fork twice this, or 2" (5cm) plus ¼" (6mm) or 2¼" (5.7cm) wide." To make the fringe fork, cut the longest straight side of a heavy coat hanger with wire cutters. Then bend it with pliers, squaring it off at one end so the tines are the desired distance apart.

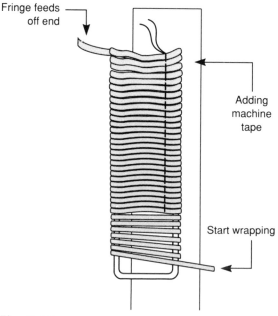

Fig. 6.14
Bend a length of heavy coat hanger into a fringe fork.

Mane and Bangs

1. Cut a piece of adding-machine tape 24″ (61 cm) long. Wrap fringe fork with yarn and straight-stitch yarn to adding-machine tape so the line of stitching is to one side to make fringe for the mane (see Fig. 6.14).

2. Cut off about 4½″ (11.5 cm) of fringe. Pull off the adding-machine tape and pin fringe across the widest part of the gusset (forehead) to make bangs, positioning the long loops toward the nose.

Sew-How: After adding-machine tape has been removed, the fringe "grows" in length a little bit.

Machine Readiness Checklist	
Stitch:	straight (29 or 30, 7500; 1 or 2, 8000)
Length:	3
Width:	0
Foot:	F satin stitch
Thread:	all-purpose to match fringe or nylon monofilament
Feed dogs:	up
Tension:	normal (auto)

Stitch fringe to gusset, centering the needle over the original stitching line. Cut another length of fringe, shorter than the first. Pin and straight-stitch it above the first row of fringe, overlapping it slightly so the long loops hide the previous row of stitching. Repeat until the crown is covered with fringe, stitching one row of fringe above the next. Cut loops after the fringe is secured to the crown.

3. Turn the head inside out. Carefully remove adding-machine tape from the unused fringe. Pin back head pieces, right sides together, sandwiching fringe in the seam allowance. Stop fringe 1½″ (3.8 cm) from the neck opening (Fig. 6.15). Stitch seam.

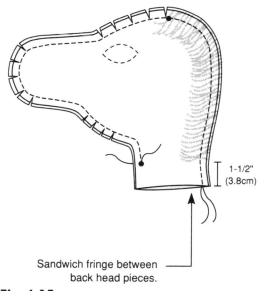

Sandwich fringe between back head pieces.

1-1/2″ (3.8cm)

Fig. 6.15
Sandwich fringe between the two head pieces. Stop fringe 1½″ (3.8cm) from the neck opening and stitch.

Sew-How: You may have some fringe left. It will be used to thicken the top of the mane.

---

4. Turn up the raw neck edge ½″ (1.3cm) to the wrong side and press. Gather over a 10″ (25.5cm) length of pearl cotton around the neck opening (see Fig. 8.22) guiding ⅛″ (3mm) from fold.

5. Turn the head right side out. Take the remainder of the fringe and fold it in half on the stitching line. Starting at the top of the mane, sandwich loose fringe around the fringe stitched in the seam. Straight-stitch loose fringe to the mane, backstitching at beginning and end. Cut yarn loops. **Note:** If machine stitching is too cumbersome, use a double thread and hand stitch this extra fringe to the mane.

6. Stuff the head with fiberfill. The neck opening should be large enough for you to reach your hand in to stuff fill into the corners. If it isn't, use a ruler or a wooden spoon to push fill in place.

Bridle

1. Put ribbon around the end of the nose so it fits snugly. Cut and seam it into a circle. Put the larger length of ribbon at right angles to create the reins. Seam it into a circle. Pin the bridle together where the ribbons intersect, long ribbon beneath short ribbon circle, so the seam on the small ribbon is under the chin and the seam of large ribbon is under the intersection (Fig. 6.16). (You may have to put the bridle on the horse for proper positioning.)

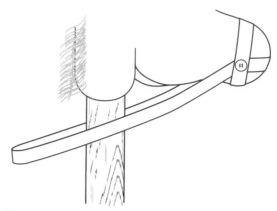

Fig. 6.16
To make the bridle, put a circle of ribbon around the nose and seam it together. Put a longer length of ribbon at right angles to the first. Pin where ribbons intersect, so the seam on the first ribbon is under the chin, and the seam of the large ribbon is under the intersection. Machine stitch buttons at each intersection.

2. In order to stitch the buttons in place, remove the bridle and machine stitch a button on each side where the ribbons intersect (see Figs. 8.17, 9.30, 9.31).

3. Hand tack the bridle at each seam line so it won't slip off when the hobbyhorse is played with.

4. Put the broom handle up in the head. You may have to stuff extra fiberfill around the broom handle to secure it.

5. Draw up pearl cotton to gather the neck around the broom handle, and tie securely.

TRANSFERABLE LEARNINGS

The information and techniques you have learned by making the fabric blocks and hobbyhorse have given you the skills necessary to sew many other projects. You have learned to:

• Enlarge and draw a pattern from a reduced version using graph paper and a curve—this process is useful for enlarging other patterns. Using a curve is also helpful when making some pattern alterations.

• Stitch, turn, stuff, and close three-dimensional shapes. Techniques are the same for stuffed toys, some pillows, a hassock, or a beanbag chair.

• Insert a gusset. Use this technique in garment construction, as well as for slipcovers, pillows, and cushions.

• Use paper-backed fusible web to make any fabric fusible.

• Properly fuse one fabric to the other with heat, moisture, and pressure.

• Appliqué using a straight stitch on a nonraveling fabric. Use this technique with leather, vinyl, or suede. Use a satin stitch for those fabrics that ravel.

• Sew a dart. Darts are used in other projects to create shape so that a pattern piece conforms to the shape of the body.

• Use the fringe foot to make eyelashes.

• Make yarn fringe using the fringe fork. You can make fringe trim this way to match any fabric, rather than searching for fringe trim by the yard.

• Gather over a cord for even gathers. This also adds strength to the gathering stitch so thread won't break. This technique can be used to gather almost any medium-to-heavy fabric.

I hope that in addition to your exploring another spoke in our World of Sewing, your family members or friends will enjoy playing with the blocks and hobbyhorse you made as you stitched your way through this chapter.

In the next chapter you will further your sewing knowledge by making some gifts. The key rings are great for anyone and take as long to make as it would take to shop for something—and each is personalized for the recipient. The fabric game board also makes a welcome gift, offering peaceful travel time in a car or plane and fun on family vacations.

SEW GIFTS

When people know you sew, even if it's only once in a while, friends and family sometimes expect a handmade gift. In this chapter, we'll make a few quick gifts using a little ribbon or fabric scraps—you probably have most of the supplies on hand. We will also make a fabric game board and game piece pouch, a welcome gift for family members or friends.

Step One:
PLAN YOUR PROJECTS

Everyone has a set of keys, so let's stitch some decorative key rings. To make one of these key rings I bought a simple metal key ring from the hardware store; the others are kits from a cross-stitch shop. The rest of the supplies required are listed under each project.

These small embroideries showcase your stitchery, so use rayon, or acrylic embroidery thread because they have a lot of shine and fill in better than all-purpose thread.

The game board is made of cotton-blend prints and solids, cotton/polyester hem facing (available in 2½-yard [2.3m] packages at your local fabric store), felt, grosgrain ribbon, yarn, and paper-backed fusible web. The game pouch is made from a red cotton blend, a black-and-white checked fabric, a zipper, and scraps of turquoise and yellow solids.

Sew-How: *For a perfect color match to the game board, I had to make this pouch out of knit fabrics. If you, too,* *have difficulty finding woven fabrics for your pouch, stabilize the knit by fusing a piece of stable interfacing to the wrong side of each fabric. Then it behaves like a woven fabric.*

To make your game board washable, preshrink all the fabrics, except the paper-backed fusible web and the washable polyester felt (washable polyester felt is available at most fabric stores.)

To preshrink hem facing tape without uncreasing the prefolded edges, bend the cardboard and immerse the tape in very hot tap water leaving it wrapped around the cardboard core; then roll it in a towel to remove most of the moisture. Leave the tape on the cardboard and dry on a towel.

You will also use nylon monofilament thread in both the key ring and the game board projects. This way, you don't have to rethread the top and bobbin each time you change the fabric color.

Step Two:
THREE KEY RINGS

My machine can stitch letters and numbers, a feature I thought I would use only rarely but which I have come to appreciate. If your New Home has the same capacity, make a script monogrammed key ring (Fig. 7.1).

Fig. 7.1
Key ring projects.

MAKE THE MONOGRAMMED KEY RING

I subscribe to a lot of needlecraft magazines to see how stitchery of all kinds is stitched and displayed. Although I don't hand cross-stitch, I found many great gift ideas for small stitchery in one of the cross-stitch magazines, which inspired me to seek out a cross-stitch shop in my area. Once there, I found kits of all kinds for bookmarks, paperweights, trivets, and the key ring kits described below—which provide an easy way to frame small embroideries stitched on the sewing machine so you can give them away as gifts. Take the opportunity to stop into a cross-stitch shop in your area or subscribe to needlecraft magazines for these and other ingenious gift ideas. **Note:** If you can't find key ring kits in your area, skip ahead to the "fob" key ring instructions.

Machine Readiness Checklist	
Stitch:	lettering
Length:	varies
Width:	widest
Foot:	F satin stitch
Needle:	14/90 stretch
Thread:	top, rayon or acrylic embroidery; bobbin, darning or basting
Tension:	top, loosened slightly; bobbin, normal
Fabric:	$1\frac{1}{2}''$ × $1\frac{1}{2}''$ (3.8cm × 3.8cm) grosgrain ribbon or felt
Accessories:	key ring kit, iron-on freezer wrap, vanishing marker

1. Iron freezer wrap to the wrong side of the ribbon or felt. (Make a test swatch to determine letter spacing.) Mark where to start the lettering and draw a line with the vanishing marker so the lettering is straight.

2. Program initials and stitch them slowly (see your *Instruction Book*). Remove the freezer wrap. Press top and bottom up desired amount to fit in acrylic key ring frame. (The key ring kit is similar to a watch. The stitchery fits into a small frame, then a crystal snaps in place over the top.)

MAKE THE ROUND KEY RING

The round key ring is satin-stitched with an off-center plaid design and embroidered initials in one corner.

Machine Readiness Checklist

Stitch:	zigzag (35, 7500; 4, 8000)
Length:	0.4–0.6
Width:	widest
Foot:	F satin stitch
Needle:	14/90 stretch
Thread:	red and blue rayon or acrylic embroidery
Feed dogs:	up
Tension:	top, slightly loosened; bobbin, normal
Fabric:	closely woven kettle (weaver's) cloth
Accessories:	key ring kit, iron-on freezer wrap, vanishing marker, liquid seam sealant (optional)

1. Iron freezer wrap to the wrong side of your fabric. Remove the crystal from key ring and trace the circle on your fabric. Mark a straight line to follow for the first row of satin stitching.

2. Thread top and bobbin with red thread. Satin-stitch (35, 7500; 4, 8000) one row, starting and stopping just inside the circle. Remove work from the machine and draw another line perpendicular to the first. Satin-stitch (35, 7500; 4, 8000) following that line.

3. Rethread top and bobbin with blue thread. Satin-stitch (35, 7500; 4, 8000) next to the first row of red satin stitches, starting and stopping just inside the circle. Turn your work perpendicular and repeat.

4. Rethread top and bobbin with red thread. Program the appropriate initials. Test for spacing on a scrap. Mark where to start lettering with the vanishing marker. Stitch initials and then remove freezer wrap. Pull threads to the wrong side and tie them off.

Sew-How: Put a drop of liquid seam sealant on each knot so the knots won't pull out.

5. Cut embroidery to fit inside the frame. Snap crystal over the top.

MAKE THE ''FOB'' KEY RING

If you can't find a kit like those shown above, buy a simple key ring at the hardware store and embroider a fob.

Machine Readiness Checklist

Stitch:	diamond (65, 7500; 35, 8000)
Length:	0.3–0.5
Width:	7
Foot:	F satin stitch
Needle:	14/90 stretch
Thread:	rayon or acrylic embroidery; nylon monofilament
Tension:	top, loosened slightly; bobbin, normal
Fabric:	Ultrasuede, Ultraleather, or felt; fusible interfacing; paper-backed fusible web
Accessories:	key ring, tracing paper, vanishing marker

1. Fuse interfacing to the wrong side of the fob fabric. Trace the fob pattern shown in Fig. 7.2.

2. Cut out Ultrasuede, Ultraleather, or felt using the pattern. Cut paper-backed fusible web slightly smaller than the pattern.

3. On the right side of the fabric, mark the center of one side of the fob with a dot using the vanishing marker (see Fig. 7.2).

Sew-How: *The design in the center of the fob is a flower created by decorative stitches. Before stitching your fob, practice and perfect your technique on a fabric scrap backed with interfacing.*

4. Select the diamond stitch (65, 7500; 35, 8000).

Sew-How: *This flower can be made on many New Home sewing machines because the diamond is a common stitch. Of course, you can experiment with other decorative stitches to invent your own motifs put them in your notebook.*

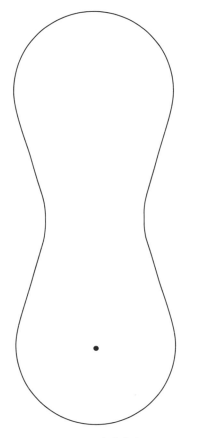

Fob pattern is full size.

Fig. 7.2
Key ring fob pattern.

New Sewer's Note: *Set iron on cotton or wool setting. Place interfacing so the rough side is against the wrong side of the fob fabric. Dampen a press cloth and fuse interfacing with firm pressure for about 10 seconds. Remove the iron, let steam escape, then press again until the fabric and press cloth are dry.*

5. Starting in the center, stitch one diamond and stop. Remove the fabric, cut the threads, and turn the fob 180 degrees. Stitch another diamond across from the first. Remove fabric, cut threads, and pivot 90 degrees. Starting in the center again, stitch another diamond. Repeat for the last diamond (Fig. 7.3). Pull threads to the wrong side and tie them off.

6. Press paper-backed fusible web to the wrong side of the fob, following manufacturer's instructions. After the fabric is cool, remove the paper and pull the fob through the key ring. Line up the cut edges and fuse the fob together.

7. Rethread top and bobbin with nylon monofilament thread. Put the A zigzag or G blind hem foot on your New Home. Decenter the needle to the left and edge-stitch $\frac{1}{8}''$ (3mm) from cut edges (see Fig. 9.10 or 9.17). Lock stitches at the end of the stitching.

Wasn't that fun? Now let's try something more challenging.

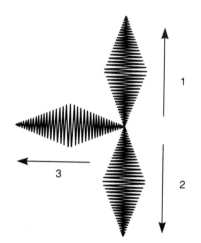

Fig. 7.3

Starting in the center, stitch one diamond and stop. Remove the fabric, cut the threads, and turn the fabric 180 degrees. Stitch another diamond across from the first. Remove the fabric, cut the threads, turn the fabric 90 degrees, and stitch another diamond. Repeat for the last diamond.

Step Three:

FABRIC GAME BOARD AND POUCH

The fabric game board is easy to pack, travels well in a car or on a plane, and can stave off back-seat wars during the family vacation. Both backgammon and checkerboard are combined in one travel game you make yourself.

Supplies:

- 2 packages black $1\frac{3}{4}''$ (4.5cm) wide hem facing (cotton/polyester blend)

- 2 packages red $1\frac{3}{4}''$ (4.5cm) wide hem facing (cotton/polyester blend)

- 27" (68.5cm) of 1" (2.5cm) red or black grosgrain ribbon

- $\frac{1}{2}$ yd. (45.5cm) paper-backed fusible web

- 16" (40.5cm) square of cotton/polyester red print fabric

- 1 yellow washable felt square

- 1 blue washable felt square

- 1 white strip and 1 black strip of woven cotton-blend fabric each at least $1\frac{1}{2}'' \times 16''$ (3.8cm × 40.5cm)

- nylon monofilament thread

- all-purpose thread in black and white

- 4 yds. (3.6m) black yarn, or size #3 or size #5 pearl cotton

• tracing paper and water-erasable marker

MAKE THE BACKGAMMON BOARD

1. Enlarge the pattern to double the size of Fig. 7.4. Trace patterns for triangles and bars.

2. Fuse a piece of paper-backed fusible web on the back of the yellow and the back of the blue felt square and on the wrong side of the black and the white cotton strips, following manufacturer's instructions.

3. Using the pattern traced in Step 1, cut twelve triangles from the yellow felt square and twelve triangles from the blue felt square.

Sew-How: To cut both colored triangles at the same time, place yellow and blue felt squares on top of one another. Use your sharp rotary cutter, mat, and see-through ruler to cut through both layers.

---

4. Cut out black and white bars.

5. Fold 16″ (40.5cm) print square in half and press a crease. Open square. Remove web paper from white strip. Center and fuse white bar over crease on the right side of the print square.

Machine Readiness Checklist

Stitch:	zigzag (35, 7500; 4, 8000)
Length:	0.4–0.6
Width:	2
Foot:	F satin stitch
Needle:	11/75 Blue Tip
Thread:	white all-purpose, cotton, rayon, or acrylic embroidery
Feed dogs:	up
Tension:	top, loosened slightly; bobbin, normal

Satin-stitch both raw edges of the white bar, centering the raw edge under the foot.

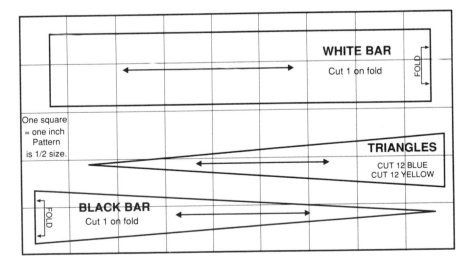

Fig. 7.4
Backgammon triangles and bar patterns. Pattern is half-size.

6. Fold square in half again in the other direction and press a crease. Open square. Remove paper-backed fusible web from the black bar; then center and fuse it over the crease on the right side of the print square. Rethread top and bobbin with black thread and satin-stitch both sides of the bar.

7. Starting on either side of the black bar, remove paper backing and position blue and yellow triangles, alternating colors as shown in Fig. 7.5. Be sure triangle points are exactly opposite one another across the board. Carefully fuse triangles on print square using a damp press cloth and steam.

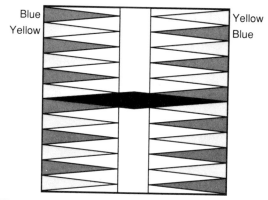

Fig. 7.5
Position blue and yellow triangles, alternating colors so the points are exactly opposite one another across the board.

8. Rethread top and bobbin with nylon monofilament thread.

Machine Readiness Checklist	
Stitch:	straight (29 or 30, 7500; 1 or 2, 8000)
Length:	2
Width:	0
Foot:	A zigzag, or G, or G adjustable blind hem
Needle:	11/75 Blue Tip
Thread:	nylon monofilament
Feed dogs:	up
Tension:	top, loosened slightly; bobbin, normal

Topstitch around each triangle, stitching $\frac{1}{8}''$ (3mm) from the cut edge. Don't cut threads between triangles. Simply lift the presser foot, turn the fabric around, and continue stitching.

Sew-How: When using the G or G adjustable blind hem foot, guide the straight edge of the appliqué to the right inside edge of the guide. If necessary, move the needle position slightly so stitching is $\frac{1}{8}''$ (3mm) from cut edge of felt (see Figs. 9.10 or 9.17).

9. With the wrong side up, press the backgammon board with steam.

10. Cut a 16″ (40.5cm) square of paper-backed fusible web and fuse it to the wrong side of the backgammon board. After cooling, remove the paper backing. This enables you to fuse the checkerboard to the back of the backgammon board.

Sew-How: Save paper from the fusible web to use as a paper press cloth. Put the paper over your work to prevent fusible web from gumming up the sole plate of your iron.

MAKE THE CHECKERBOARD

1. Cut eight 16″ (40.5cm) strips of black hem facing and eight 16″ (40.5cm) strips of red hem facing.

2. Starting in the center of the board and working out, pin black hem facing strips next to each other on one side of the board so the wrong side of the tape is against the wrong side of the backgammon board. **Note:** Leave the hems in hem facing strips.

3. Pin red hem facing strips next to each other on a side adjacent to the first, weaving them in and out of black strips as shown (Fig. 7.6).

Fig. 7.6
Pin black strips next to each other on one side of the board. Pin red strips next to each other on a side adjacent to the first, weaving them in and out of black strips.

4. Set iron on the hottest setting. Thoroughly dampen a press cloth and place it over the checkerboard.

5. Fuse checkerboard to the back of backgammon board. For a permanent bond, apply a lot of pressure and press the work until it is dry.

FINISH THE EDGE

1. Straighten the edges of your board using the rotary cutter, mat, and cutting ruler.

2. Starting in the middle of a straight edge, couch over yarn or double strand of pearl cotton.

Machine Readiness Checklist	
Stitch:	zigzag (35, 7500; 4, 8000)
Length:	2
Width:	3–4
Foot:	H cording
Needle:	11/75 Blue Tip
Needle position:	center
Thread:	all-purpose black
Feed dogs:	up
Tension:	normal (auto)
Accessories:	black yarn or pearl cotton

Thread yarn or pearl cotton through the clip in the H cording. Guide the yarn so the needle stitches into the fabric on the left and swings off the edge at the right (see Figs. 8.20 and 9.18). Stitch a gentle curve at the corners (with the needle on the inside corner, pivot fabric around it). At the join, cut yarn off, overlap the ends, and zigzag couch over them.

3. Satin-stitch (35, 7500; 4, 8000) over couched yarn or pearl cotton using a 0.4–0.6 length, 4–5 width zigzag stitch, and slightly loosened upper tension (see Fig. 8.25). Flair stitches out at the corners using the inside of the corner as a pivot point (see Fig. 4.12).

4. Satin-stitch around the edge again, using a slightly longer stitch length and the widest stitch width. This second row of satin stitches over the first helps to firm up and finish the edge of the board.

5. To smooth out the satin-stitched edge, couch over another piece of yarn around the outside edge of the game board.

Machine Readiness Checklist

Stitch:	zigzag (35, 7500; 4, 8000)
Length:	1.5–2
Width:	3
Foot:	H cording
Needle:	11/75 Blue Tip
Needle position:	center
Thread:	all-purpose black, top and bobbin
Feed dogs:	up
Tension:	normal (auto)
Accessories:	yarn or pearl cotton

Guide so the needle stitches just into the satin stitches on the left and swings over the yarn and off the edge on the right. As before, overlap yarn ends and couch over them.

6. Cut a length of grosgrain ribbon 27" (68.5cm) long and stitch it onto one end of the board by stitching-in-the-ditch along the satin-stitched edge (see Fig. 8.8). Roll the board up and tie the ribbon into a bow.

MAKE THE GAME PIECE POUCH

Supplies:

• Paper-backed fusible web scraps

• two 9" (23cm) squares of red cotton or cotton-blend fabric

• 3" × 9" (7.6cm × 23cm) strip of black-and-white checked fabric

• 2¼" (5.7cm) square of yellow fabric

• 1⅝" (4.1cm) square of turquoise fabric (Lycra spandex swim wear or knit fabric works well)

• fusible interfacing

• 10"–12" (25.5cm–30.5cm) zipper

• red all-purpose thread; yellow and turquoise rayon or acrylic embroidery thread

1. Fuse paper-backed fusible web to the back of the yellow and turquoise fabrics before cutting them out. If the red and checked fabrics are knits, fuse interfacing to the wrong side of each piece.

2. Center and fuse yellow square on checked fabric as shown (Fig. 7.7). Satin-stitch around it with a 2.5–3 width zigzag (35, 7500; 4, 8000) (see Fig. 8.25).

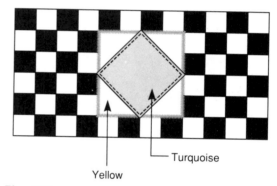

— Turquoise

Yellow

Fig. 7.7
Center and fuse yellow square on checked fabric, then satin-stitch around the edge. Turn turquoise square on end, position and fuse over the yellow square, then straight stitch ⅛" (3mm) from the edge.

3. Turn turquoise square on end; position and fuse over yellow square as shown (see Fig. 7.7). If this fabric is a knit, straight-stitch around it guiding ⅛" (3mm) from the raw edge (see Fig. 9.10 or 9.17). If it is a woven fabric, satin-stitch around it as you did for the yellow square (see Fig. 8.25).

4. Fold back a $\frac{1}{2}''$ (1.3cm) seam allowance on the two long edges of the checked fabric and press toward the wrong side. Center the checked strip on the right side of a red square and position it so it goes across the grain. Topstitch along the two folded edges with a 3 length straight stitch and red thread (Fig. 7.8).

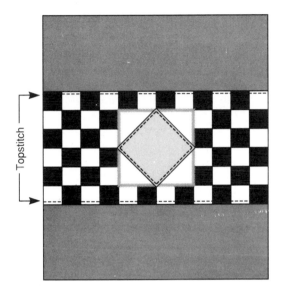

Fig. 7.8
Topstitch along the two folded edges with a 3 length straight stitch.

INSERT THE ZIPPER

1. Place the zipped zipper along one 9" (23cm) edge of the decorated square, right sides together, so the zipper is parallel to the checkered strip; align the edge of the zipper tape with the cut edge. **Note:** The pull should be at one end of the zipper, out of the way (Fig. 7.9).

Stitch close to coil

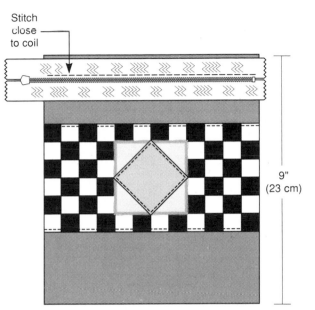

9" (23 cm)

Fig. 7.9
Place decorated pouch piece and zipper right sides together, aligning edge of zipper and fabric edge. Pull should be to one end, out of the way. Stitch close to coil.

2. Using your E zipper foot and a 3 length straight stitch (29 or 30, 7500; 1 or 2, 8000), stitch zipper to fabric, sewing next to the zipper coil. Press seam away from the coil as shown in Fig. 7.10. (See Figs. 9.7, 9.8.)

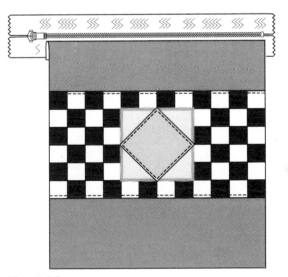

Fig. 7.10
Press seam away from coil.

3. Repeat for the other edge of the zipper on the plain fabric square, being sure the cut edge is aligned with the edge of the zipper tape and is across the grain and even with the first red square (Fig. 7.11). This is called an exposed zipper application because the zipper coil is exposed.

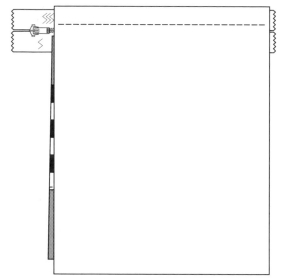

Fig. 7.11
Repeat for other side.

4. Unzip the zipper slightly. Tack the top of the zipper so the two sides of the coil are together ½″ (1.3mm) inside the cut edge of the pouch (Fig. 7.12). Cut excess zipper tape off so it is even with the edge of the fabric.

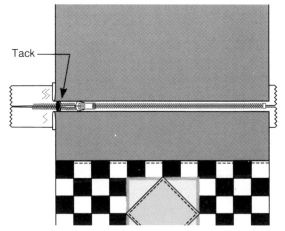

Fig. 7.12
Tack top of zipper coil so the pull will not come off track. Cut excess tape off, even with fabric.

Sew-How: *If you should accidentally slide the pull off the coil before tacking over it, remove the metal stop at the bottom of zipper. Then slide the pull back on track from the bottom up. Remember to replace the metal stop or tack across the bottom of the zipper.*

5. With the zipper still unzipped about 3″ (7.6cm), place the pouch right sides together and straight-stitch around the remaining three sides of the pouch using a ½″ (1.3mm) seam allowance. Backstitch over the zipper coil a few times to secure both ends of the seam. Open the zipper all the way; then turn the pouch right side out and press.

Sew-How: *To make the zipper easier to pull, loop a couple of strands of #3 pearl cotton through the hole in the tab (see color pages).*

MAKE GAME PIECES

If you don't have an extra set of game pieces, make your own out of red and black felt. Each player needs fifteen game pieces for backgammon (but only twelve for checkers), so make thirty pieces.

Machine Readiness Checklist

Stitch:	straight-edge scallop (60, 7500; 38, 8000); zigzag (35, 7500; 4, 8000)
Length:	0.3–0.5
Width:	widest for scallop; 2 for satin stitch
Foot:	F satin stitch
Function:	pattern turn-over for scallop
Needle:	11/75 Blue Tip or 14/90 stretch
Thread:	yellow and white cotton or acrylic embroidery
Tension:	top, loosened slightly; bobbin, normal
Fabric:	2 felt squares each of black and red
Accessories:	paper-backed fusible web; disappearing dressmaker's chalk or soap sliver

Sew-How: To center the crown in each square, use the L quilter and guide along the edge of each square (Fig. 7.13).

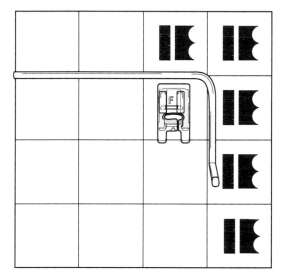

Fig. 7.13
Center crown on each square using the L quilter along the edge of each square.

1. Fuse a piece of fusible web on one black felt square and one red felt square.

2. Mark fifteen $1\frac{1}{4}$–2″ (3.2–5cm) squares on remaining black and remaining red felt squares using a soap sliver or disappearing dressmaker's chalk.

3. On twelve squares of each color, sew a decorative stitch to create the crowns for the checkers (optional). I used a straight-edge scallop stitch (60, 7500; 38, 8000) and yellow thread for the top and a 2 width satin stitch and white thread for the bottom of each crown.

4. Remove web paper; then fuse a plain black piece of felt on the back of black decorated pieces. Repeat stitching and fusing procedure for red felt piece. Cut squares apart. Trim each square into a circle to finish each game piece.

Put game pieces in the pouch, roll the pouch in the game board, and tie the ribbons into a bow.

TRANSFERABLE LEARNINGS

The information and techniques you have learned and practiced in making the gifts in this chapter have given you skills necessary to sew other projects. You have learned how to:

• Stitch and center lettering on a project.

• Use nylon monofilament thread top and bobbin so you don't have to rethread for different colors of fabric in the same project.

• Appliqué using a straight stitch on fabrics that don't ravel, such as felt, leather, knits, suede, and synthetic leather or suede. Appliqué using a satin stitch on fabrics that ravel.

• Use paper-backed fusible web to make any fabric fusible.

• Use the G or G adjustable blind hem foot to topstitch evenly from a cut or finished edge—helpful when topstitching a pocket, lapel, front tab, belt loop, waistband, tote bag strap, and so on.

• Move needle position rather than the fabric to stitch precisely where you want to.

• Couch over a piece of yarn or pearl cotton using the H cording foot and zigzag stitch (35, 7500; 4, 8000) as a way to add dimension under a satin stitch.

• Satin-stitch an edge twice, with a progressively wider and longer zigzag stitch to create a better finish to an edge.

• Couch over a piece of yarn or pearl cotton on the outer edge of satin stitching to finish an uneven edge cleanly. This technique is often used on European table linens, napkin edges, and cut work. It's also a way to finish an edge on a fabric that is too thick to seam and turn to the right side in the conventional way (for example, denim, leather, canvas, and heavy duck cloth).

• Use an exposed zipper in a pocket or a seam.

• Use the L quilter to guide fabric evenly when you can't guide using the lines on the needle plate. This is helpful when stitching even rows of straight and decorative stitching, and when machine quilting.

Now that you've stitched your way through the projects in Part II, I hope you have learned to sew . . . better. Are you motivated to use the many stitches, presser feet, and accessories available to you? I hope so. I also hope that you've had fun stitching along with me, that you have a bunch of completed projects to give away or to keep, and that you're inspired to learn more about the World of Sewing.

Besides collecting fabric and other sewing paraphernalia, I also collect sewing and needlecraft books. In listing them in the bibliography, I feel as if I'm introducing you to dear friends. I encourage you to get to know them better as you further refine your skills. They're not only a helpful reference library but also a continuous source of inspiration.

Good-bye for now, and happy sewing.

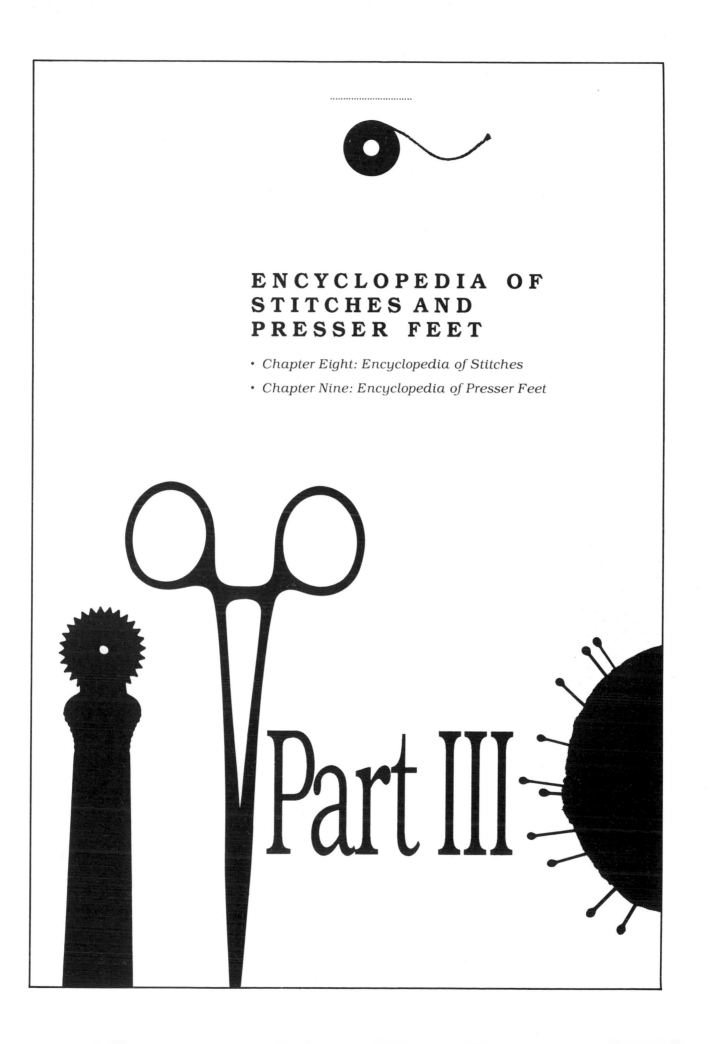

ENCYCLOPEDIA OF STITCHES AND PRESSER FEET

Part III

PART III

ENCYCLOPEDIA OF STITCHES AND PRESSER FEET

DO YOU KNOW how many stitches are built in to your New Home sewing machine or are available and how to use them? Do you know what feet and accessories came with your machine and what they are for?

Part III, the Encyclopedia of Stitches and Presser Feet, answers these questions. We will explore the most common New Home stitches and presser feet, what they look like, what they are designed to do, and their practical and decorative uses.

When I first began experimenting with machine stitches and presser feet, I started keeping stitch samples and notes in a large, three-ring binder with clear, pocket-type pages (available from office supply stores). My notebook is organized by stitches and feet, similar to this encyclopedia. I continue to add to this notebook, so I have lots of ideas to choose from for future projects. It's one of the most valuable parts of my sewing room.

As you read through this encyclopedia, why not keep your own notebook, too? Cut your light-colored fabric scraps into 6–9" (15–23cm) squares, ready to experiment with. Or use demo cloth, available through your local sewing machine dealer. The fabric is on a roll, firmly woven, and starched so the stitches show up well, plus it's easy to write on. This way you aren't hunting for fabric and you can write machine settings on the sample before it goes into your notebook.

As you experiment and get to know your machine better, keep everything—your successes, failures and your new discoveries. Why keep your failures? So you don't make the same mistake twice. Then refer to your notebook of ideas for your next project.

Now find some fabric, your box of accessories, and your *Instruction Book*. Then sit down in front of your machine with me and discover the world of stitches and presser feet.

ENCYCLOPEDIA OF STITCHES

Most encyclopedias are organized alphabetically. This one is not. Instead it is organized into groups of utility, decorative, and embroidery stitches.

For each stitch in this encyclopedia, I give the stitch name and the Memory Craft model 7500 and 8000 stitch numbers (see Table 8.1). For example, the patchwork stitch is 45 on the Memory Craft 7500, and 25 on the Memory Craft 8000; the diamond is 65 on the 7500, and 35 on the 8000. Refer to Fig. 8.1, which shows the model 8000 stitches, and compare the stitches on your New Home with the ones pictured.

Table 8.1 New Home Memory Craft Stitch Reference Chart Models 7500 and 8000

Model 7500	Model 8000	Stitch Name
1	N/A	bridging
2	58	decorative (overlock)
3	66	loop
4	49	Turkish hemstitch
5	56	briar
6	57	smocking
7	63	Venetian hemstitch
8	67	running stems
9	107	running leaves (open)
10	106	running leaves (closed)

Table 8.1 New Home Memory Craft Stitch Reference Chart Models 7500 and 8000 (*cont.*)

Model 7500	Model 8000	Stitch Name
11	60	smocking key
12	65	Swiss hemstitch
13	59	double overlock
14	104	four-leaf clover
15	101	sculpture (seed) stitch
16	53	sand stitch
17	102	shading (outline) stitch
18	103	shading (fill-in) stitch
19	74	row of tulips
20	N/A	clover
21	N/A	dog (Memory Lock)
22	97	branch
23	N/A	broken satin stitch
24	54	double smocking
25	47	southwestern arrow
26	105	leafing vine
27	N/A	running cross stitch
28	N/A	loop de loop
29	1	straight stitch (left needle position)
30	2	straight stitch (center needle position)

Table 8.1 New Home Memory Craft Stitch Reference Chart Models 7500 and 8000 (*cont.*)

Model 7500	Model 8000	Stitch Name
31	3	Lock-a-matic stitch
32	15	triple strength
33	16	(outline) stretch
34	17	saddle stitch
35	4	zigzag
36	18	multiple zigzag
37	19	knit stitch
38	5	overcast stitch
39	22	double overedge stitch
40	23	(special) overlock
41	6	blind hem
42	20	stretch blind hem
43	21	zigzag appliqué
44	24	(heirloom) appliqué
45	25	patchwork
46	26	wide cording (rick-rack)
47	27	scallop
48	28	(heirloom) scallop
49	N/A	blanket stitch
50	45	argyle
51	55	heirloom smocking
52	48	wheat
53	87	decorative
54	86	decorative
55	46	decorative
56	29	tapered scallop
57	30	half-ball
58	31	triangle
59	37	satin stitch scallop
60	38	straight-edge scallop
61	39	smocking scallop
62	32	ribbon stitch
63	33	tapered leaf
64	34	ball

Table 8.1 New Home Memory Craft Stitch Reference Chart Models 7500 and 8000 (*cont.*)

Model 7500	Model 8000	Stitch Name
65	35	diamond
66	40	arrowhead
67	41	elongated ribbon
68	43	triple domino
69	42	domino
N/A	44	satin wave
70	100	fern
71	85	decorative
72	96	scalloped heart
73	98	decorative
74	90	decorative
75	92	decorative
76	91	decorative
77	62	open cube
78	64	decorative
79	99	snowflake (Memory Lock)
80	88	decorative
81	89	decorative
82	61	Greek key
83	69	decorative
84	70	cross stitch (Memory Lock)
85	73	tulips
86	72	open hearts
87	71	stars
88	75	ducks
89	81	airplane (Memory Lock)
90	79	butterfly (Memory Lock)
91	78	penguin (Memory Lock)
92	77	alligator (Memory Lock)
93	80	bird (Memory Lock)
94	N/A	fish (Memory Lock)

Table 8.1 New Home Memory Craft Stitch Reference Chart Models 7500 and 8000 (cont.)

Model 7500	Model 8000	Stitch Name
95	82	decorative (Memory Lock)
96	N/A	decorative (Memory Lock)
97	83	open circle (Memory Lock)
98	84	daisy (Memory Lock)
99	115	moustache (Memory Lock)
100	N/A	southwestern cross
101	52	bamboo
102	51	open ribbon
103	50	open chain
104	93	open rose
105	94	open grapes
106	95	decorative
107	12	bartack buttonhole
108	13	rounded buttonhole
109	14	keyhole buttonhole
110	8	eyelet
111	9	darn
112	10	bartack
113	11	basting
114	113	satin leaf
115	114	decorative
116	108	decorative vine
117	112	decorative
118	111	satin stitch hearts
119	110	decorative
120	109	decorative
121	N/A	decorative (smile)
122	68 & 116	space
N/A	36	locking stitch

Sew-How: For easy reference, photocopy Fig. 8.1 and keep it near your machine. Another great way to acquaint you with the variety of stitches available on your machine is to make a stitch sampler (see the exercises in Chapter 1).

FORWARD CYCLE VERSUS REVERSE CYCLE STITCHES

Stitches are classified in two ways—forward cycle and reverse cycle. "Forward cycle" means the stitches feed through the machine in one direction, and the needle may also move from side to side automatically; the zigzag (35, 7500; 4, 8000), multiple zigzag (36, 7500; 18, 8000), and blind hem (41, 7500; 6, 8000) stitches are examples.

"Reverse cycle" stitches, sometimes referred to as stretch stitches, are made when the needle zigzags as the feed dogs move the fabric forward and backward. Because of the way they are made, reverse cycle stitches stretch and return to shape when sewn on a knit fabric. Examples of these stitches are the knit stitch (37, 7500; 19, 8000), overlock (2, 7500; 58, 8000), single overlock (38, 7500; 5, 8000), and special overlock (40, 7500; 23, 8000). In some decorative stitches on the Memory Craft machines, both the forward and reverse cycle functions are used in the same stitch. An example is the vine (116, 7500; 108, 8000).

Stitches are also divided further into utility and decorative classifications.

UTILITY AND DECORATIVE STITCHES

The utility stitches are used most often for basic sewing and mending. Other utility stitches are the buttonholes and the special-purpose stitches.

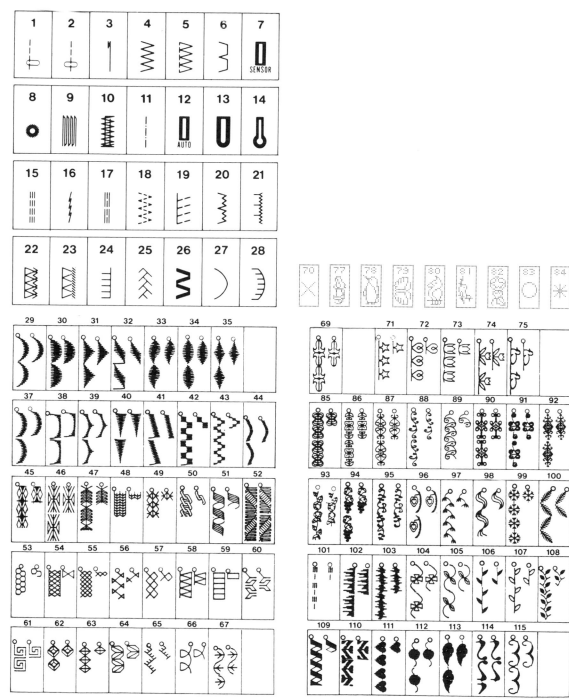

Fig. 8.1
Memory Craft 8000 stitch reference chart.

Decorative stitches are used to embellish a piece of fabric, ribbon, or trim. Examples are stitches 45–106 and 114–121 on the Memory Craft 7500 and 24–115 on the 8000. I have grouped the decorative stitches into categories, and at the beginning of each heading I explain what each group of stitches is used for. For more stitch applications and imaginative projects, ask your local dealer for the Memory Craft Design Books.

UTILITY STITCHES

FORWARD CYCLE UTILITY STITCHES

- Straight Stitch
- (Outline) Stretch Stitch
- Zigzag Stitch
- Multiple Zigzag Stitch
- Blind Hem Stitch
- Stretch Blind Hem Stitch
- Zigzag Appliqué Stitch

Let's start by taking a closer look at the most common utility stitch—the straight stitch.

STRAIGHT STITCH (29 and 30, 7500; 1 and 2, 8000)

- Lock-a-Matic
- Basting
- Easestitching
- Edgestitching
- Staystitching
- Stitch-in-the-Ditch
- Straight Seams
- Topstitching
- Twin Needle Hem
- Twin Needle Tucks (Pintucks)
- Understitching

The straight stitch is used primarily to sew straight seams on woven fabrics. The stitch length is changed depending on the weight of the fabric. Generally, for a finer fabric, a shorter stitch length is used. For heavier fabrics, a longer stitch length is used. When you turn on the Memory Craft 7500 or 8000, a straight stitch in left needle position is automatically selected at 2.2 stitch length—a length used for many fabrics. Why in left needle position? Because in left needle position there is support around three sides of the needle to help prevent skipped stitches and puckering (see Fig. 9.5). On computerized Memory Craft models, the seam allowance marks on the needle plate are measured from left rather than center needle position. Some mechanical models measure from center needle position.

For a straight stitch in center needle position, select stitch 30 (7500) or 2 (8000).

Make a stitch sample for your notebook with each stitch length sewn on the same piece of fabric so you can see how they differ. Label each length. Try stitching on different weights of fabric (Fig. 8.2).

Fig. 8.2
Try various stitch lengths on a piece of fabric, label each, and put in your notebook.

Sew-How: To keep your stitches straight and to count the number of stitches per inch, stitch various lengths on 1" (2.5cm) gingham. If the fabric puckers, iron a piece of plastic-coated freezer wrap to the wrong side of a single layer of gingham. If your fabric still puckers, shorten the stitch length. If the fabric waves out of shape, lengthen the stitch.

Lock-a-Matic Stitch (31, 7500; 3, 8000)

New Home sewing machines have a straight stitch function called the Lock-a-Matic stitch. Start sewing at the beginning of the seam and the machine takes four stitches forward, then four stitches back. At the end of the seam simply push the reverse (backstitch) key and again the machine will take four stitches back, then automatically stop and lock off the stitch.

The Memory Craft 8000 also has a locking stitch that works similarly, but instead of taking four stitches forward and back, the needle takes six stitches in place to "lock" the seam. To end the seam, push the reverse key and the stitch will stop and lock off with six straight stitches again.

Use this feature at the beginning or end of a seam to secure it and to eliminate the need to hand-tie the stitches.

The following applications of the straight stitch are commonly used in pattern instructions.

Basting

Basting is a line of temporary stitching used to join pattern pieces to check fit and appearance of the seam before final stitching. For easy removal, set your New Home as follows:

Machine Readiness Checklist	
Stitch:	straight (29 or 30, 7500; 1 or 2, 8000)
Length:	4–5
Width:	0
Foot:	A zigzag
Needle:	appropriate for the fabric
Thread:	all-purpose top and bobbin; contrasting color in the bobbin
Tension:	top, loosened slightly; bobbin, normal

With right sides together, baste the seam at the ⅝" (1.5cm) or ¼" (6mm) seam line. Fit the garment and make adjustments as necessary. To remove the basting stitches, pull bobbin thread—it's easy to find because you used a different color in the bobbin (Fig. 8.3). After basting, re-member to reset your top tension to nor-mal or auto and change your bobbin thread to match the top.

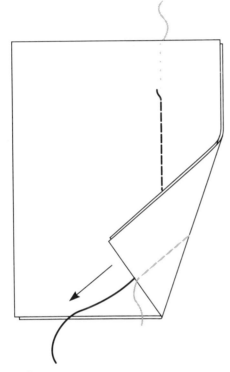

Fig. 8.3
Baste using contrasting bobbin thread and a loosened upper tension. Pull bobbin thread to remove stitches.

Easestitching

Many projects require flat pieces of fabric to fit curved areas. By easestitching, you can manipulate the flat fabric to fit.

In easestitching, a longer fabric edge is joined to a shorter one without folds or gathers being visible from the right side of the project. Easestitching is used for setting in sleeves, in a two-piece sleeve at the elbow, for easing a skirt or pants waistline into a waistband, and in other areas as described in the pattern.

Machine Readiness Checklist	
Stitch:	straight (30, 7500; 2, 8000)
Length:	2.2 (fine fabrics)–3.5 (heavy fabrics)
Width:	0
Foot:	A zigzag
Needle:	appropriate for the fabric
Needle position:	center or far right
Thread:	all-purpose
Feed dogs:	up
Tension:	normal (auto); for more ease, tighten upper ten-sion

1. On a single layer of the fabric to be eased, stitch between notches, guiding the raw edge at the ⅝" (1.5cm) seam line marked on your needle plate. Because you are sewing in center needle position and guiding the raw edge by the ⅝" (1.5cm) seam line, easestitches are inside the seam allowance and won't show once the seam is stitched. On models that measure from center needle position, move the needle to the far right for the same effect.

2. Pin fabric pieces together, matching notches. Pull bobbin thread to adjust ease as needed (Fig. 8.4).

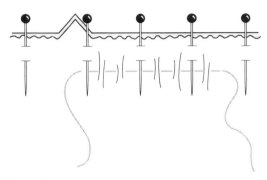

Fig. 8.4
Pin fabric together and pull bobbin thread to adjust ease.

Sew-How: For more ease, try the ease-stitch "plus" method. Set your machine as described above, but slightly tighten the upper tension. As you sew, hold your index finger behind the foot so the fabric bunches up (Fig. 8.5). Hold fabric until you can't hold it firmly any longer, release, and repeat. The fabric eases automatically without tucks or gathers. This is great for easing a set-in sleeve or the edge of a circular or curved hemline.

Edgestitching

Edgestitching is a line of stitching $\frac{1}{8}$" (3mm) or less from the finished edge and is generally stitched with thread matching the fabric. Edgestitch a collar, cuff, top of a waistband, hem edge, belt edges, around a front facing, the edge of a pleat, or to stitch a tuck.

Machine Readiness Checklist	
Stitch:	straight (29, 7500; 1, 8000)
Length:	normal for the fabric
Width:	0
Foot:	G blind hem or G adjustable blind hem
Needle:	appropriate for fabric
Needle position:	left
Thread:	all-purpose
Feed dogs:	up
Tension:	normal (auto)

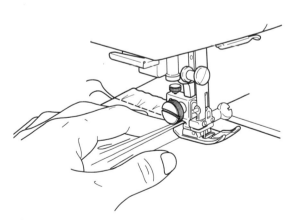

Fig. 8.5
Hold your index finger behind the foot so fabric bunches up to easestitch "plus."

1. Press edge to be edgestitched. Place edge of fold so it guides against the inside right edge of the guide in either foot (Fig. 8.6).

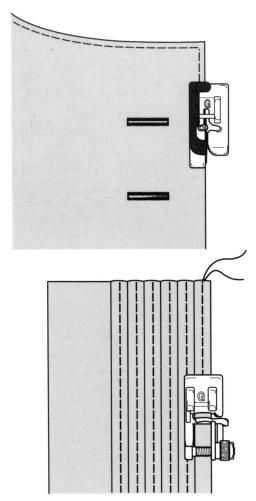

Fig. 8.6
Edgestitch a collar, cuff, top of waistband, belt edges, the edge of a pleat, or edgestitch around front facing. To make a tuck, place edge of fold against the guide in the G blind hem or G adjustable blind hem foot and stitch.

─────────────

Sew-How: *Because of the guide in the center of the G blind stitch foot, you cannot edgestitch in center needle position without missing the fabric. Therefore, for more versatility, use the G adjustable blind hem foot.*

─────────────

2. Set your needle position so the needle is the desired distance from the edge and edgestitch. The foot enables you to edgestitch uniformly from the fabric edge (see Figs. 9.10, 9.17).

Staystitching

Staystitching is a line of stitching on a single layer of fabric just inside the seam allowance which keeps curved and bias-cut edges from stretching out of shape as the fabric is handled during construction. Areas commonly staystitched are necklines, shoulders, and waistlines.

To staystitch, use a 2-length straight stitch and stitch ½" (1.3cm) from the raw edge on a single layer of fabric (Fig. 8.7). To prevent the fabric from distorting, staystitch in the direction of the arrows as shown.

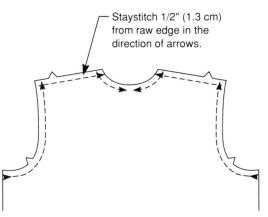

Staystitch 1/2" (1.3 cm) from raw edge in the direction of arrows.

Fig. 8.7
To prevent fabric from stretching out of shape, staystitch curved and bias-cut edges ½" (1.3cm) from raw edge.

─────────────

Sew-How: *When you pin a straight piece to a curved pattern piece (as you would when putting a collar on a neckline) staystitch around the curve ½" (1.3cm) from the raw edge. Then clip the curved seam line almost to the staystitching. The neckline can be straightened out so the pattern pieces fit better and the fabric will not ravel past the staystitching.*

─────────────

Stitch-in-the-Ditch

Tack facings or finish waistbands by stitching-in-the-ditch:

1. Use the G blind hem or G adjustable blind hem foot (Figs. 9.10, 9.17) and a 3-length straight stitch.

2. With the right side up, place the crack of the seam under guide in the foot, and adjust the needle position so the needle stitches in the "ditch" of the seam (Fig. 8.8).

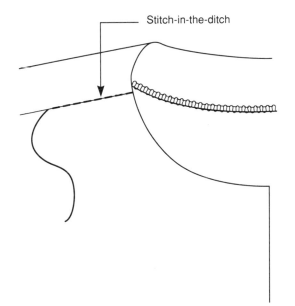

Stitch-in-the-ditch

Fig. 8.8
Stitch-in-the-ditch to tack down facings or finish waistbands.

3. Pull threads to the wrong side and tie them off.

Straight Seams

The straight stitch is used to sew a seam that will be pressed open on a woven fabric.

Machine Readiness Checklist	
Stitch:	straight (29, 30, or 31, 7500; 1, 2, or 3, 8000)
Length:	2.2–3.5
Width:	0
Foot:	A zigzag
Needle:	11/75 Blue Tip
Thread:	all-purpose
Feed dogs:	up
Tension:	normal (auto)
Fabric:	varies

With right sides together, sew a seam, stitching ⅝" (1.5cm) from the raw edge. To set the stitches, press over them so seam is flat and together. Then press seam open.

Sew-How: *If your seam line puckers, the thread may be too heavy for the fabric. Try using machine-embroidery thread with a finer needle, or shorten the stitch length.*

Topstitching

Topstitching is a line of stitches sewn on the top side of a project parallel to the finished edge or to a seam line. Topstitching differs from edgestitching in that it's not sewn as close to the finished edge, and a longer stitch length is usually used. Topstitching can also be done with decorative top threads such as silk twist or polyester topstitching thread, or with two threads through the same needle. Generally topstitching is used to embellish and is not necessary for the construction of a project (Fig. 8.9).

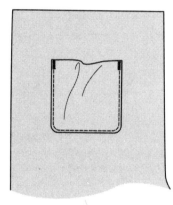

Fig. 8.9
Topstitching on a pocket.

Sew-How: *Topstitching is often easier when you move the needle position rather than moving the fabric one way or the other. Older model New Home machines have infinite needle positions between right and left needle position. Newer models have fifteen needle positions adjusted by touching the stitch width key.*

Machine Readiness Checklist	
Stitch:	straight (29 or 30, 7500; 1 or 2, 8000)
Length:	3–5
Width:	0
Foot:	A zigzag
Needle:	11/75 Blue Tip, 14/90 topstitching for heavy threads
Thread:	two threads through the same needle; silk twist or topstitching
Feed dogs:	up
Tension:	normal (auto) for two threads through same needle; tighten top slightly for heavier threads

---

Sew-How: *Be consistent. Use the same stitch length to topstitch all parts of a project. Also, varying thicknesses may create stitch length inconsistencies, so experiment on scraps to fine-tune your stitch length. If you have a mechanical machine, stop at a corner so the needle has hit its dead lowest point and is on its way out of the fabric. This way, the stitch cycle is complete so you don't run the risk of skipping a stitch. Computerized machines that can stop sewing with the needle in the fabric do this automatically.*

Interface three weights of fabric. Fold each in half on the lengthwise grain and topstitch each using different stitch lengths. Make a note of the best stitch length for topstitching each fabric. Put these samples in your notebook.

Twin Needle Hem

Twin needles are used on top- and front-loading bobbin machines only. If your bobbin goes in the side of your machine, the needles sit in the machine incorrectly and will not work.

This fast, professional-looking way to hem a knit makes the hem look as if it has been knitted into the fabric (Fig. 8.10). For stretchy knits such as sweater knits, stretch terry, and velour, lengthen stitch to 4–4.5.

Fig. 8.10
Twin needle hem on a knit fabric looks as if it has been knitted into the fabric.

Machine Readiness Checklist

Stitch:	straight (30, 7500; 2, 8000)
Length:	2.5–3.5
Width:	0
Foot:	A zigzag
Needle:	twin, size 2.0/80(12)
Needle position:	center
Thread:	all-purpose to match fabric
Tension:	normal (auto); for more pronounced tuck, tighten upper tension
Fabric:	woven or knit

Sew-How: To prevent threads from tangling through the upper tension, place one spool so thread pulls from the front of the spool; place the other spool so the thread pulls from the back of the spool. Note that the Memory Craft 7500 and 8000 have auxiliary spool pins that attach on the top inside cover of the machine. See your Instruction Book for specific instructions.

1. Fold hem up desired amount and press.
2. With the right side up, place fabric under foot the width of the hem, so foot is resting on a double layer of fabric. Stitch.
3. Trim excess fabric away from the underside.

Sew-How: To keep from cutting a hole when trimming away the fabric close to the stitch, use a pair of scissors with one rounded or pelican-shaped blade. Position the scissors so the rounded blade is between the hem allowance and the wrong side of the project.

Twin Needle Tucks (Pintucks)

Set your machine as described above under Twin Needle Hem using the F appliqué or the pintuck foot (Fig. 9.35). For a more pronounced tuck, tighten the upper tension, and cord the tuck with pearl cotton. See Pintuck foot in Chapter 9 for instructions on corded pintucking.

Stitch tucks with thread matching the fabric to create texture down the front of a knit sweatshirt, top, or dress. Pintuck the front of an heirloom blouse or christening gown. Run multiple rows around the hem of a skirt for more body (Fig. 8.11).

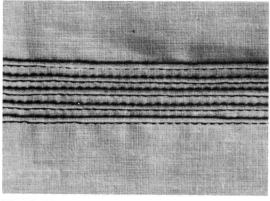

Fig. 8.11
Twin needle pintucks.

With the right side up, sew on a single layer of fabric. The bobbin thread shares itself between the two top threads creating a zigzag stitch on the underside and a tuck on the right side of the fabric. For stretchy knits, lengthen stitch to 4–4.5

Understiching

Understiching prevents the inside layer of fabric from rolling to the outside and is generally done on a facing edge.

After stitching and trimming the seam, press seam allowance toward the facing. With the right side up, stitch ⅛″ (3mm) from the seam line using a straight stitch appropriate for the fabric (Fig. 8.12).

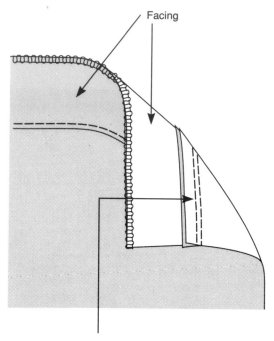

Fig. 8.12
Understitching prevents facing from rolling toward the outside.

Understitching a facing first makes it easier to topstitch later. However, you may not always want to topstitch, so instead of using a straight stitch to understitch a facing, use a multiple zigzag stitch on a 1.5 length and a 4–5 width (see Fig. 8.37). This stitch flattens the bulk and makes the seam allowance lie flat so it may not be necessary to topstitch.

(OUTLINE) STRETCH STITCH (33, 7500; 16, 8000)

· Seaming Knits
· Outline Stretch Stitch as a Hem Stitch
· Roll and Whip Edges
· Attach Entredeux

Seaming Knits

The stretch stitch, sometimes referred to as the outline stretch stitch, is recommended for seaming knits where the seam allowance will be pressed open and for seaming very fine knits where the seam will be trimmed to ¼″ (6mm) (Fig. 8.13). Note that this stitch guides in center needle position on the Memory Craft models, so make the appropriate adjustments when guiding for a ⅝″ (1.5cm) seam allowance.

Fig. 8.13
The (outline) stretch stitch.

Machine Readiness Checklist	
Stitch:	(outline) stretch (33, 7500; 16, 8000)
Length:	2.5
Width:	1
Foot:	A zigzag
Needle:	appropriate for fabric or 11/75 Blue Tip
Tension:	normal (auto)

Place right sides together and stitch on the ⅝″ (1.5cm) seam line. Press seam flat and together, then press the seam open. For a ¼″ (6mm) seam, sew at the ¼″ (6mm) seam line, overcast the seam allowance together using the multiple zigzag stitch (1–1.5 length, 5 width; see Fig. 8.32 later in this chapter), then press seam to one side toward the front of the garment.

Sew-How: The (outline) stretch stitch is a great problem-solver stitch; if you have a difficult, slippery fabric, this stitch will generally produce a satisfactory seam.

Outline Stretch Stitch as a Hem Stitch

Another application for the (outline) stretch stitch is to hemstitch a linen collar, cuff, napkin, or tablecloth.

Machine Readiness Checklist	
Stitch:	(outline) stretch (33, 7500; 16, 8000)
Length:	2.5
Width:	1–1.5
Foot:	A zigzag
Needle:	wing
Thread:	darning (see Sources of Supply)
Feed dogs:	up
Tension:	normal (auto)
Fabric:	tightly woven cotton or linen

1. Using all-purpose thread and a 11/75 Blue Tip needle, finish hem edge with the multiple zigzag stitch (1–1.5 length, 5 width). Fold hem up desired amount and press.

2. Using a wing needle, rethread top and bobbin with darning (basting) thread. Topstitch hem so the foot is resting on a double layer of fabric.

Roll and Whip Edges

In lace insertions in French hand-sewn projects, the fabric must be secured to the lace so the lace will not pull off the fabric. To secure an edge, roll and whip with the (outline) stretch stitch.

Machine Readiness Checklist

Stitch:	(outline) stretch (33,7500; 16, 8000)
Length:	2
Width:	2–3
Foot:	F satin stitch
Needle:	9/60 universal
Thread:	top and bobbin, darning or #50 machine embroidery
Feed dogs:	up
Tension:	top, loosened slightly; bobbin, normal
Fabric:	cotton batiste
Accessories:	edging lace

1. Place edging lace on batiste, right sides together, leaving a ¼″ (6mm) seam allowance on the fabric.

2. Baste lace to the fabric using the A zigzag foot and 2.2 length straight stitch. Trim seam allowance to ⅛″ (3mm) (Fig. 8.14A).

3. Snap on the F satin stitch foot. Place the fabric under the foot, centering the stitched edge of lace under the arrow in the foot and stitch (Fig. 8.14B). The needle swings off the edge at the right to "roll and whip" the lace to the fabric.

4. Lengthen the stitch to 2.5–3 and stitch over the seam again from the right side. This helps stabilize the seam and allows it to lie flat (Fig. 8.14C).

Attach Entredeux

Entredeux is a trim used in French hand-sewn projects. Here's how to attach it:

1. Without trimming the seam allowance away, place batiste and entredeux right sides together.

2. Baste entredeux to fabric, stitching-in-the-ditch as close to the holes of the entredeux as possible (see Fig. 8.8).

Sew-How: Try using the G blind hem foot (Figs. 9.10, 9.17) to stitch-in-the-ditch, guiding the blade along the ridge in the entredeux. Remember to adjust the needle position to avoid hitting the blade in the foot.

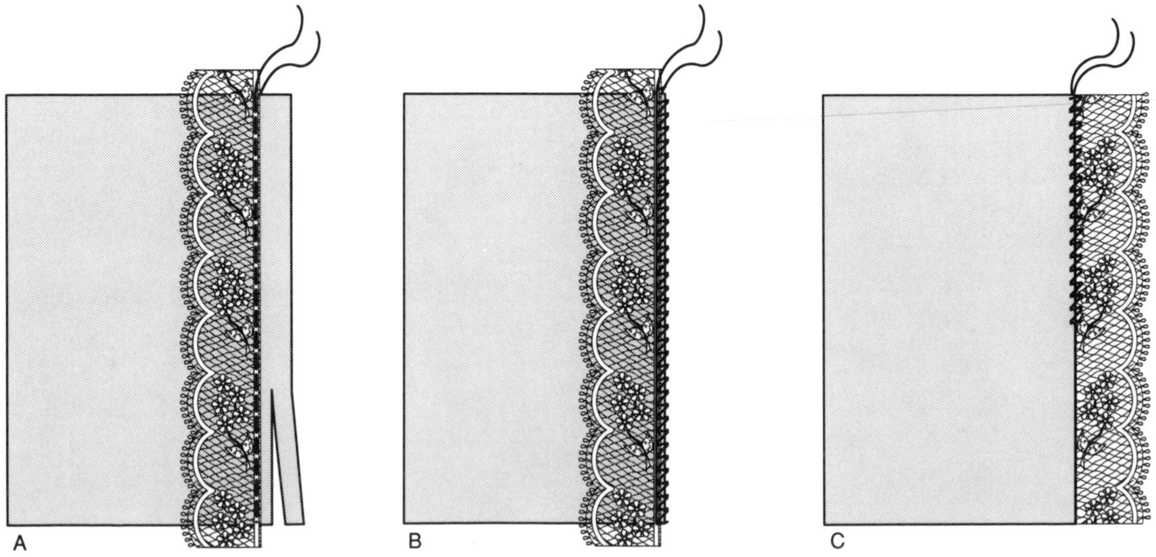

Fig. 8.14
Attaching a lace insertion on French hand-sewn projects. A, Straight stitch along lace heading, right sides together. B, Roll and whip the fabric edge using the (outline) stretch stitch. C, Stitch over the seam again from the right side.

3. Trim seam allowance to ⅛" (3mm) and press seam toward the fabric.

4. Set your New Home as described above under Roll and Whip Edges, and roll and whip along both edges of the entredeux, letting the needle stitch in the holes of the trim (Fig. 8.15).

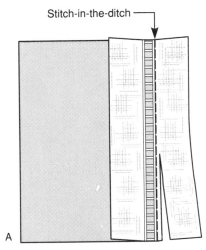

Stitch-in-the-ditch

Trim to 1/8" (3mm)

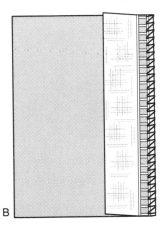

Fig. 8.15
Attach entredeux to fabric. A, Place right sides together, then straight stitch-in-the-ditch next to the entredeux. Trim seam allowance to ⅛" (3mm). B, Roll and whip the edges together with the (outline) stretch stitch.

ZIGZAG STITCH (35, 7500; 4, 8000)

· Button Sewing

· Button and Belt Loops

· Couching with the Zigzag Stitch

· Gathering over a Cord

· ⅝" (1.5cm) Knit Seam

· Overcast a Raw Edge

· Satin Stitch

· Satin Stitch Lettuce or Rolled Edge

· Tapered Satin Stitch

· Speed Basting

· Thread Tacks

On older mechanical machines you add stitch width to a straight stitch to get a zigzag stitch. On newer models, select the stitch by touching the zigzag key.

The zigzag stitch is used to sew buttons, embroider, make belt loops, gather over a cord, stitch a knit seam, overcast a raw edge, satin stitch, tack down a facing, plus much more.

To acquaint yourself with the stitch, sew row after row of zigzag stitches, experimenting with the stitch width and length (Fig. 8.16). Record settings and keep your experiments in your notebook. Once you have a basic familiarity with the zigzag, you will master the following techniques.

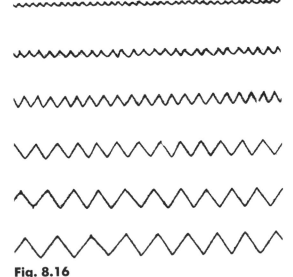

Fig. 8.16
Zigzag stitch on varying widths and lengths.

Button Sewing

Use the zigzag stitch to sew a button on by machine (see Fig. 9.30). Unlike commercial machines that use a one-thread chain stitch to attach buttons, the conventional sewing machine has a top and bobbin thread so buttons are stitched securely. Sewing buttons by machine is also faster than sewing them on by hand.

Machine Readiness Checklist

Stitch:	zigzag (35, 7500; 4, 8000)
Length:	0
Width:	2–4 (test on your button)
Foot:	F satin stitch, button sewing, or none
Program function (7500 only):	M/memory + M/memory + lock-off + M/memory
Needle:	appropriate for fabric
Needle position:	left (if possible)
Thread:	all-purpose
Feed dogs:	down
Tension:	normal (auto) or loosened slightly to make a thicker shank
Accessories:	transparent tape or glue stick, Fray-Check, tapestry hand needle or wooden matchstick

1. Mark button placement. Place button by taping it on or by dabbing the back with the glue stick.

Sew-How: A thread shank between the button and the fabric allows room for the buttoned fabric. To make a thread shank, either use the button sewing foot (Fig. 9.30) and place a tapestry needle or wooden matchstick between toes of the foot, or tape a needle between the holes of the button before placing the button on the fabric (Fig. 8.17).

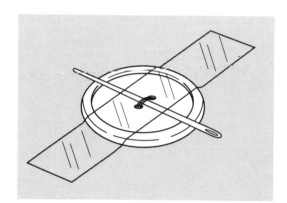

Fig. 8.17
Button taped to fabric with tapestry needle between the holes.

2. Turn the flywheel by hand so the machine needle stops in the left hole of the button and lower the presser bar lever.

3. Turn the flywheel by hand to check the needle clearance; adjust your zigzag width if necessary. Then stitch.

4. Stitch five or six zigzag stitches. Move the width to 0 so the needle is positioned over a hole in the button, then take a few straight stitches in place to anchor threads.

Sew-How: For button sewing, the Memory Craft 7500 is programmed to stitch, then automatically lock off with a straight stitch in the left hole. To sew a straight stitch in left needle position on the 8000, touch stitch 1 then the reverse key to lock off the threads.

5. Remove fabric and pull off enough thread to wrap a shank between the button and fabric (Fig. 8.18).

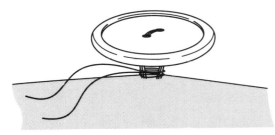

Fig. 8.18
Wrap a thread shank between the button and fabric.

6. After wrapping shank, pull threads to the back, tie, and clip them off at the fabric. Put a drop of liquid fabric sealant on threads to secure them.

Button and Belt Loops

Rather than hand crocheting belt or button loops, zigzag over pearl cotton or multiple strands of thread.

Machine Readiness Checklist	
Stitch:	zigzag (35, 7500; 4, 8000)
Length:	0.5–0.8
Width:	3–5
Foot:	H cording
Needle:	11/80 Blue Tip
Thread:	all-purpose
Feed dogs:	up
Tension:	normal (auto)
Accessories:	pearl cotton to match thread or multiple strands of thread, large-eyed tapestry needle

1. Place a double strand of pearl cotton or multiple strands of thread under the clip and in the center of the foot so 2" (5cm) extend behind the foot (see Fig. 9.18).

2. Hold top and bobbin thread tails behind the foot and zigzag over the cord by pulling it through the foot so the stitches cover cord (Fig. 8.19).

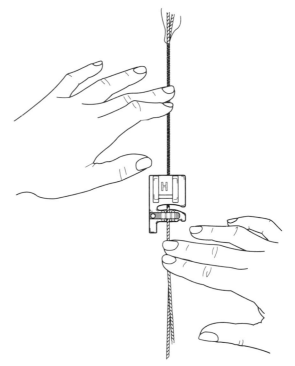

Fig. 8.19
Zigzag over pearl cotton to make belt and button loops.

3. Thread stitched cord through tapestry needle to insert in seam where desired. Knot both ends so loop will not pull out.

Sew-How: For a stretchy loop, zigzag over elastic thread instead of pearl cotton.

Couching with the Zigzag Stitch

Couching is a way to attach cord, floss, yarn, or ribbon to the surface of a fabric for an edge finish or decorative treatment.

Machine Readiness Checklist	
Stitch:	zigzag (35, 7500; 4, 8000)
Length:	1–2
Width:	wide enough to clear cord
Foot:	H cording
Needle:	11/75 Blue Tip
Thread:	all-purpose to match cord or nylon monofilament
Feed dogs:	up
Tension:	normal (auto)
Fabric:	medium-weight woven
Accessories:	tear-away stabilizer or iron-on freezer wrap

Place cord, floss, yarn, or ribbon on the right side of a single layer of fabric. Zigzag over cord to attach to the fabric (Fig. 8.20). If the fabric is lightweight, place tear-away or iron-on freezer wrap to stabilize the fabric.

Fig. 8.20
Yarn couched down with a zigzag stitch.

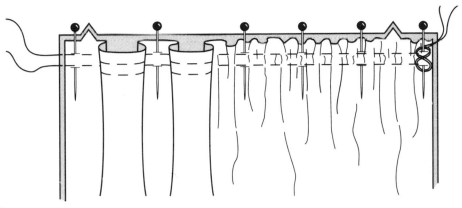

Fig. 8.21
Two rows of straight stitches pulled into gathers.

Gathering over a Cord

To gather fabric, pattern instructions usually say to stitch two rows of straight stitches and then pull (Fig. 8.21). While this is the preferred method for fine fabrics such as batiste, the threads often break when they are pulled on midweight to heavy fabrics. To circumvent this problem, zigzag over a cord.

Machine Readiness Checklist	
Stitch:	zigzag (35, 7500; 4, 8000)
Length:	2–3
Width:	2–3 or wide enough to clear cord
Foot:	H cording
Needle:	appropriate for the fabric
Needle position:	center
Feed dogs:	up
Tension:	normal (auto)
Accessories:	#8 or #5 pearl cotton or nylon fishing line

1. Place pearl cotton or fishing line under the center groove in the foot so the cord extends 2–3″ (5–7.5cm) behind. (Sewers I met in Nebraska who make square-dance dresses gather over fishing line because it is strong and slippery to make yards and yards of ruffles.)

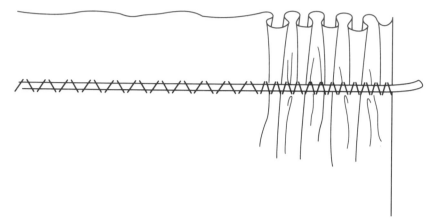

Fig. 8.22
Zigzag over cord and pull gathers up.

2. Guiding ½" (1.3cm) from the raw edge and on the wrong side of a single layer of fabric, zigzag over cord, being careful not to catch cord in the stitching (Fig. 8.22).

3. Pull gathers up and adjust from both ends. Once fabric has been gathered to desired length, knot or anchor cord so gathers don't pull out. Although it is not necessary, you may remove the cord after stitching.

Sew-How: If gathering a long ruffle, cut the cord or pearl cotton the length of the finished ruffle plus 4" (10cm). Mark the finished length of ruffle on the cord by marking 2" (5cm) from both ends of the cord. Then mark the cord and fabric to be ruffled into fourths between the pins. Anchor the beginning end of the cord by wrapping it around a pin. Zigzag over the cord as described above. While stitching, guide cord with your right hand while pushing gathers down the cord with your left, matching the marks on the fabric with the marks on the cord. This way, the ruffle is gathered to the exact length needed without wasting a lot of cord. Twist cord around a pin at the other end of the ruffle so it won't slide off the cord.

⅝" (1.5cm) Knit Seam

If a straight stitch is used to construct a knit, the thread often breaks. Instead, stitch the seam with a tiny zigzag stitch.

Machine Readiness Checklist	
Stitch:	zigzag (35, 7500; 4, 8000)
Length:	1–2
Width:	1
Foot:	A zigzag
Needle:	11/75 Blue Tip
Thread:	all-purpose
Feed dogs:	up
Tension:	normal (auto)
Fabric:	wool jersey or mid-weight knit

1. Place right sides together and stitch seam at the ⅝" (1.5cm) seam line (Fig. 8.23).

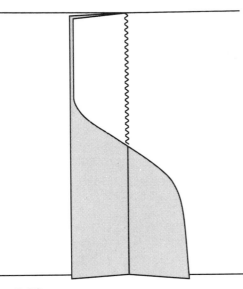

Fig. 8.23
Use tiny zigzag to sew a ⅝" (1.5cm) seam on a knit.

2. Press seam flat and together to blend the stitches. Then press seam open.

Sew-How: This stitch is difficult to rip, so baste the seam together first (see Speed Basting on page 167) to check the fit.

Overcast a Raw Edge

Although it isn't always necessary to finish the seams, overcasting a raw edge prevents raveling and makes the project look more professional. The zigzag stitch can be used to overcast a raw edge; however, many fabrics curl or tunnel under the stitch. To minimize this curling, try the following method.

Sew-How: The multiple zigzag (36, 7500; 18, 8000), overcast stitch (38, 7500; 5, 8000), and special overlock (40, 7500; 23, 8000) are preferred stitches for overcasting. If you have one of those stitches available, skip ahead to pages 171, 185, and 187 and read how to use them for overcasting.

Machine Readiness Checklist	
Stitch:	zigzag (35, 7500; 4, 8000)
Length:	1.5–2
Width:	4–5
Foot:	C overedge
Needle:	appropriate for fabric
Thread:	all-purpose
Feed dogs:	up
Tension:	normal (auto)

1. Place single layer of fabric under the foot so the raw edge is even with the guide in the foot.

2. Overcast edge, guiding the fabric so the needle swings off the edge on the right (Fig. 8.24).

Fig. 8.24
Finish raw edge with a zigzag and the C overedge foot.

Machine Readiness Checklist	
Stitch:	zigzag (35, 7500; 4, 8000)
Length:	0.3–0.5
Width:	2, 4, 5
Foot:	F satin stitch or F appliqué
Needle:	appropriate for fabric
Needle position:	center
Thread:	cotton, rayon, or acrylic embroidery
Feed dogs:	up
Tension:	top, loosened slightly; bobbin, normal
Fabric:	tightly woven cotton or cotton blend
Accessories:	iron-on freezer paper or tear-away stabilizer

Satin Stitch

- Satin Stitch Lettuce or Rolled Edge
- Tapered Satin Stitch

The satin stitch looks like a narrow satin ribbon stitched around appliqués and is used to monogram and embroider. Stitch different widths of satin stitches for your notebook.

Iron freezer paper or pin stabilizer to the back of a single layer of fabric. Set your machine for a 2-width satin stitch. Stitch and examine, then adjust the stitch length so the stitches are next to, but not on top of, each other (Fig. 8.25). Use the satin stitch for appliquéing, block monograms, flower stems, satin stitched edges, and cut work.

Fig. 8.25
Varying widths of satin stitching.

Satin Stitch Lettuce or Rolled Edge

The lettuce edge looks like the edge of a lettuce leaf when stitched on a knit. It's used on lingerie, ribbing edges, and children's clothing. When used on a woven, it looks like a rolled hem found on the edge of placemats, napkins, and scarves. When a woven is worked on the bias and stretched, it becomes a lettuce edge.

Machine Readiness Checklist	
Stitch:	zigzag (35, 7500; 4, 8000)
Length:	0.3–0.5
Width:	4–5
Foot:	F satin stitch or F appliqué
Needle:	11/75 Blue Tip
Thread:	all-purpose, cotton, or acrylic embroidery
Feed dogs:	up
Fabric:	single knits (e.g., interlock, jersey, tricot, ribbings)
Tension:	top, loosened slightly; bobbin, normal
Accessories:	round-nosed or pelican scissors

Method One

This technique works beautifully on nylon tricot or any single knit. When stretched across the grain, single knits curl to the right side.

1. To make the fabric roll, stretch the raw edge across the grain. Place rolled edge under the foot, holding the fabric in front of and behind the foot (Fig. 8.26).

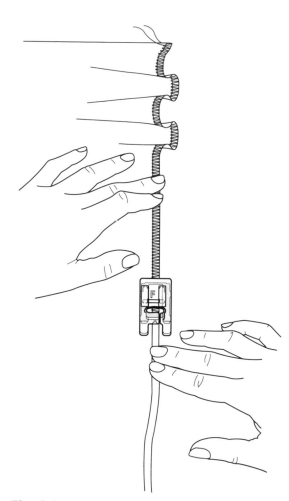

Fig. 8.26
Zigzag over curled edge, holding fabric in front of and behind the foot.

2. Guide fabric so the needle stitches over the roll on the left and off the raw edge at the right.

Sew-How: To prevent the roll from becoming too thick, pull across the grain, grasping the fabric as close to the edge as possible.

Method Two

This is recommended for woven fabrics and single knits that run or are very stretchy (e.g., ribbing, interlock, wool jersey, and Lycra spandex).

1. Fold and press at least a $\frac{1}{2}''$ (1.3cm) hem.

2. Place fold halfway under the foot, right side up, so the needle catches the fabric on the left and swings off the fold at the right. Do not stretch the fabric while sewing. The stitches automatically push the fabric out of shape, creating a ripple.

3. Carefully trim the excess fabric to the stitching line.

4. After trimming, stretch the fabric across the grain and the edge ripples even more.

Tapered Satin Stitch

Use a tapered satin stitch to create leaves, stems, and tapered monograms.

Machine Readiness Checklist	
Stitch:	zigzag (35, 7500; 4, 8000)
Length:	0.5—0.8
Width:	0—5—0
Foot:	F satin stitch
Needle:	11/75 Blue Tip or 14/90 stretch
Thread:	top, cotton, rayon, or acrylic embroidery; bobbin, darning
Feed dogs:	up
Tension:	top, loosened slightly; bobbin, normal
Fabric:	firmly woven
Accessories:	iron-on freezer wrap or tear-away stabilizer

Starting at a 0 width, begin sewing fast while quickly moving from a narrow width to the widest width then back again. Practice by making a sampler and putting it in your notebook.

Speed Basting

This is a fast, easy method of basting knits together, and the stitches pull out quickly after fitting.

Machine Readiness Checklist	
Stitch:	zigzag (35, 7500; 4, 8000)
Length:	4–5
Width:	4
Foot:	A zigzag
Needle:	appropriate for fabric
Thread:	top, all-purpose; bobbin, color that contrasts, top thread
Feed dogs:	up
Tension:	top, loosened; bobbin, normal
Fabric:	knits

1. Speed baste the seam at seam line indicated on pattern.

2. Check fit, reset your machine for the appropriate stitch and tension, then permanently stitch the seam. Remove basting stitches by pulling bobbin thread (Fig. 8.27).

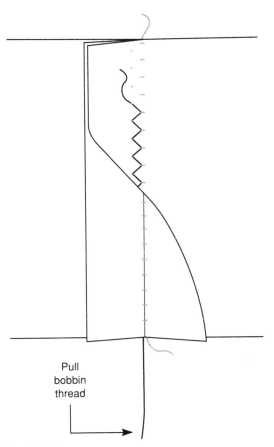

Fig. 8.27
Remove speed basting by pulling bobbin thread.

Sew-How: Use water-soluble basting thread on the bobbin as a temporary seam. The stitches dissolve in water.

Thread Tacks

Tack a facing, bow, or small appliqué like this:

Machine Readiness Checklist	
Stitch:	zigzag (35, 7500; 4, 8000)
Length:	0
Width:	3–5
Foot:	A zigzag or F satin stitch
Needle:	14/90 denim for heavy fabrics, 11/75 Blue Tip for light to midweight fabrics
Feed dogs:	down
Tension:	normal (auto)
Accessories:	liquid seam sealant

1. Place item to be tacked under the foot. Take four to five zigzag stitches. Move the width to 0 (Fig. 8.28).

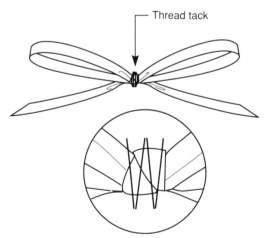

— Thread tack

Fig. 8.28
Attaching a ribbon or yarn with thread tack.

2. Stitch a few straight locking stitches, remove the fabric, and pull threads to the back. Clip threads close to the fabric and dab them with seam sealant.

MULTIPLE ZIGZAG (36, 7500; 18, 8000)

- Attaching Elastic
- Mending
- Overcasting a Raw Edge
- Patching
- Tacking
- With Twin Needles
- Understitching

Next to the straight and zigzag stitches, I feel the multiple zigzag, often referred to as the three-step zigzag, is most useful. The stitch takes three short stitches to the left, and three short stitches to the right—there is a sharp point where the stitch changes direction. Use this stitch for attaching elastic, mending, overcasting a raw edge, patching, tacking down facings or trims, twin needle cable stitching, understitching, and much more.

Attaching Elastic

Pattern instructions usually say to stretch the elastic while attaching it to the fabric. When the needle stitches through the elastic, it causes the rubber to break down and the elastic to stretch out of shape. You can avoid this pitfall with the following method because the fabric is stretched rather than the elastic. For this reason, it works only on knits.

Machine Readiness Checklist

Stitch:	multiple zigzag (36, 7500; 18, 8000)
Length:	1–1.5
Width:	4–5
Foot:	A zigzag
Needle:	11/75 Blue Tip
Thread:	all-purpose
Feed dogs:	up
Tension:	normal (auto)
Fabric:	sweatshirt fleece, velour, stretch terry, or other knit fabrics
Accessories:	vanishing marker, pencil with an eraser on the end

Note: To do this technique properly, you must have about ½″ (1.3cm) of fabric on either side of the elastic. Therefore, when cutting fabric out, add ½″ (1.3cm) to the top opening where elastic is to be stitched. This method also works the same no matter where the elastic is applied. However, for this example, the instructions are written as if you were applying elastic to the waistline.

1. Cut elastic 3–5″ (7.5–12.5cm) shorter than waistline measurement. Mark it into eighths with the vanishing marker. Mark garment waistline into eights.

Sew-How: *Double-check the length of waistline elastic before cutting to be sure it fits over your hips.*

2. Pin elastic to wrong side of fabric, matching eighth-marks and placing it ½″ (1.3cm) from cut edge. Do not join elastic ends.

3. Place work under the foot and sew a couple of stitches to anchor elastic. Using index finger of both hands simultaneously, start sewing while pulling the fabric out sideways, exactly where the needle enters the fabric. Take four or five stitches, reposition your fingers, and repeat until the fabric is eased in place and elastic ends overlap (Fig. 8.29).

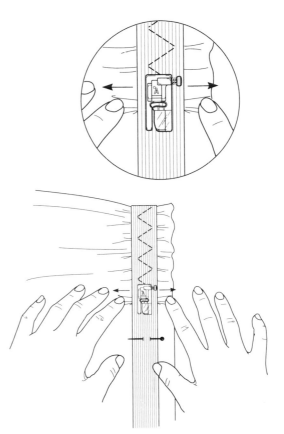

Fig. 8.29
Pin elastic to wrong side, ½″ (1.3cm) from cut edge. Pull fabric out sideways where the needle enters the fabric, and sew four to five stitches. Repeat until fabric is eased into elastic.

Sew-How: *For a firmer grip at the right, pull on the fabric using the eraser end of a pencil.*

4. Fold fabric over elastic so the multiple zigzag shows on the inside.

5. Place waistline under foot, wrong side up so the needle will be stitching just under the elastic. Place index finger to the left side of the foot. Sew to the left of the elastic while wiggling the fabric back and forth with the index finger of your left hand (Fig. 8.30). The wiggling prevents the elastic from stretching out and eliminates unnecessary puckers, tucks, or gathers from being stitched in the right side of the work.

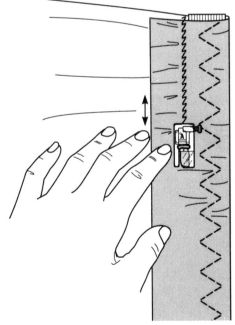

Fig. 8.30
"Wiggle" fabric into place with left index finger.

6. Trim excess fabric away up to the stitch.

Mending

Mend a run or tear with the multiple zigzag stitch.

Sew-How: I mend old denim jeans using a gray color thread on the bobbin and a blue to match the fabric on the top. Then I tighten the upper tension slightly. The mend is almost invisible because the gray thread pulls slightly to the surface of the fabric, giving a faded look to the stitch to match the denim.

1. Fuse a strip of interfacing to the underside of tear. Center the run or tear under the foot and sew (Fig. 8.31). The stitches form over and across the tear, keeping the fabric flat and helping pull raveled threads in place.

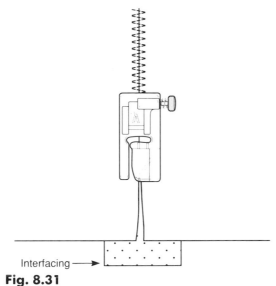

Fig. 8.31
Center run or tear under foot and mend with the multiple zigzag stitch.

2. If necessary, turn the fabric around and stitch another row of multiple zigzags next to the first until tear is repaired.

Overcasting a Raw Edge

Overcasting a raw edge with the zigzag stitch often causes tunneling. Because the multiple zigzag takes three short stitches over and three back, it keeps raw edges flat. Overcast almost any type of fabric with this stitch.

Machine Readiness Checklist	
Stitch:	multiple zigzag (36, 7500; 18, 8000)
Length:	0.8–1.5 (use shorter length on fine fabrics, longer length on heavy fabrics)
Width:	5–7
Foot:	A zigzag

Place raw edge under the foot so the right swing of the stitch is just off the edge.

Sew-How: *After cutting, overcast raw edges before putting the project together. To overcast quickly, butt one pattern piece up next to the other without lifting the foot. When you're done, pattern pieces will look like a kite tail (Fig. 8.32). Then cut threads between the pieces before construction.*

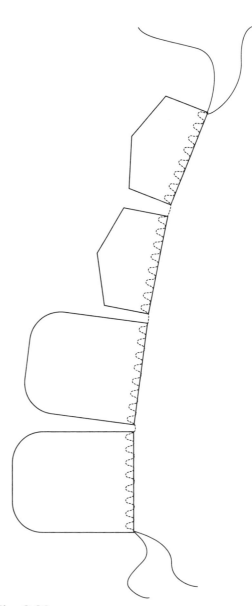

Fig. 8.32
To save time, butt one pattern piece up to the next when overcasting.

Patching

The old-fashioned way to patch was to turn the raw edges in on the patch and stitch it over the hole by hand. This method is so slow, I found my mending pile getting unmanageable. Save time and put a patch on to stay with this method.

Machine Readiness Checklist	
Stitch:	multiple zigzag (36, 7500; 18, 8000)
Length:	0.5–0.8
Width:	7
Foot:	A zigzag or Teflon
Needle:	14/90 denim for medium to heavy fabrics; 11/75 Blue Tip for lightweight fabrics
Thread:	all-purpose, cotton darning, or basting (see Sources of Supply)
Feed dogs:	up
Accessories:	glue stick

1. Cut patch large enough to cover the hole so the frayed fabric is covered. Don't turn under edges. Because the mending stitches are so close, the edges won't fray. This method also cuts down on bulk.

2. Pin or glue-stick patch over hole. Starting at one corner, guide fabric so the right swing of the needle clears the raw edge of the patch. Sew to the corner, stopping with the needle on the far right side of the stitch (Fig. 8.33).

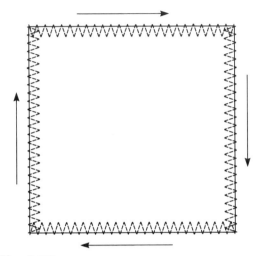

Fig. 8.33
Stitch patch so the stitches cross each other at the corners.

3. Pivot patch and stitch second side. The stitches should cross each other in the corner for extra reinforcement.

4. Repeat for other two sides. Pull threads to the back and tie them off. Trim damaged fabric from the wrong side of the patch.

Sew-How: If you have a free-arm machine, you can patch a knee or elbow without ripping out the seam and without removing the fabric as long as your model has the continuous reverse feature (see your Instruction Book). To do this, sew the first two sides of the patch as described above, then use the continuous reverse to sew the second two sides of the patch.

Tacking

Tack down a facing, ribbon, or yarn tie when tying a quilt, or attach a small appliqué.

Machine Readiness Checklist	
Stitch:	multiple zigzag (36, 7500; 18, 8000)
Length:	0
Width:	3–7
Foot:	A zigzag or F satin stitch
Feed dogs:	down
Needle position:	left (if possible)

1. Place facing, yarn, ribbon, or appliqué on background or fashion fabric and under the foot.

2. Stitch across and back in the same place five or six stitches (Fig. 8.34). Move width to 0 and stitch in one place.

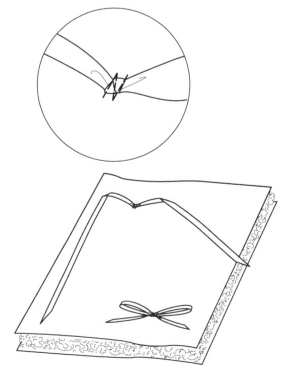

Fig. 8.34

Stitch across and back a few times to tack down a facing, ribbon, or yarn tie in a quilt.

Sew-How: *On the New Home Memory Craft models, push the lock-off or reverse key so stitches lock off automatically.*

3. Pull threads to the back and cut or tie them off.

Multiple Zigzag with Twin Needles

Use thread matching the fabric to create a cable in a solid-colored fabric. I've used five to seven rows of cable stitching down the front of a stretch terry cloth sweatshirt and centered down each sleeve.

Machine Readiness Checklist	
Stitch:	multiple zigzag (36, 7500; 18, 8000)
Length:	1–2
Width:	3 (wide enough for needles to clear the hole in the foot and needle plate)
Foot:	F satin stitch
Needle:	twin, size 2.0/12 (80) or 2.5/12 (80)
Thread:	all-purpose
Feed dogs:	up
Tension:	top, increase slightly for sharper tuck; bobbin, normal
Fabric:	stretch terry, velour, wool jersey, some midweight T-shirt knits
Accessories:	vanishing marker or dressmaker's chalk

1. Using the vanishing marker or dressmaker's chalk, mark where the center cable is to be stitched.

2. Sew the first row of cable stitches over the line marked in Step 1. Turn the fabric around and stitch the second row next to the first about a presser-foot-width away (Fig. 8.35). (If you were to sew every line the same way, the fabric would distort.)

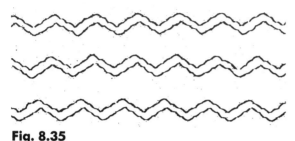

Fig. 8.35
Use twin needles with the multiple zigzag to create a cable on a soft knit.

3. Continue to sew row after row of cable stitching, working from the center row of cable stitches out, until you have the desired effect.

Sew-How: Once you have mastered this technique, match the stitches, back to back, and use this design as the center row of cabling (Fig. 8.36).

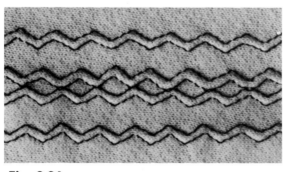

Fig. 8.36
Match twin needle, multiple zigzag cable stitches back to back.

Understitching

Understitching prevents the inside layer of fabric from rolling to the outside and is generally done on a facing edge. You can understitch with the straight stitch, but the multiple zigzag flattens the bulk of a faced edge better, so it's not always necessary to topstitch.

Machine Readiness Checklist	
Stitch:	multiple zigzag (36, 7500; 18, 8000)
Length:	1–1.5
Width:	5–7
Foot:	A zigzag

1. After stitching, trimming, and grading the seam, press seam allowance toward facing.

2. With the right side up, place the foot so the right edge of the needle hole is at the seam line, and understitch (Fig. 8.37).

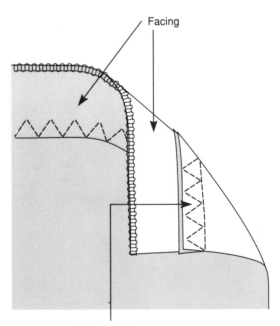

Facing

Understitching

Fig. 8.37
Understitch facings with the multiple zigzag to prevent them from rolling out of place.

Sew-How: The purpose of grading a seam (trimming one seam allowance narrower than the other) is to minimize bulk and to help a seam allowance that is not pressed open to lie properly. When grading a seam, the fabric always falls to the narrow seam allowance.

Sew-How: Rather than using hem tape to finish the hem edge of a woven fabric, overcast the hem edge with the multiple zigzag (36, 7500; 18, 8000), decorative overlock (2, 7500; 58, 8000), or serge finish. By doing so you save time, minimize bulk, and have one less thing you need to find to match your fabric.

BLIND HEM STITCH (41, 7500; 6, 8000)

- Blind Hemming Woven Fabrics
- Couched Saddle Stitch
- Shell Tuck and Corded Shell Tuck

Blind Hemming Woven Fabrics

The blind hem stitch, sometimes referred to as the blind stitch, enables you to hem woven fabrics quickly. There are two New Home G blind hem feet (see Figs. 9.10, 9.17)—one is adjustable, and one has a fixed black metal blade. I prefer the type with the metal blade for blind hemming because the blade helps you guide the fabric and creates slack in the stitch so the stitch is almost invisible.

Machine Readiness Checklist	
Stitch:	blind hem (41, 7500; 6, 8000)
Length:	2–2.5
Width:	0.7–1
Foot:	G blind hem
Needle:	9/65 universal
Thread:	all-purpose
Feed dogs:	up
Tension:	top, loosened slightly on fine fabrics; bobbin, normal
Fabric:	a variety of woven fabrics to practice and to make samples for your notebook

1. Measure hem, and cut raw hem edge so it is even. Then finish the raw edge as described in the Sew-How above. Pin hem up desired amount, placing pins perpendicular to and ¼" (6mm) from hem edge (Fig. 8.38).

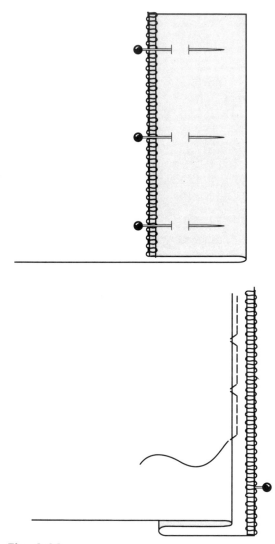

Fig. 8.38
Top, Place pins perpendicular to and ¼" (6mm) from hem edge. Bottom, Fold hem back to where the pins enter the fabric. Needle stitches on extension, then takes a small bite into the fold.

Sew-How: For circular hems "easestitch plus" around the finished edge (see Fig. 8.5).

2. With gentle steam and a press cloth, press hem without pressing over pins.

3. Fold hem allowance to the outside, folding the hem back to where the pins enter the fabric. Place hem under foot so the body of the garment is to the left, and the ¼" (6mm) extension is to the right of the needle.

4. Begin stitching so the needle takes a few stitches on the extension, then a small bite into the fold, picking up a thread or two at the left. Remove pins before stitching over them. The less fabric the needle catches, the more invisible the hem. On lightweight fabrics, loosen the top tension slightly.

5. Press hem from the right side with steam and a press cloth.

Sew-How: Although it's not necessary to use finer thread when hemming, it does give more invisible results. I like #50 weight cotton embroidery thread (see Sources of Supply).

Couched Saddle Stitch

This topstitching technique is used commonly on ready-to-wear coats and suits and is easy to duplicate.

Machine Readiness Checklist

Stitch:	blind hem (41, 7500; 6, 8000)
Length:	1–1.5
Width:	1.5
Foot:	H cording
Needle:	11/75 Blue Tip
Thread:	nylon monofilament top and bobbin
Feed dogs:	up
Tension:	normal (auto)
Fabric:	wool coating, fleece, or suiting
Accessories:	#3 or #5 pearl cotton, strand of embroidery floss, or fine yarn

---

Thread pearl cotton or floss into the center groove of the H cording foot and topstitch. The straight stitches bury themselves in the fabric next to the floss, while the zigzag creates an indentation so each stitch looks $\frac{1}{4}$" (6mm) long (Fig. 8.39). For a longer look to the topstitch, lengthen the stitch.

Fig. 8.39
Couched saddle stitch.

Shell Tuck and Corded Shell Tuck

Shell tuck the edge of a half-slip, skirt lining, neck edge, facing, or trim with the blind hem stitch.

Machine Readiness Checklist

Stitch:	blind hem (41, 7500; 6, 8000)
Length:	1.5–2
Width:	1.3–7
Foot:	B transparent buttonhole or F satin stitch
Needle:	appropriate for the fabric
Thread:	all-purpose or cotton embroidery
Feed dogs:	up
Tension:	top, tightened slightly; bobbin, normal
Fabric:	nylon tricot, cotton knits, lining fabrics
Accessories:	#3 or #5 pearl cotton

Memory Craft 6000, 7000, 7500 Notes:
Stitching a shell tuck with the bulk of the fabric to the right can be awkward. Instead, push the pattern turn-over key and guide the fabric so the bulk is to the left.

---

1. Turn up a hem and press. **Note:** If shell tucking a ribbing edge, do not press over folded edge because it may distort the ribbing.

2. If using a standard blind hem stitch, place folded edge under the foot so the bulk of the fabric is to the right. If using the pattern turn-over function, place folded edge under the foot with the bulk to the left. Place fold halfway under the foot and stitch (Fig. 8.40). To prevent skipped stitches, the needle must swing completely off the folded edge.

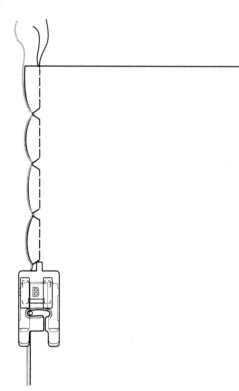

Fig. 8.40
To shell tuck with the standard blind hem stitch, place folded edge under foot with bulk to the right. To cord tuck, guide cord under the left groove in the B transparent buttonhole foot.

Sew-How: To cord the shell tuck, lay a strand of pearl cotton under the foot and along the fold, then stitch. Note that the cord guides under the left groove if you are using the blind hem stitch; the cord guides under the right groove if you are using the pattern turn-over function. Again, the needle must swing off the fabric and over the cord.

---

3. You can trim the excess fabric to the stitch; however, the edge may curl on a single knit. To avoid this, sew a row or two of decorative stitching or a twin needle tuck a presser-foot-width from the shell tuck; then trim excess fabric to the stitch.

STRETCH BLIND HEM STITCH (42, 7500; 20, 8000)

· Blind Hemming Knits
· Narrow Decorative Edge

Blind Hemming Knits

The stretch blind hem stitch is designed for hemming knit fabrics. Notice the narrow zigzag stitches between the wider ones (Fig. 8.41). This enables the stitch to stretch with the fabric, so you are less likely to catch your heel in a knit hemline and rip it out.

Fig. 8.41
The stretch blind hem stitch in two widths.

Machine Readiness Checklist	
Stitch:	stretch blind hem (42, 7500; 20, 8000)
Length:	0.6–1
Width:	0.7–1.3
Foot:	G blind hem or G adjustable blind hem
Needle:	11/75 Blue Tip
Thread:	all-purpose
Tension:	top, loosened slightly for lightweight fabrics; bobbin, normal
Fabric:	knit jersey, double knit, velour, or stretch terry cloth

1. Measure hem, and cut raw hem edge so it is even. Pin hem up desired amount, placing pins perpendicular to and ¼" (6mm) from hem edge (see Fig. 8.38).

Sew-How: *Because the stretch blind hem stitch is made of zigzag stitches, it is not necessary to overcast the raw hem edge of the knit fabric.*

---

2. With gentle steam and a press cloth, press hem without pressing over pins.

3. Fold hem allowance to the outside, folding the hem back to where the pins enter the fabric. Place hem under foot so the body of the garment is to the left, and the ¼" (6mm) extension is to the right of the needle.

Sew-How: *The fabric is guided the same for both blind hem and stretch blind hem stitches (see Fig. 8.38).*

---

4. Begin stitching so the needle takes a few stitches on the extension, then a small bite into the fold, picking up a thread or two at the left. Remove pins before stitching over them. The less fabric the needle catches, the more invisible the hem, so use the narrowest width possible. On lightweight fabrics you may want to loosen the bobbin tension, too.

5. Press hem from the right side with steam and a press cloth.

Sew-How: *Although it's not necessary, the finer the thread used when hemming, the more invisible the results. I like #50 weight cotton embroidery thread (see Sources of Supply).*

Narrow Decorative Edge

The stretch blind hem stitch can also be used on a shorter stitch length and a wider width to create a stitch that looks like an eyelash or hand buttonhole stitch. Use it to topstitch an appliqué, create eyelashes on a puppet or toy (see Chapter 6), or cord the stitch for a two-toned decorative effect (Fig. 8.42).

Fig. 8.42
Narrow decorative edge with the stretch blind hem stitch.

Machine Readiness Checklist	
Stitch:	stretch blind hem (42, 7500; 20, 8000)
Length:	0.3–0.4
Width:	1.2–7
Foot:	F satin stitch
Needle:	11/75 Blue Tip
Thread:	all-purpose or cotton, rayon, or acrylic embroidery (for a faster fill-in, use two threads through the same needle)
Feed dogs:	up
Tension:	top, loosened slightly; bobbin, normal

Fold and press a narrow ½" (1.3cm) hem. Place fold under the foot so the stitches on the right fall just off the edge of the fold.

Sew-How: *If you are using the stretch blind hem stitch to appliqué, guide the straight edge of the stitch along the edge of the appliqué so the stitches on the left cover the raw edge. For an edge finish, fold under at least ½" (1.3cm) hem and press.*

ZIGZAG APPLIQUÉ STITCH (43, 7500; 21, 8000)

Corded Edge Finish

For a wider edge finish than is possible with the stretch blind hem stitch on some models, use the zigzag appliqué stitch (Fig. 8.43).

Fig. 8.43
Corded edge finish with the zigzag appliqué stitch.

Machine Readiness Checklist	
Stitch:	zigzag appliqué (43, 7500; 21, 8000)
Length:	0.3–0.5
Width:	2–7
Foot:	H cording
Needle:	appropriate for fabric
Thread:	all-purpose or cotton, rayon or acrylic embroidery
Feed dogs:	up
Tension:	normal (auto)
Accessories:	#5 pearl cotton

1. Press a narrow ½" (1.3cm) hem. Place a strand of pearl cotton under the center or left groove of the clip in the cording foot.

Sew-How: *For a 3–4 width, use the center groove of the foot; for a 5 width or wider, use the far right or far left groove in the foot.*

---

2. Place the fabric under the foot so the stitches zigzag off the fold and over the cord on the right.

3. Trim away excess hem allowance to the stitch. Use this on the edge of a ruffle, place mat, cuff, front tab, or the edge of a collar or pocket.

REVERSE CYCLE UTILITY STITCHES

- Decorative (Overlock) Stitch
- Triple Strength Stitch
- Saddle Stitch
- Knit Stitch
- Overcast
- Double Overedge
- (Special) Overlock
- Appliqué Stitch
- Patchwork Stitch
- Wide Cording (Rickrack) Stitch

Reverse cycle stitches, often referred to as stretch stitches, are created by the feed dogs moving the fabric forward and backward as the needle zigzags from side to side. The combination of the needle swing and the feed dog action creates stitches such as the decorative (overlock) stitch (2, 7500; 58, 8000), which we will look at first.

DECORATIVE (OVERLOCK) STITCH (2, 7500; 58, 8000)

· Overcast a Raw Edge
· One-Step ¼″ (6mm) Seams

The decorative stitch, sometimes called the overlook stitch, resembles a 3-thread serger overlock. It is used on knits and wovens to overcast raw edges and to stitch and finish a ¼″ (6mm) seam in one operation. It is also used to topstitch T-shirts, sweatshirts, swim wear, and other active sportswear.

Overcast a Raw Edge

This edge finish is recommended for loosely woven fabrics.

Machine Readiness Checklist	
Stitch:	decorative (overlock) (2, 7500; 58, 8000)
Length:	2–2.5
Width:	4–7
Foot:	A zigzag or C overedge for fine- to midweight fabrics, F satin stitch for heavy or lofty fabrics
Needle:	appropriate for the fabric
Thread:	all-purpose
Feed dogs:	up
Tension:	normal (auto)

To overcast a raw edge, place raw edge under foot so the needle catches into the fabric on the left and swings just off the raw edge and over the guide in the foot on the right (Fig. 8.44).

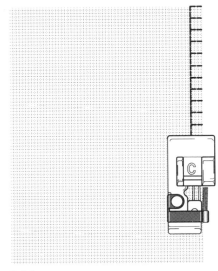

Fig. 8.44
Overcast a raw fabric edge with the decorative (overlock) stitch. The C foot distorts the stitch so that it looks like this.

One-Step ¼″ (6mm) Seams

Use this method on midweight knits and some wovens. As always, test on a swatch first.

Machine Readiness Checklist	
Stitch:	decorative (overlock) (2, 7500; 58, 8000)
Length:	2–2.5
Width:	5–7
Foot:	F satin stitch or C overedge
Needle:	11/75 Blue Tip for knits; 12/80 universal for wovens
Thread:	all-purpose
Feed dogs:	up
Tension:	normal (auto)

1. For a project cut with ¼″ (6mm) seam allowances, place right sides together so raw edges are to the right inside edge of the guide in the presser foot. The needle stitches into the seam allowance on the left and swings off the raw edge on the right (Fig. 8.45).

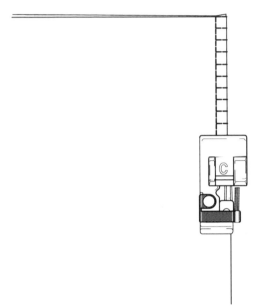

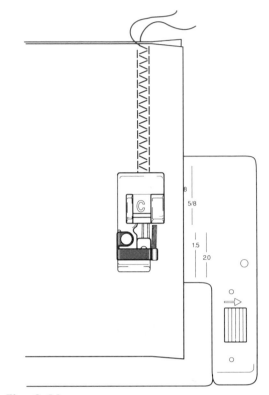

Fig. 8.46
Guide seam allowance by the ½″ (1.3cm) line in the needle plate and trim the fabric up to the stitch.

Fig. 8.45
Stitch a ¼″ (6mm) seam allowance with the decorative (overlock) stitch so the stitch swings off raw edge on the right.

Sew-How: For a project with ⅝″ (1.5cm) seam allowances, place fabric under foot, guiding the raw edge by the ½″ (1.3cm) line in the needle plate (Fig. 8.46). If you guide by the ⅝″ (1.5cm) line in the needle plate, the stitch cheats you out of ⅛″ (3mm) at each seam allowance. That doesn't sound like much, but multiply ⅛″ (3mm) by eight cut edges and you have removed 1″ (2.5cm) from the total circumference. Your garment may be too snug for comfort. Trim excess fabric up to the stitch.

TRIPLE STRENGTH STITCH (32, 7500; 15, 8000)

This stitch was thought of as the original stretch stitch because it is strong enough to stretch with a knit seam and recovers well after stretching. However, it is almost impossible to rip out if you make a mistake. The triple strength stitch takes two stitches forward and one back and is used to reinforce areas of stress such as underarm and crotch seams. It can also be used as a topstitch (Fig. 8.47).

Fig. 8.47
Triple strength or saddle stitch as a topstitch on jeans.

Sew-How: The triple strength stitch must be adjusted so the needle stitches back into the same holes. If your stitching line is rough and the stitch uneven, check your Instruction Book *to see how the stitch length can be balanced or fine-tuned, using the feed balance dial.*

SADDLE STITCH (34, 7500; 17, 8000)

To outline an appliqué or duplicate the look you see on jeans and leather goods, use the saddle stitch. The needle takes two short stitches back and one longer stitch forward to cover the two back-stitches, which gives the stitch its bold look.

KNIT STITCH (37, 7500; 19, 8000)

- $\frac{1}{4}''$ (6mm) Seams on Stretchy Knits
- Reverse Embroidered Blanket Edge Finish
- Fagoting

$\frac{1}{4}''$ (6mm) Seams on Stretchy Knits

The knit stitch is designed for use on midweight and heavy, super-stretchy fabrics. It can also be used on heavy woven fabrics as a seam finish. Use it for $\frac{1}{4}''$ (6mm) seams on sweater knits, stretchy terry cloth, ribbing, Lycra spandex swim wear, and biking fabrics.

Often seams on these fabrics require stabilizing so they will not droop or stretch out of shape. To stabilize, incorporate elastic thread, yarn, or pearl cotton in the seam.

Machine Readiness Checklist	
Stitch:	knit (37, 7500; 19, 8000)
Length:	2–2.5
Width:	4–5
Foot:	A zigzag for fine fabrics; H cording for mid-weight to heavy fabrics
Needle:	appropriate for fabric
Thread:	all-purpose
Feed dogs:	up
Tension:	normal (auto)
Pressure:	2 for heavy fabrics
Fabric:	stretch terry, velour, sweater knits
Accessories:	elastic thread, yarn, or pearl cotton

1. For a project cut with $\frac{1}{4}''$ (6mm) seam allowances, place right sides together so raw edges are to the right inside edge of the needle hole in the presser foot. Put needle in fabric and raise the foot. (For a project with $\frac{5}{8}''$ [1.5cm] seams, see Sew-How under Decorative [Overlook] Stitch on page 182.)

2. Cut a length of elastic thread, yarn, or pearl cotton the length of the seam, and place it under the foot. Put the foot down and stitch (Fig. 8.48). The needle stitches into the seam allowance on the left and off the raw edge at the right. If you use the H cording foot, slip the cord or elastic thread in the middle channel and sew. The clip keeps the cord from moving around under the stitch.

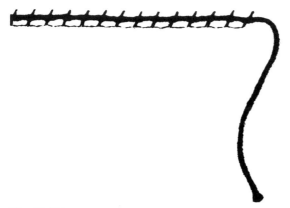

Fig. 8.48
To stabilize a knit seam, place a strand of elastic thread, yarn, or pearl cotton under foot and stitch with the knit stitch.

Reverse Embroidered Blanket Edge Finish

Instead of using trim, braid, or bias tape to finish and decorate an edge, try this striking edge finish on a wool coating or fleece.

Machine Readiness Checklist	
Stitch:	knit stitch (37, 7500; 19, 8000)
Length:	2.5
Width:	4–7
Foot:	F satin stitch
Needle:	appropriate for fabric
Thread:	top, all-purpose to match pearl cotton; bobbin, #5 pearl cotton
Feed dogs:	up
Tension:	top, normal (auto); bobbin, bypassed
Fabric:	wool coating or fleece, heavy wool flannel, other plush fabrics to make samples for your notebook
Accessories:	#5 pearl cotton to match or contrast fabric, adding machine tape

1. Wind a bobbin with pearl cotton by threading it through one of the holes in the bobbin. Then put the bobbin on the bobbin winder so the end of the pearl cotton is through the top of the bobbin. Let the bobbin turn a few times until the pearl cotton is secured around it. Stop, then clip the tail off at the bobbin so it won't get tangled. Then finish winding the bobbin until it is full.

2. Place the bobbin in the race as you would a bobbin wound with all-purpose thread, *but do not thread it into the bobbin tension.*

3. Place the fabric *right side down* and so the cut edge is to the inside edge of the right toe of the foot. Sew. The last stitch to the right should fall just off the edge of the fabric.

4. Now, if you can, push the pattern turn-over key, and repeat as described above. This time the straight stitches lie along the cut edge (Fig. 8.49). Aren't the results sensational?

Fig. 8.49
Reverse embroidered knit stitch used as a blanket edge finish.

Fagoting

Fagoting is a method of joining two pieces of fabric with a stitch, resulting in a lacy look to the seam. Fagoting can be used on christening gowns, blouses, tablecloths, or anywhere there is a seam. This technique has a bold crocheted look. Make samples for your notebook using a variety of fabrics and weights of pearl cotton, embroidery floss, ribbon, or ribbon floss.

1. Set your machine as described above for the blanket edge finish and, if possible, using the pattern turn-over key.

 2. On the edges that will be fagoted together, finish the raw edge using all-purpose thread and the multiple zigzag stitch (or serge finish), then fold and press a $\frac{1}{2}''$ hem.

3. Place the fabric so the right side is down against the adding machine tape. Then place the fabric so the folded hem edge is half under the presser foot. This way half of the stitch will form on the fabric, and the other half will form on the paper.

4. Sew one row of stitches the length of the fabric to be fagoted together. Turn the fagoted fabric around, then place the second piece of fabric under the foot so the fold is halfway under the foot. Stitch so the straight part of the stitch is formed in the center on the adding machine tape.

5. Remove the adding machine tape. The two pieces of fabric should be joined with a beautiful row of stitching (Fig. 8.50).

Fig. 8.50
Reverse embroidered knit stitch used for fagoting.

OVERCAST (38, 7500; 5, 8000)

• Lingerie Elastic Application

The overcast stitch can also be used to overcast a raw edge or for a one-step $\frac{1}{4}''$ (6mm) seam finish as described above for the decorative (overlock) stitch, but my favorite application is for attaching lingerie elastic.

Lingerie Elastic Application

Machine Readiness Checklist	
Stitch:	overcast (38, 7500; 5, 8000)
Length:	2.0–2.5
Width:	3–5
Foot:	F satin stitch
Needle:	11/75 Blue Tip or 10/70 universal
Thread:	all-purpose or nylon lingerie
Feed dogs:	up
Tension:	normal (auto)
Fabric:	nylon tricot or cotton single knit
Accessories:	½″ (1.3cm) lingerie elastic, vanishing marker

Note: To do this technique properly, leave about ½″ (1.3cm) of fabric on either side of the elastic. It works only on knits or loosely woven fabrics cut on the bias. Cut lingerie with ½″ (1.3cm) extra fabric at the top of waistline and at panty legs where elastic is to be sewn.

1. Measure elastic to fit comfortably around the waist or legs—usually 2–5″ (5–12.5cm) smaller than garment opening. Mark elastic and opening into eighths using the vanishing marker.

2. Pin elastic to opening on the right side, ½″ (1.3cm) down from the raw edge. Overlap and pin elastic ends at the side seams.

Sew-How: Lingerie elastic wears longer when sewn on the outside of the garment because the fabric underneath protects it from perspiration and body oils.

3. Place work under presser foot so the left side of the stitch falls on the fabric and the right side swings onto the elastic. Take a couple of stitches to anchor elastic.

4. Using index fingers of both hands simultaneously, start sewing while pulling the fabric out sideways, exactly where the needle enters the fabric. Take four or five stitches, reposition your fingers, and repeat until the fabric is eased into place and elastic ends overlap (Fig. 8.51).

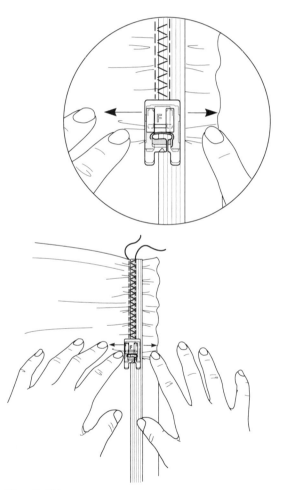

Fig. 8.51
Place work so left side of stitch falls on the fabric and right side swings onto elastic. Pull fabric sideways where needle enters fabric and take four or five stitches. Repeat until fabric is eased into elastic.

5. Trim away excess fabric to the stitch. Stitch a ribbon over elastic ends to cover the overlap.

DOUBLE OVEREDGE
(39, 7500; 22, 8000)

As with the overcast stitch, the double overedge is used for overcasting a raw edge. The extra zigzag stitches keep threads from raveling on a loosely woven fabric (Fig. 8.52).

Fig. 8.52
Finish edge of loosely woven fabric with the double overedge stitch.

Machine Readiness Checklist	
Stitch:	double overedge (39, 7500; 22, 8000)
Length:	2.5
Width:	5
Foot:	C overedge
Needle:	appropriate for the fabric
Thread:	all-purpose
Feed dogs:	up
Tension:	normal (auto)

Guide the raw edge against the guide in the foot. The stitch is tricked into thinking the fabric extends past the guide by stitching through the brush on the foot (see Fig. 9.6), creating a beautifully finished edge.

(SPECIAL) OVERLOCK
(40, 7500; 23, 8000)

The overlock stitch, sometimes called the special overlock, is an industrial-type overcasting stitch used to finish a raw edge on a loosely woven fabric and to stitch and finish a seam in one operation.

Machine Readiness Checklist	
Stitch:	(special) overlock (40, 7500; 23, 8000)
Length:	2
Width:	7
Foot:	M special overcast
Needle:	appropriate for fabric
Feed dogs:	up
Tension:	top, loosened slightly; bobbin, normal

1. Place fabric under the M special overcast foot so the raw edge or edges are against the guide in the foot.

Memory Craft Notes: On some Memory Craft models, this stitch sews backward first, so start sewing $\frac{1}{4}''$ (6mm) from the end of the fabric.

2. The needle sews over the prong farthest to the right, forming a thread chain over the edge of the fabric. After sewing a short distance, check to see that the thread chain is forming without any loops. If loops appear, tighten the upper tension slightly until you get the desired result (Fig. 8.53).

Fig. 8.53
Special overlock stitch.

APPLIQUÉ STITCH
(44, 7500; 24, 8000)

· Hand-Look Appliqué

· Fine Seam-and-Overcast

· Delicate Edge Finish

This simple stitch, sometimes called a picot or heirloom appliqué stitch, can be used in a variety of ways. First, it can be used to simulate a hand appliqué stitch. If possible on your machine, push the pattern turnover key, and it becomes a fine seam-and-overcast, perfect for seaming batiste, organdy, organza, handkerchief linen, nylon tricot, and lining fabrics. Use it as a delicate edge finish on lightweight wovens and knits (Fig. 8.54).

Fig. 8.54

Use the appliqué stitch for a hand-look appliqué work or a fine seam-and-overcast.

Hand-Look Appliqué

Machine Readiness Checklist	
Stitch:	appliqué (44, 7500; 24, 8000)
Length:	2–2.5
Width:	2.5–3.5
Foot:	F satin stitch or A zig-zag
Needle:	10/70 universal
Thread:	100% cotton machine embroidery to match base fabric
Feed dogs:	up
Tension:	top, loosened slightly; bobbin, normal
Fabric:	lightweight woven
Accessories:	glue stick

1. Cut out appliqué shape, adding $\frac{1}{4}''$ (6mm) seam allowances.

2. Turn appliqué seam allowance to the wrong side and press.

Sew-How: If the appliqué has a lot of curves, try this shortcut: Cut out shape from appliqué fabric using a $\frac{1}{4}''$ (6mm) seam allowance. Cut out shape plus seam allowances from a piece of paper-backed fusible web. Place the right side of the fabric against the rough side of web, then stitch around appliqué shape using a $\frac{1}{4}''$ (6mm) seam allowance. Clip or notch around curves as needed, or trim around appliqué using pinking shears. Cut a slit through the center of the paper and web. Peel off paper from the web, then turn appliqué through the slit. Fuse appliqué to the base fabric. This way the seam allowance is turned to the wrong side, then fused so the edge of the appliqué is smooth and easy to stitch around.

3. Glue-stick the appliqué to the base fabric if you haven't done the above Sew-How technique to affix appliqué to the base fabric. (Apply the glue stick to the appliqué when the fabric is warm for a better stick.)

4. Guide your work so the straight part of the stitch falls just off the folded edge of the appliqué. Stitch around appliqué, matching stitches at the beginning and end. Pull threads to the back and tie them off.

Sew-How: For a shadow appliqué, cut appliqué the exact size needed. Glue-stick appliqué to the base fabric. Lay a piece of sheer fabric over appliqué, and stitch around appliqué so the stitch is along the raw edge. The fabric will not ravel because the sheer fabric overlays the appliqué. The overlay also softens the appliqué color.

Fine Seam-and-Overcast

Machine Readiness Checklist	
Stitch:	appliqué (44, 7500; 24, 8000)
Length:	2–2.5
Width:	2.5–3.5
Function:	pattern turn over (if possible)
Foot:	A zigzag
Needle:	10/70 universal
Thread:	100% cotton sewing
Tension:	top, loosened slightly; bobbin, normal
Fabric:	organza, organdy, batiste, tricot, handkerchief linen

1. Cut out pattern pieces with a $\frac{5}{8}''$ (1.5cm) seam allowance.

2. If possible, push the pattern turn over key so the straight part of the stitch is on the left. If this is not possible, place the fabric under the foot with the bulk to the right.

3. Place right sides together, and stitch the seam at the $\frac{5}{8}''$ (1.5cm) seam line. Trim away seam allowance to the stitch.

Sew-How: For a French seam, place wrong sides together and stitch as instructed above. Press seam to one side, then fold right sides together to encase the seam allowance. Stitch next to the encased seam with a short straight stitch, guiding the seam allowance in the left channel of the B transparent buttonhole foot.

Delicate Edge Finish

Apply a piece of straight-edge lace using the appliqué stitch, guiding the straight part of the stitch along the straight edge of the lace.

Hem a napkin, placemat, or collar using the wing needle, fine thread, and the appliqué stitch. To do this, fold and press hem. Topstitch so the straight part of the stitch is parallel to the hem edge and the needle bites over and off the folded edge. Trim excess hem allowance to the stitch. Also try this delicate edge finish on a hem or at the edge of a collar, cuff, or tuck.

Machine Readiness Checklist	
Stitch:	appliqué (44, 7500; 24, 8000)
Length:	1.5–2.5
Width:	2.5–7
Foot:	B transparent buttonhole, M special overcast
Needle:	10/70 universal
Thread:	100% cotton machine embroidery
Feed dogs:	up
Tension:	top, loosened slightly; bobbin, normal
Fabric:	shirt-weight cotton, handkerchief linen

1. For a hem edge, fold and press a narrow $\frac{1}{2}''$ (1.3cm) hem and press.

2. Place the fold under the B transparent buttonhole foot so the fold is against the right inside edge of the left groove. The needle takes one stitch on the fabric and a couple of stitches over the fold to create a delicate thread chain.

Sew-How: When using the M special overcast foot, adjust the width so the right swing of the needle swings over the center wire.

3. If this technique was used at a hem edge, trim away excess hem fabric to the stitch.

PATCHWORK STITCH (45, 7500; 25, 8000)

Like the bridging stitch (1, 7500; N/A, 8000), the patchwork stitch is similar to the hand feather stitch used to piece crazy quilts. Use it as a decorative top-stitch on children's clothes, gifts, and table linens.

Reverse Embroidery

The patchwork stitch is also beautiful when stitched with pearl cotton. Reverse embroidery is done with the decorative thread in the bobbin, so remember to sew with the right side down.

Machine Readiness Checklist

Stitch:	patchwork (45, 7500; 25, 8000). On the 7500 also try 1, 47, 48, 49, 73, and 84. On the 8000 try 27, 28, and 98.
Length:	2.5; varies
Width:	4–7
Foot:	F satin stitch
Needle:	11/75 Blue Tip or appropriate for fabric
Thread:	top, all-purpose to match pearl cotton; bobbin, pearl cotton
Feed dogs:	up
Tension:	top, normal (auto) or slightly tightened; bobbin, bypassed
Fabric:	medium-weight knit or woven
Accessories:	water-erasable marker

---

1. Wind a bobbin with pearl cotton as explained above on page 184, guiding the pearl cotton evenly on the bobbin by hand as the bobbin turns on the winder.

2. For Memory Craft models, place bobbin in bobbin case without threading it through the tension. For machines with removable bobbin cases, slightly loosen the tension screw on the bobbin case by turning the screw counterclockwise, then thread the bobbin case with pearl cotton as you would with all-purpose thread. The pearl cotton should pull through the tension smoothly with a slight drag on it. Put bobbin case in the race as normal, then bring bobbin thread up by turning the flywheel one complete turn.

3. Test sew on a scrap and adjust the top tension so the pearl cotton does not loop. Mark where you want to sew on the wrong side of the fabric, and guide by the line. Turn your work over. Aren't the results beautiful (Fig. 8.55)? This is an easy way to create a trim, braid, or appliqué.

Fig. 8.55
Reverse embroidered patchwork stitch.

WIDE CORDING (RICKRACK) STITCH (46, 7500; 26, 8000)

This stitch is more a decorative than a utility stitch, but it can be used as a decorative seaming technique, so it is discussed here. Use this stitch on a 2–4 width where you would attach narrow rickrack. Try the following seaming technique to add a little interest to your next project.

Wide Cording (Rickrack) Stitch as Decorative "Ladder" Seam

Machine Readiness Checklist

Stitch:	wide cording (rickrack) (46, 7500; 26, 8000)
Length:	2.5
Width:	4–5
Foot:	fringe
Needle:	11/75 Blue Tip
Thread:	all-purpose or cotton to match fabric
Feed dogs:	up
Tension:	top, loosened sightly; bobbin, normal
Fabric:	suit-weight linen

 1. Overcast raw edges with the multiple zigzag, or serge finish (see Fig. 8.32).

2. Place the fabric right sides together and sew at the ⅝″ (1.5cm) seam line. The wide cording (rickrack) stitch forms over the blade in the fringe foot (see Fig. 9.33).

3. From the right side, pull the seam open so the ladder stitches are seen (Fig. 8.56). For a fagoted seam, press seam open. For a closed ladder seam, press seam to one side. Make a sample of each for your notebook.

Fig. 8.56
Wide cording (rickrack) stitch used as a decorative ladder seam.

BUTTONHOLES

· Bartack Buttonhole

· Rounded Buttonhole

· Keyhole Buttonhole

Today's New Home sewing machines and their buttonhole feet make sewing buttonholes easier than ever. In this section, we will look at the basic automatic bartack buttonhole, a corded buttonhole, and the speciality buttonholes available on the Memory Craft models (Fig. 8.57).

Fig. 8.57
From top to bottom, bartack, rounded, and keyhole buttonholes.

BARTACK BUTTONHOLE (107, 7500; 12, 8000)

Most New Home sewing machines built in the last 15 years make an automatic bartack buttonhole in one, two, or four steps without your having to turn the fabric. Each model has its own method. Check your *Instruction Book*.

Corded Buttonholes

Corded buttonholes look better and wear longer than ordinary buttonholes. Use them on coats, suits, and areas that receive a lot of stress and wear.

1. Set your New Home to make a bartack buttonhole (107, 7500; 12, 8000).

2. Select a pearl cotton, embroidery floss, or multiple strand of thread to match the fabric and thread. Place the cord over the prong on the back of the J sliding, N or R sensor buttonhole foot. Clip the ends of the cord between the prongs in the front of the foot. If you are using the B transparent buttonhole foot, loop the cord on the prong in the back of the foot and bring cord under the grooves. Regardless of the presser foot used, the loop should be at the stress point of the buttonhole.

3. Stitch the buttonhole making sure the zigzag stitches cover the cord but don't pierce it. Do not pull the cord while making the buttonhole because the cord moves with each stitch.

Sew-How: Some New Home models sew the sides of the buttonhole in the same direction, resulting in a better-looking buttonhole. This way, one side of the cord is stitched through, so simply pull the other side of the cord to snug it up to the bartack.

4. Pull the loop to the bartack. Then pull free ends of the cord to the back or between the facing and fashion fabric to tie them off (Fig. 8.58).

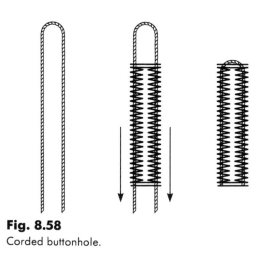

Fig. 8.58
Corded buttonhole.

Sew-How: To cut buttonholes open, use the back of your ripper to score the fabric between the two rows of stitching (Fig. 8.59). This opens the cutting space. Then use a buttonhole cutter and block to cut the buttonhole open. If you don't have a buttonhole cutter, use the ripper, sometimes called a buttonhole knife, to cut the buttonhole open. Put the point of the ripper in the middle of the buttonhole, then bring it up through the fabric in front of the bartack as if it were a pin (Fig. 8.60). Cut. Repeat for the other end of the buttonhole, cutting from the center out. This way you don't inadvertently cut through the bartack. Trim out any fraying threads; then put a little liquid seam sealant on the inside of the buttonhole.

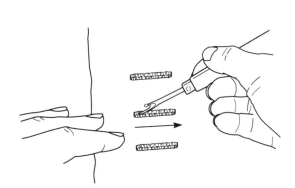

Fig. 8.59
Use the back of your ripper to score the cutting space and separate the two sides of the buttonhole.

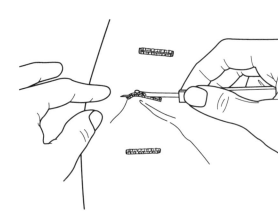

Fig. 8.60
Use a ripper to cut the buttonhole open.

Memory Craft Notes: *After making the first bartack, lift the foot and pull the pearl cotton loop up to the first bartack. Stitch the second side, then cross pearl cotton ends over one another at the other end of the buttonhole and bartack. Clip cord off at the fabric. The reinforced bartack stitches over the cord so it won't pull out when the buttonhole is used.*

ROUNDED BUTTONHOLE (108, 7500; 13, 8000)

This buttonhole is designed for light blouse-weight fabrics and children's clothing and is programmed on a 4 width. If you widen the width to 5–5.5, it can also be used as a lapel buttonhole on a tailored suit or jacket.

KEYHOLE BUTTONHOLE (109, 7500; 14, 8000)

This buttonhole is recommended for use on tailored jackets, coats, and men's wear. Although it is programmed on a 7 width, you can use it on a narrower width. I prefer it on a 5.5 width on most projects. Make samples for your notebook to find your favorite width setting.

Sew-How: *For the full effect of a keyhole buttonhole, the eye end must be trimmed out close to the stitches. This is difficult to do with a pair of scissors, so use an eyelet cutter. It has a wooden handle and a sharp eyelet-shaped blade. To use it, push straight down through the fabric against a wooden block.*

SPECIAL-PURPOSE STITCHES

- Eyelet
- Darn
- Bartack
- Basting

EYELET (110, 7500; 8, 8000)

You can make eyelets easily on the New Home 7000, 7500, and 8000 Memory Craft models. Use them to embellish a piece of fabric or run cord, ribbon, or trim through them. Other places to use eyelets are belts, down the front and cuffs of a tuxedo shirt so studs can pass through them, or at the top of a shower curtain.

Sew-How: *Rather than trimming away the fabric from the center of the eyelet with a pair of scissors, use an eyelet cutter (explained in the Sew-How opposite under Keyhole Buttonhole).*

DARN (111, 7500; 9, 8000)

- Darning
- Decorative Treatments

Darning

With the darn stitch you can darn the length of the tear, up to 2cm, and change direction by pushing the reverse key (7500) or size/set key (8000). The stitch then takes sixteen passes vertically over the hole and automatically stops and locks off.

Machine Readiness Checklist	
Stitch:	darn (111, 7500; 9, 8000)
Length:	varies with model
Width:	0
Foot:	J or R buttonhole
Function:	pattern turn over, M/Memory (7500); size/set key (8000)
Needle:	appropriate for fabric
Thread:	cotton darning or embroidery
Feed dogs:	up
Tension:	normal (auto)

Sew-How: To get the top thread under the presser foot, grasp both threads in one hand while pushing the needle up/down key twice. This makes the needle complete a stitch. Then, holding the bobbin thread with both hands, pass the bobbin thread under the foot to pull the top thread under the foot.

1. Place fabric under the foot and lower the presser foot so the threads are to the left.

2. Press the foot control and begin to darn. If you want the line of stitching to be less than 2cm long, press the reverse or size/set key when you reach the length you want. The machine then makes sixteen rows of darning from left to right.

3. To reinforce the darn on the 7500, press the pattern turn over key. The machine will stitch sixteen rows from right to left. The darn should look like Fig. 8.61. If it doesn't, then you must fine-tune by pushing the stitch length key or adjusting the feed balance. Complete instructions for your model are in your *Instruction Book.*

Fig. 8.61
Darn stitch.

Decorative Treatments

You can achieve some interesting decorative effects by distorting the darn stitch. By lengthening the stitch, you get a darn that looks like it has been stitched on the bias. Cross that darn with another color of thread and create another motif. Elongate by turning the feed balancing dial to plus (+) or minus (−) to achieve a flame stitch. Experiment and put your results in your notebook (Fig. 8.62).

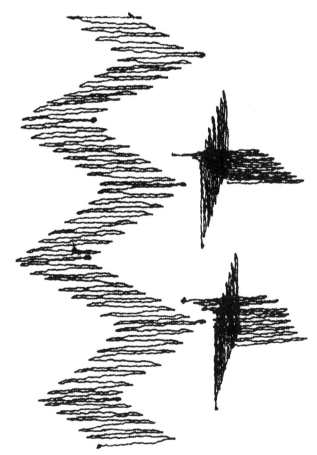

Fig. 8.62
Decorative variations of the darn stitch.

Sew-How: For a "pucker-proof" mend, darn, or decorative treatment, stretch your work in a hoop, or back it with tear-away or iron-on freezer wrap before sewing.

BARTACK
(112, 7500; 10, 8000)

Use the programmed bartack to reinforce pocket corners or the bottom of fly-front zippers and plackets or to tack drapery pleats or attach belt loops.

Machine Readiness Checklist	
Stitch:	bartack (112, 7500; 10, 8000)
Length:	1–2.5
Width:	1–5
Foot:	F satin stitch
Needle:	appropriate for the fabric
Thread:	all-purpose
Feed dogs:	up
Tension:	normal (auto)

Place pocket corner or area in need of reinforcement under the foot and sew. The stitch sews back first, then forward in vertical straight stitches, and finally overcasts with a row of zigzag stitches, so place fabric appropriately. The density and width can be changed by pressing the width and length keys. Sew the length of the bartack needed, stop, then press the reverse or size/set key. (The maximum length of the bartack from end to end is 2cm.) The bartack can also be repeated just by pressing the foot control again on the 8000 or the M/Memory key on the 7500.

BASTING
(113, 7500; 11, 8000)

For a longer basting stitch, use the stitch-by-stitch basting feature. This is a great way to baste quilt layers together or to machine-stitch tailor tacks.

Machine Readiness Checklist	
Stitch:	basting (113, 7500; 11, 8000)
Length:	preset
Width:	0–7 (this changes the needle position)
Foot:	P embroidery
Needle:	11/75 Blue Tip
Thread:	all-purpose
Feed dogs:	down
Tension:	top, normal (auto) or loosen to 0–2.5; bobbin, normal
Pressure:	2

Step on the foot control and the machine takes one stitch, then stops until you press the foot control again. To baste a long area, push the foot control, slide the fabric under the presser foot the desired distance, press the foot control again, and so on until the area has been basted together.

DECORATIVE STITCHES

New Home sewing machines have a wide array of decorative stitches to choose from. I have broken them down into the following groups by stitch application:

• Heirloom Lace Work Stitches
• Machine Embroidery Stitches
• Open Decorative Stitches
• Satin Stitch Variations
• Showcase Stitches
• Character Stitches
• Showcase Satin Stitches
• Letters, Numbers, and Punctuation

Decorative stitches on the New Home Memory Craft models are closed or open or have both closed and open motifs incorporated into one stitch. Closed means the stitches are close together and are variations of the satin stitch such as the tapered leaf (63, 7500; 33, 8000), ball (64, 7500; 34, 8000), and diamond (65, 7500; 35, 8000). Open decorative stitches are those where the beauty is in seeing the stitch and the fabric under it, such as the bamboo (101, 7500; 52, 8000) and the open chain (103, 7500; 50, 8000). Combination decorative stitches have both closed and open elements in one stitch, such as the argyle stitch (50, 7500; 45, 8000) and the vine (116, 7500; 108, 8000). Use decorative stitches to create borders on a front tab, pocket top, belt, or pair of suspenders. Decorate a napkin, placemat, or table cloth. Use them on children's clothes, gifts, toys, and games.

One of the most valuable samples in my notebook is a piece of pillow ticking on which I stitched row after row of decorative stitches, using varying lengths and widths and experimenting with the twin needle.

HEIRLOOM LACE WORK STITCHES

• Bridging Stitch
• Loop Stitch
• Hemstitches
• Briar Stitch
• Smocking Stitch
• Running Stems, Running Leaves, Smocking Key, and Four-Leaf Clover
• Double Overlock

Generally, lace work stitches are open decorative stitches that have a lacy look to them when stitched on the fabric. Many can also be used in heirloom sewing and for hemstitching using a wing needle and darning thread (see specific stitches for instructions) (Fig. 8.63).

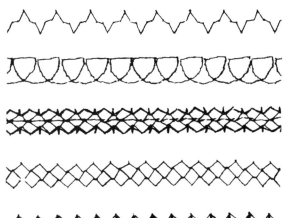

Fig. 8.63
Examples of heirloom lace work stitches.

BRIDGING STITCH (1, 7500; N/A 8000)

• Edge-to-Edge Piecing
• Fagoting

The bridging stitch resembles a hand stitch that was commonly used on crazy quilts years ago. It is used to piece together straight-cut edges of leather, vinyl, Ultraleather, or Ultrasuede. It is also used for piecing straight-edge lace or ribbon or to join two pieces of fabric or for fagoting.

Edge-to-Edge Piecing

This is a great way to join leather scraps together to make a belt, tote, or handbag. Also join straight-edge ribbon and lace.

Machine Readiness Checklist	
Stitch:	bridging (1, 7500: N/A 8000)
Length:	0.7–1.5
Width:	5–7
Foot:	A zigzag for fabric: Teflon for leather, suede, or vinyl
Needle:	appropriate for fabric
Thread:	appropriate for fabric
Feed dogs:	up
Tension:	normal (auto)
Fabric suggestions:	leather, suede, straight-edge lace or trim, straight seam allowances folded back and pressed
Accessories:	liquid seam sealant

1. With right side up, center the straight edge of leather, suede, lace, trim, or fabric under the foot.

2. Pull threads to the wrong side and tie them off. Drop liquid seam sealant on the knot.

3. For extra reinforcement, press a strip of fusible interfacing over the wrong side of the join.

Fagoting

Fagoting is a method of attaching fabric to fabric, or fabric to trim, with a row of stitching. For even spacing, use the G blind hem foot.

Machine Readiness Checklist	
Stitch:	bridging (1, 7500; N/A, 8000)
Length:	0.7–1.5
Width:	6–7
Foot:	G blind hem
Needle:	appropriate for fabric
Thread:	all-purpose or 100% cotton
Feed dogs:	up
Tension:	normal (auto)

1. Fold seam allowance of two pieces of fabric to the wrong side and press.

2. With the right side up, snug the fold of the left fabric piece against the guide in the G foot. Place the fold of the right fabric piece even with the bump on the right side of the guide. The space created between the two pieces of fabric by the foot keeps the spacing even.

3. Begin stitching. The needle catches a stitch in the fold on the left, then catches a stitch in the fold at the right. Continue stitching until fagoting is complete. Pull thread ends to the back and tie them off.

Use fagoting in heirloom sewing on a front yoke, down a sleeve, or at a hem.

LOOP STITCH (3, 7500; 66, 8000)

This open decorative stitch can be used to create borders and trims. My favorite use, however, is to stitch with #5 pearl cotton in the bobbin and match it up back to back over adding machine tape as described for the knit stitch (see Figs. 8.49, 8.50).

To make small button loops, use #5 pearl cotton in the bobbin and stitch half on and half off the fabric using adding machine tape under the fabric.

HEMSTITCHES
(4, 7, 12, 13, 27, 44, 48, 7500; 49, 63, 65, 59, 24, 28, 8000)

Hemstitches should not be confused with blind hem stitches; hemstitches look like a row of holes found at hems and edges of heirloom linen napkins, table linens, and linen fingertip and hand towels. Hemstitching can also be used as a lace insertion on French hand-sewn projects.

The holes are the predominant feature of these stitches, which are made with fine thread and a wing needle, which has wings on either side and pokes a large hole in the fabric. The stitch takes a few passes in and out of the same hole, which binds the hole open so it will not close after the fabric is cleaned or laundered. Fine thread is used so it will not fill up the holes with each stitch.

Although your New Home sewing machine has many of the hemstitches pre-programmed on a 7 stitch width, I prefer a 2–3 width on most of them. Make stitch samples for your notebook and write your preferred width setting for each stitch.

Stitch 4 (7500) or 49 (8000) is known as the Turkish hemstitch and is a beautiful topstitch on linen and other coarsely woven fabrics. Use stitch 7 (7500) or 63 (8000), the Venetian hemstitch, on a 1.5 length and a 3–4.5 width to make corded entredeux. Using the B transparent buttonhole foot, lay a fine cord under both sides of the stitch and it looks like purchased entredeux.

Stitch 13 (7500) or 59 (8000), the double overlock, is a beautiful hemstitch when sewn on handkerchief or suit-weight linen.

Stitch 12 (7500) or 65 (8000) is the Swiss hemstitch because, when used on batiste, it looks like fine Swiss hand loom.

Stitch 27 (7500), the running cross stitch; stitch 44 (7500) or 24 (8000), the appliqué stitch; and stitch 48 (7500) or 28 (8000), the (heirloom) scallop, also look like Swiss hand loom lace when stitched with the wing needle and darning thread. Combine these stitches on a strip of batiste and create your own lace trims.

BRIAR STITCH
(5, 7500; 56, 8000)

Use the briar stitch like the bridging stitch or patchwork stitch for reverse embroidery, fagoting, and edge-to-edge joining (see Figs. 8.49, 8.50).

SMOCKING STITCH
(6, 7500; 57, 8000)

This stitch can be used to stitch and finish a $\frac{1}{4}''$ (6mm) seam in one step on a lightweight knit as described on pages 181–182 for the (decorative) overlock stitch, as a decorative topstitch using two threads through the same needle, and to stitch overlapped seams in lacy fabrics as described here.

Machine Readiness Checklist

Stitch:	smocking (6, 7500; 57, 8000)
Length:	1–2.5
Width:	4–7
Foot:	A zigzag for fine fabrics, F satin stitch for heavier fabrics
Needle:	10/70 universal or 11/75 Blue Tip
Thread:	all-purpose or 100% cotton to match fabric
Feed dogs:	up
Tension:	normal (auto)
Fabric:	lace or lacy fabric
Accessories:	glue stick

---

1. On a flat surface, overlap a $\frac{5}{8}''$ (1.5cm) seam allowance by overlapping the wrong side of one fabric pattern piece against the right side of another.

Sew-How: *Use the glue stick to hold the seam together before stitching.*

---

2. Topstitch with the smocking stitch. Because the stitch is open looking, the lacy fabric shows through the stitch.

3. Carefully trim seam allowances to the stitch on both sides of the overlapped seam.

Sew-How: *The sand stitch (16, 7500; 53, 8000) can also be used in much the same way as the smocking stitch.*

RUNNING STEMS, RUNNING LEAVES, SMOCKING KEY, AND FOUR-LEAF CLOVER AS DECORATIVE STITCHES

These stitches (8, 9, 10, 11, 14, 7500; 67, 107, 106, 60, 104, 8000) can be used to create borders on a piece of ribbon, trim, or a flat piece of fabric.

Machine Readiness Checklist

Stitch:	one of those mentioned above
Length:	varies
Width:	varies
Foot:	F satin stitch
Needle:	14/90 Blue Tip
Thread:	rayon or acrylic embroidery
Feed dogs:	up
Tension:	Memory Craft, normal (auto); other models: top, loosened slightly; bobbin, normal
Fabric:	variety of woven strips cut into 4″ (10cm) widths
Accessories:	vanishing or water-erasable marker, iron-on freezer wrap

---

1. Cut freezer wrap into 4″ (10cm) widths. Iron it on the back of your fabric strips.

2. Draw a line down the center of the length of the fabric strip.

3. Sew a decorative stitch using the line as a guide. Decorate the strips with a variety of decorative stitches. Use them as strip samplers for your notebook and for borders and trims.

DOUBLE OVERLOCK (13, 7500; 59, 8000)

Use the double overlock for lapped seams or as a way of encasing narrow $\frac{1}{8}''$ (3mm) elastic, as described here. Also use it as described above as a hemstitch.

Machine Readiness Checklist	
Stitch:	double overlock (13, 7500; 59, 8000)
Length:	1–2.5
Width:	5–7
Foot:	F satin stitch
Needle:	appropriate for fabric
Thread:	all-purpose or nylon lingerie to match fabric
Feed dogs:	up
Tension:	normal (auto)
Fabric:	lightweight knit (tricot) or woven (handkerchief linen)
Accessories:	$\frac{1}{8}''$ (3mm) elastic

Sew-How: This is an easy way to attach elastic at the cuff of a little girl's dress sleeve. To do this, leave the sleeve open, attach the elastic 1" (2.5cm) above the finished edge of the sleeve, then seam the sleeve, catching elastic ends in the seam. The cuff shirrs in with a ruffle below the elastic.

1. With the sole off the foot shank, thread elastic up and over between the toes of the foot, and through the needle hole, so the elastic is under the heel of the foot.

2. Snap sole in place. Guiding on the wrong side of the fabric, take a few multiple zigzag stitches on a 0 length to anchor the beginning end of the elastic. Select the double overlock stitch and sew, encasing the elastic with the stitch, without stitching through the elastic.

Sew-How: If you pull the elastic slightly while sewing, the fabric will shir.

3. Slide stitches down elastic for desired fullness. Stitch seam, catching elastic ends in the seam.

MACHINE EMBROIDERY STITCHES

- Sculpture Stitch
- Sand Stitch
- Shading (Outline) Stitch and Shading (Fill-in) Stitch
- Broken Satin Stitch

Free-machine stitches are used to add depth and dimension and to help you to master free-machine embroidery (Fig. 8.64). Most of them are also used on a 2 pressure setting. Check your *Instruction Book.*

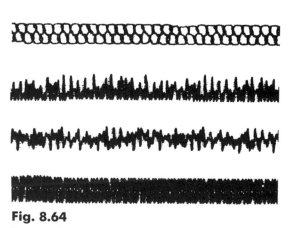

Fig. 8.64
Free-machine stitches, top to bottom: sculpture stitch, sand stitch, shading (outline) stitch, shading (fill-in) stitch, and broken satin stitch.

SCULPTURE (SEED) STITCH (15, 7500; 101, 8000)

After you have appliquéd, satin stitched, couched, or freely embroidered a design, outline or sculpture it for dimension and contrast. The sculpture stitch also looks like a string of seed pearls, so use it alone as a topstitch or to outline a shape that will be filled in.

SAND STITCH (16, 7500; 53, 8000)

The sand stitch resembles the smocking stitch, but rather than squares, the needle stitches complete circles, one next to the other. Use this intricate stitch to create cobblestones, seed pods, or to texture a shape or design.

SHADING (OUTLINE) STITCH (17, 7500; 102, 8000) AND SHADING (FILL-IN) STITCH (18, 7500; 103, 8000)

These stitches make free-machine embroidery a lot easier; they are used to outline and fill in designs while you freely move the fabric under the P embroidery foot. Or use these stitches with the F satin stitch foot for a quick, neat outline on an appliqué.

Machine Readiness Checklist	
Stitch:	(outline) shading (17, 7500; 102, 8000) and (fill-in) shading (18, 7500; 103, 8000)
Length:	0.4
Width:	2.5–7
Foot:	F satin stitch; P embroidery
Needle:	11/75 Blue Tip or 14/90 stretch
Thread:	top, cotton, rayon, or acrylic embroidery; bobbin, darning or basting
Feed dogs:	up; down
Tension:	top, loosened slightly; bobbin, normal
Pressure:	2
Accessories:	vanishing or water-erasable marker, embroidery hoop or tear-away stabilizer or iron-on freezer wrap

1. Try this technique with fabric stretched in a hoop and tear-away underneath, then without the hoop and stabilized with iron-on freezer wrap.

2. Draw a leaf shape on your fabric with the marker.

3. Place the fabric under the presser foot, then lower it. Take one stitch so the bobbin thread pulls up through the fabric. Bring the bobbin thread through the surface of the fabric and take a couple of stitches to lock off the threads. Clip off loose threads at the fabric.

4. Begin moving the fabric slowly while stitching quickly and outline the right side of the leaf with the straight edge shading stitch so the straight part of the stitch touches the line. To outline the left side of the leaf push the pattern turn-over key.

Sew-How: When you select either of these patterns, the visual screen may tell you to raise the feed dogs, even though the Instruction Book tells you to lower the feed dogs. I found that there was a difference in the look of the stitch with the feed dogs lowered and preferred them to be in the up position. Test for the desired effect.

5. To fill in the design, use the shading (fill-in) stitch (18, 7500; 103, 8000) and move the fabric smoothly from side to side. Experiment by moving the fabric in different directions and keep your samples for your notebook. For more information on free-machine embroidery techniques see Chapter 3 and *Know Your New Home* by Jackie Dodson with Judi Cull and Vicki Lyn Hastings (Chilton, 1989).

BROKEN SATIN STITCH (23, 7500; N/A, 8000)

This stitch can be stitched freely with the P embroidery foot and the feed dogs lowered, or with the F satin stitch foot to create even more texture. Use it to make stems or branches or as an interesting edge finish.

OPEN DECORATIVE STITCHES

• Reverse Embroidered Blanket Stitch
• Cross Stitch or Smocking Stitch for Russian Embroidery

Open decorative stitches (6, 19–28, 47–55, 80–84, 7500; 27, 28, 45–48, 54, 55, 57, 61, 69, 70, 74, 86–89, 97, 105, 8000) also known as tracery patterns, can be used to embellish everything from children's clothing to lingerie (Fig. 8.65). They can also be programmed with other stitches, letters, and numbers and matched back-to-back. Make a sampler of open decorative stitches for your notebook and vary the width, length, and pattern turn over function; also try them with twin needles.

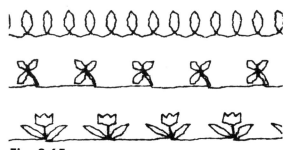

Fig. 8.65
Examples of open decorative stitches.

Sew-How: The following techniques are methods of reverse embroidery; see bobbin winding and threading instructions for the knit stitch, page 184.

REVERSE EMBROIDERED BLANKET STITCH (49, 7500; N/A, 8000)

Try this on the edge of a belt or front tab or on the edge of wool fleece.

Machine Readiness Checklist	
Stitch:	blanket stitch (49, 7500; N/A 8000)
Length:	2.5
Width:	7
Foot:	F satin stitch
Needle:	appropriate for fabric
Thread:	top, all-purpose or cotton embroidery; bobbin #8 pearl cotton or ribbon thread
Feed dogs:	up
Tension:	top, normal (auto); bobbin, bypassed
Accessories:	firmly woven fabric, iron-on freezer wrap, vanishing or water-erasable marker

1. Sewing with the right side down against the feed dogs, guide the right edge of the presser foot along the raw edge.

2. Turn your work over. Doesn't it look like a bound blanket edge? Trim away the fabric to the stitch.

CROSS STITCH (84, 7500; 70, 8000) OR SMOCKING STITCH (6, 7500; 57, 8000) FOR RUSSIAN EMBROIDERY

This technique looks like hand needle punch and can be done with the cross stitch (84, 7500; 70, 8000) or smocking stitch (6, 7500; 57, 8000). Use this to fill in a solid shape or to add a textured line to your embellishments.

Machine Readiness Checklist	
Stitch:	cross stitch (84, 7500; 70, 8000) or smocking stitch (6, 7500; 57, 8000)
Length:	1.5–2.5
Width:	3–3.5
Foot:	F satin stitch
Function:	feed balance dial to +
Needle:	appropriate for fabric
Thread:	top, all-purpose or cotton embroidery; bobbin, #5 or #8 pearl cotton, embroidery floss, or ribbon thread
Feed dogs:	up
Tension:	top, normal (auto); bobbin, bypassed
Fabric:	woven cotton
Accessories:	vanishing or water-erasable marker, iron-on freezer wrap

1. Iron freezer wrap onto the wrong side of a piece of woven fabric. Draw your design on the freezer wrap.

2. Sewing with the fabric upside down, start stitching on the outside of the design, guiding around and around to the center, until you have filled in the design with stitching.

Sew-How: It is easy to stitch too densely, so experiment on a scrap to sense how close each row of stitching should be and adjust the feed balance dial as needed.

3. Turn your work over. Aren't the results lovely? Experiment with different flosses, metallics, and cords for additional textures.

SATIN STITCH VARIATIONS

The satin stitch variations (56–69, 7500; 29–35, 37–44, 8000) are closed decorative stitches. Notice that the patterns are also underlined on the pattern selection keys on the Memory Craft 7000 and 7500. This means that each stitch can be elongated up to five times the original length while maintaining the proper stitch density (Fig. 8.66). This is also possible with stitches 29–35 and 37–44 on the Memory Craft 8000 by touching the screen.

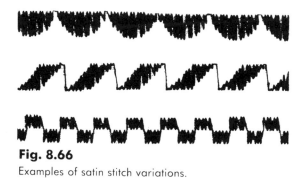

Fig. 8.66
Examples of satin stitch variations.

To do this, select the desired stitch, then press the pattern elongater key. Each time you press this key on the 7000 and 7500, the L1, L2, L3, L4, or L5 show up in the manual width indicator window to indicate the pattern is elongated 1, 2, 3, 4, or 5 times; on the 8000, you will see X-1, X-2, X-3, X-4, or X-5. To clear the elongation command, push the "clear program" or "clear" key.

Make a satin stitch variation sampler for your notebook using each stitch elongated 2, 3, 4, and 5 times its original configuration.

CORDED SATIN STITCH SCALLOP (59, 7500; 37, 8000)

This decorative treatment is lovely on the edge of a collar, front tab, sleeve hem, or anywhere you would like a hand-crocheted look to an edge.

Machine Readiness Checklist	
Stitch:	satin stitch scallop (59, 7500; 37, 8000)
Length:	0.4–0.5
Width:	5–7
Foot:	F satin stitch
Function:	elongation (experiment for desired results)
Thread:	cotton machine embroidery
Feed dogs:	up
Tension:	normal (auto)
Fabrics:	closely woven or stabilized knit
Accessories:	construction paper to match fabric, or adding machine tape or tear-away stabilizer, #8 or #5 pearl cotton to match thread

1. Place a strip of construction paper, adding machine tape, or tear-away partly under folded edge, with the right side of the fabric up. Place folded edge of fabric under the foot so half of the foot is resting on the fabric and half on the paper. Place the needle in the fabric, then raise the foot.

2. Place a strand of pearl cotton at the cut in the F satin stitch foot so about 2" (5cm) is behind the foot.

3. Begin sewing so that the point of the scallop catches on the edge of the fold and the rest of the scallop forms off the fabric on the paper or tear-away, over the cord (Fig. 8.67).

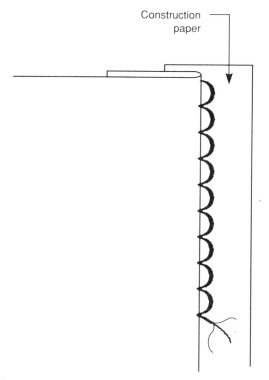

Construction paper

Fig. 8.67
Guide so the point of the scallop catches on the fold and the rest of the scallop forms off the fabric on the adding machine tape or construction paper.

Sew-How: *I found on wider widths, I had to sew slowly and manually guide the pearl cotton under the stitch while sewing.*

Remove the stabilizer by carefully ripping if off the stitches. Scallops should look like a hand-crocheted edge. **Note:** Depending on how large or how elongated a scallop you make, the space created between the fabric and scallop may be large enough to slip over a small button.

SHOWCASE STITCHES

Showcase stitches (70–79, 100–106, 7500; 46, 50–52, 62, 64, 85, 90–96, 98–100, 8000) are intricate open decorative stitches that can be used as a single motif to decorate a pocket, or in combination for an edge finish or border (Fig. 8.68).

Fig. 8.68
Examples of showcase stitches.

Program the fern (70, 7500; 100, 8000) with the pattern turn over function so it forms back-to-back embroidery on batiste. Use it to create a flower with leaves, or use it in a jungle scene.

The showcase border stitches (71, 74, 75, 76, 104, 105, 106, 7500; 85, 90, 91, 92, 93, 94, 95, 8000) are beautiful when stitched as a lone motif. Use them on a pocket top to create your own designer signature. Add beading to create a bar pin or small pendant (see *Know Your New Home* by Jackie Dodson with Judi Cull and Vicki Lyn Hastings, Chilton 1989, for pendant ideas).

The scalloped heart (72, 7500; 96, 8000) can be used to stitch and finish an edge in one step on a collar, cuff, or front tab. Use a light to midweight woven fabric such as batiste or broadcloth. Interface the upper collar, then place *wrong* sides together and baste collar pieces together, guiding $\frac{1}{2}''$ (1.3cm) from the raw edge. Stitch the scalloped heart, guiding $\frac{5}{8}''$ (1.5cm) from the raw edge. Carefully trim excess fabric to the scallop, and the edge is finished.

Stitches 73, 77, 78, and 79 (7500); 98, 62, 64, and 99 (8000) are great border motifs. Stitch samplers for your notebook.

Use the southwestern cross stitch (100, 7500; 46, 8000) for a western border, the bamboo (101, 7500; 52, 8000) to make bamboo in a forest or jungle scene, and use the open ribbon (102, 7500; 51, 8000) and the open chain (103, 7500; 50, 8000) to create and decorate original wrapping paper and greeting cards.

CHARACTER STITCHES

The character stitches (85–99, 7500; 71–73, 75, 77–84, 115, 8000) are fun to use on children's clothing or to create your own labels or designer signature. Stitch each on a sampler. Notice how intricate they are and plan for enough space when using them on a project (Fig. 8.69).

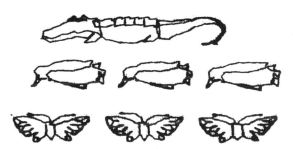

Fig. 8.69
Examples of character stitches.

SHOWCASE SATIN STITCHES

These stitches (114–121, 7500; 108–114, 8000) are bold and beautiful. I have used them instead of trim by stitching directly on the fabric, or as a braid over narrow ribbon or multiple strands of pearl cotton or embroidery floss. Also use them to create colorful soft jewelry (see *How To Make Soft Jewelry* by Jackie Dodson, Chilton, 1991).

Stitches 114, 117, and 120 (7500); 113, 112, and 109 (8000) are designed so the needle takes a few stitches over and back to create the solid looking shape. This minimizes puckering and skipped stitches for truly beautiful results. Use stitch 115 (7500) or 114 (8000) alone or as a bold border stitch. Stitch 121, the half circle, is great for smiles. Stitch it under stitch 99 (7500), 115 (8000), the mustache, to embroider Santa or other happy characters.

SPACE

Sometimes you need some space between stitches to create two-color embroidery, or to separate words or letters. To do this, use the program space key (122–123, 7500; 68, 116, 8000). The space stitches are long and easily removed after stitching.

LETTERS, NUMBERS, AND PUNCTUATION

The New Home Memory Craft models have block and script letters and numbers. Unlike many other brands, they also have upper and lower case for both fonts. See your *Instruction Book* for programming instructions.

Rather than telling you how to program the alphabet and numbers, I will give you some ideas on where to use lettering.

1. Nancy Zeiman, host of the popular TV program "Sewing with Nancy," embroiders the pattern number in the hem of the garment. If someone asks what pattern number it is, she takes a quick peek.

2. Stitch the name and birth date of your baby on a ribbon, and stitch it in the hem of the christening gown. This ribbon can be the "something old" or "something blue" when the child grows up and marries and can be stitched in the hem of the bride's wedding gown. I made one for my son and stitched it in the waistband of his christening suit, so when the time comes, I hope his bride will want it stitched into the hem of her gown.

3. Stitch name tags for a child's birthday party or name cards for an adult's tea or dinner party.

4. Make your own designer labels, or label clothing that will be sent to the cleaner's, laundry, or summer camp.

5. Incorporate lettering into a decorative border sewn at a hem, pocket, placket, waistband, or the length of suspenders.

Memory Craft Notes: The New Home 7500 and 8000 can store up to sixty-two stitches or characters. This means you can spell out a name, then run a couple decorative stitches between the name on the same program. The 8000 also has a "recall" function where the patterns, letters, or numbers are entered in with the "store" key, then recalled immediately by pressing the "recall" key. The patterns in "store" are stored for about three days even when the power is switched off. Also note that the first set of stored stitched patterns will be erased if you store a second set of stitch patterns. Finally, the 8000 can store a program from Memory Card #1 (monogramming) as long as the card is in the machine.

EMBROIDERY

MEMORY CARD STITCHES

The New Home Memory Craft 8000 has revolutionized embroidery sewing with the introduction of the copyrighted Memory Card embroidery designs similar to what has been available only on industrial embroidery sewing machines until now.

To create 5" × 2⅔" (12.5cm × 7cm) professional-style embroidery, insert one of the Memory Cards, touch the message key on the Visual Touch Screen and follow the directions. This user-friendly system enables even the novice to create professional shaded embroidery in minutes. Currently there are four Memory Cards available, with others to come.

Memory Card #1 is a complete monogram series with upper- and lowercase alphabets in block, script, and Old English, with punctuation and numerals. Memory Card #2 offers a variety of flower and sports designs to create emblems, as well as signs of the zodiac. Memory Cards #1 and #2 come with the purchase of the Memory Craft 8000 (Fig. 8.70).

Memory Card #3 is a flower series with more intricate design shading in up to five colors. Memory Card #4, the Variety Series, offers an even greater assortment of animal, marine, and sports designs. Other Memory Cards featuring a host of designs will be introduced periodically.

To create these large embroidery designs, a special hoop or frame that comes with the machine fits into a carriage located behind the free-arm. To create the design, the needle stays in one place while the carriage moves the frame back and forth to create the shaded satin stitches. The machine is even programmed to skip a few stitches on the first pass where satin stitches would normally cross if you were creating a similar design or monogramming by free-machine stitching. This ensures even stitch density and consistency of the design. The carriage also slows down automatically to stitch the wider satin stitches to ensure perfect stitch quality.

Fig. 8.70
Memory Card #1 and #2 stitch sampler.

Janome, the parent company of New Home, has developed a special line of static-free acrylic embroidery thread for the Memory Card designs available in 24 colors through New Home dealers (Fig. 8.71). (See "Rules for Thread Selection" in Chapter 1).

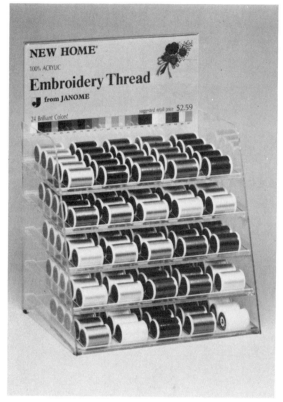

Fig. 8.71
Static-free acrylic embroidery thread.

New Home makes a workbook and video tape to help 8000 owners use these incredible designs. The *Instruction Book* and *Craft Sewing Ideas* book also come with the purchase of the machine so I will not duplicate this information in this encyclopedia other than to show you some of the applications (Fig. 8.72).

Fig. 8.72
Memory Craft embroidery applications.

If you are a Memory Craft 8000 owner, be sure to take your after-purchase lessons at your New Home dealer so that you can learn to make the best use of the Memory Card designs on your new machine.

I hope this chapter has encouraged you to use more than just your basic stitches, and that you have a notebook full of inspiration to use on future projects.

In the next chapter, you will investigate what I call the "undiscovered treasures of sewing"—the presser feet. You'll see what the tops and undersides look like to better understand why and how each foot works. You'll see how a presser foot used with different stitches creates different effects. The information is also cross-referenced with the stitches in this chapter. So find that dusty box of accessories and start your treasure hunt.

ENCYCLOPEDIA OF PRESSER FEET

Today's top-of-the-line New Home Memory Craft sewing machines come with ten or eleven standard presser feet. Why so many? To help you sew better. But which one is used for what purpose? This encyclopedia suggests ways to use each foot for practical and decorative applications. But first, you need to understand the anatomy of the presser foot.

There are two parts to a presser foot—the shank and the foot or sole. The shank holds the foot in place and provides a hinge so the foot can tip on and off varying thicknesses of fabric.

The purpose of a presser foot is to hold the fabric firmly against the feed dogs, aid in proper stitch formation, and protect your fingers from the needle. Presser feet are also designed for different uses, so let's take a closer look at one.

The underside of the foot has a toe and heel (Fig. 9.1). The underside is the most

important part because it helps guide the fabric and stitches so they feed smoothly over the feed dogs. The toe or toes are on the front of the foot in front of the needle. The heel is on the back of the foot behind the needle. Let me show you how important the presser foot can be.

When I taught machine embroidery, I showed the class a satin stitch—a wide zigzag stitch sewn very close together. When finished, satin stitching should look like a narrow strand of satin ribbon and have a smooth, rounded appearance, like the stitches you see on monogrammed towels.

Everyone tried it. But one of the students used her button sewing foot and wondered why the fabric wouldn't move. Look at the underside (Fig. 9.2). Notice the flat bottom, the short toes, and the rubber sleeve to prevent the button from slipping. You can imagine why this woman was having some difficulty—the foot could not move over the satin stitches.

Underside

Fig. 9.1
Underside toe and heel of presser foot.

Underside

Fig. 9.2
Underside of button sewing foot.

The proper foot to use is the F satin stitch foot (Fig. 9.3). The underside has a wide channel the length of the foot, which allows the stitches to form and the fabric to move smoothly under it without flattening the stitches into the fabric. Before we get ahead of ourselves, let's take a look at the six best and most common New Home feet.

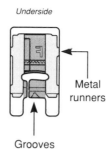

Fig. 9.3
Underside of the F satin stitch foot with wide channel the length of the foot.

THE SIX MOST COMMON FEET

- A Zigzag
- C Overedge
- E Zipper
- F Satin Stitch
- G Blind Hem
- J Sliding Buttonhole

A ZIGZAG FOOT

This foot is made of metal with transparent material between the toes for stability and visibility. The underside is smooth and flat with a slight indentation behind the needle hole—no grooves or ridges (Fig. 9.4). It is designed to stitch very fine or very heavy fabric because it holds the fabric firmly against the feed dogs.

Has your machine ever "eaten" the fabric? This foot helps prevent the problem by giving support around the needle to prevent it from pulling and pushing fabric up and down with every stitch. On fine fabrics it helps prevent puckering, and on heavy fabrics it helps prevent skipped stitches.

The A zigzag foot also has a leveling button to help you sew uneven or very heavy fabric without breaking a needle or skipping stitches. To use it when approaching a thickness, stop with the needle in the down position. Lift the presser foot; with the little finger of your right hand push in the leveling button until it snaps; then lower the foot while continuing to push the button. The foot becomes rigid on top of the thickness for a couple of stitches, then releases so the foot can pivot. Also use this leveling technique when starting to sew a thick seam.

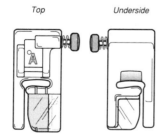

Fig. 9.4
The A zigzag foot with smooth, flat underside.

Application: Most inexperienced sewers leave this foot on all the time, but it can make sewing harder. When you teach yourself to sew better, you will use this foot for about 30 percent of garment construction and 30 percent of decorative sewing. Use this foot for most practical construction sewing, on light to mid-weight knits and wovens when using utility stitches—straight (29, 7500; 1, 8000), zigzag (35, 7500; 4, 8000), multiple zigzag (36, 7500; 18, 8000), knit stitch (37, 7500; 19, 8000) and many open decorative stitches such as the briar (5, 7500; 56, 8000), smocking (6, 7500; 57, 8000), and running leaves (9, 7500; 107, 8000). If you have the New Home 7500, push the "program check" key to see which foot is recommended on the visual screen for the selected stitch. On the 8000, just look at the Visual Touch Screen for the recommended foot.

Sew-How: *Notice that New Home sewing machines automatically are set in left needle position. The lines in the needle plate are measured and marked from left needle position as well. This way, the needle hole in the foot and needle plate provide support around three sides of the needle rather than two sides, as is the case when the needle is in the center position (Fig. 9.5). This support around the needle helps eliminate puckering and skipped stitches on fine fabrics.*

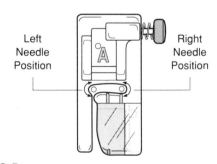

Fig. 9.5
In left or right needle position, the needle hole provides support around three sides of the needle to prevent puckering and skipped stitches.

C OVEREDGE FOOT

Have you overcast a raw edge with a zig-zag or the overcast stitch (38, 7500; 5, 8000) and ended up with the fabric tunneled under it? Then use the C overedge foot. On a 3.5 or wider width, the stitch forms over the bars on the right, keeping thread tension even during stitch formation to prevent tunneling (Fig. 9.6).

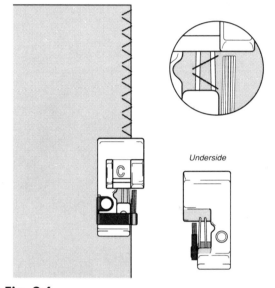

Underside

Fig. 9.6
The C overedge foot has bars on the right and a short channel behind the bars on the underside. The stitch forms over the bars to keep the fabric flat and to prevent tunneling.

Snug the raw edge against the inside of the black guide that houses the brush. When the needle passes through the brush, it simulates a piece of fabric tricking the needle into believing the raw edge of the fabric is farther to the right than it really is. This pulls off slightly more thread so the stitches lie flat on the edge of the fabric to prevent puckering.

Application: When overcasting, use this foot with the zigzag (35, 7500; 4, 8000), overcast stitch (38, 7500; 5, 8000), decorative (overlock) (2, 7500; 58, 8000) or any stitch that causes fabric tunneling on a 3.5 width or wider. Use it not only for overcasting seams, but also for ¼" (6mm) seams stitched with the stitches mentioned above.

E ZIPPER FOOT

If you have avoided a pattern because it called for a zipper, the E zipper foot will help (Fig. 9.7). To use it, you snap it on and off so the toe of the foot is on the right or left. This way you can stitch either side of the zipper without riding over the zipper coil.

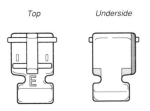

Fig. 9.7
To use the standard E zipper foot, either decenter the needle, or snap the foot on and off and move it for stitching either side of the zipper without riding over the coil.

To attach this foot to the shank, snap it on from the back. Note that it appears to be wobbly when the foot is up, but when it is down, it rests on three feed dogs, which provide a lot of support for perfect zipper insertion.

Sew-How: The E zipper foot for the 6000 operates similarly, but is wider because it has a channel for an invisible zipper centered on the underside (Fig. 9.8). This foot fits all Memory Craft models.

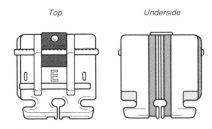

Fig. 9.8
The E zipper foot for the 6000 fits Memory Craft models and operates similarly to the standard E zipper foot. However, the foot is wider because it has a channel for an invisible zipper centered on the underside.

Application: Use the zipper foot to sew in zippers. Use it with the L quilter to cover and attach cord or piping in a pillow or slipcover.

F SATIN STITCH FOOT

The F satin stitch foot is transparent, has a wide channel carved out the length of the underside, metal runners under each toe, and shorter toes than the A zigzag foot (Fig. 9.9). This channel allows you to sew decorative stitches (e.g., satin stitch patterns, 56–69, 7500; 29–44, 8000) in a straight line without flattening the stitches into the fabric. Because the channel is straight, it is sometimes difficult to sew these stitches in a curve or around an appliqué. To turn smooth curves and corners use the F appliqué foot (described later in this chapter).

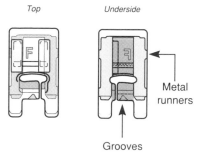

Fig. 9.9
The F satin stitch foot has a wide channel on the underside to allow you to sew decorative stitches in a straight line without flattening the stitches into the fabric.

Application: Use this foot to embroider with many of the decorative stitches on midweight to heavy fabrics. Also use it to finish corded hems and edges with the satin stitch.

G BLIND FOOT

The underside of the blind hem foot has a metal guide in the center and three lines struck on the underside. This way when the fabric is folded for blind hemming, the fold is snugged against the guide, while the textured lines prevent unnecessary slippage (Fig. 9.10).

Top   Underside

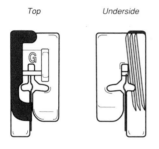

Fig. 9.10
The G blind hem foot has a metal guide and three lines struck on the underside. During blind hemming, the fabric snugs against the guide in the foot for accuracy and the lines prevent unnecessary slipping. Then the needle swings over the guide, creating slack in the upper tension so the "pick" of the stitch is almost invisible.

The blind hem stitch (41, 7500; 6, 8000) and stretch blind hem stitch (42, 7500; 20, 8000) are preprogrammed for use with the blind hem foot so the needle won't pick up too much fabric when blind hemming. While stitching, the needle swings over the guide creating slack in the upper thread tension so the "pick" of the stitch is almost invisible on most fabrics. (See Fig. 8.38.)

Also use this foot to stitch-in-the-ditch (see Fig. 8.8). Center the guide in the "ditch" in the seam. The guide on the underside spreads the seam, allowing you to stitch perfectly in the ditch.

Application: Invisible blind hemming, stitching-in-the-ditch, and edgestitching (see Fig. 9.17).

J SLIDING BUTTONHOLE FOOT

This foot can make a buttonhole as short as $\frac{1}{4}$" (6mm) and as long as $1\frac{1}{4}$" (3cm), which enables you to make all the buttonholes the same size without a lot of elaborate measuring (Fig. 9.11). If you

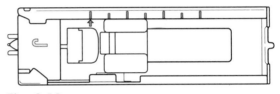

Fig. 9.11
The J sliding buttonhole foot can make a buttonhole as short as $\frac{1}{4}$" (6mm) or as long as 1-$\frac{1}{4}$" (3cm) without a lot of elaborate measuring.

have a one-step buttonhole function, follow the instructions in your *Instruction Book.* If you have a two- or four-step buttonhole function, adjust the buttonhole length as follows:

1. Slide the white slide to the back of the foot.

2. Place the button on the foot so one edge of the button is against the slide and the other edge of the button is against the white inset in the front of the foot.

3. Cut a cardboard template to fill the space from the back of the white side to the back of the foot. Snap the cardboard into the back of the foot, remove the button, and make a test buttonhole, bartacking when the slide touches the template.

4. Cut the buttonhole open to be sure it fits the button. If you need a longer buttonhole, slightly trim the cardboard. For shorter buttonholes, cut another longer cardboard template. Mark templates with the correct buttonhole lengths for future use.

Sew-How: *When making a buttonhole on an uneven surface as over a hidden seam allowance, hold the foot with your index finger and thumb on top of the slide and in front and back of the shank. This levels the foot so you don't get a buildup of stitches going up or a* *space between the stitches coming off a bump.*

Application: Use this foot to make buttonholes or corded buttonholes on medium to heavy fabrics (see Fig. 8.58).

OTHER NEW HOME FEET AND ACCESSORIES

- B Transparent Buttonhole
- D Hemmer
- F Appliqué
- G Adjustable Blind Hem
- H Cording and One-Groove Cording
- K Craft
- L Quilter
- M Special Overcast
- N and R Buttonhole Sensor
- P Embroidery
- Bias Binder
- Button Sewing
- Flower Stitcher and Eyelet Maker
- Fringe
- Gathering
- Pintuck
- Piping
- Roller
- Ruffler
- Side Cutter
- Straight Foot for Center Needle Position
- Teflon
- Tricot
- Walking

Because New Home models have different maximum width adjustments (e.g., 5mm or 7mm width), be sure to tell your dealer which model you own when you are purchasing extra presser feet and accessories. This way your dealer will order the one to fit your machine.

B TRANSPARENT BUTTONHOLE FOOT

This foot has two narrow channels in the heel on the underside (Fig. 9.12). There is also a prong on the heel to hold pearl cotton so you can easily cord a buttonhole. Corded buttonholes (see Fig. 8.58) are more durable and generally look better than uncorded buttonholes.

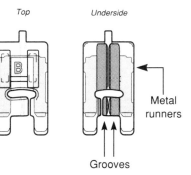

Fig. 9.12
The B (transparent) buttonhole foot has two narrow channels in the heel on the underside so the two sides of the buttonhole are parallel. The prong is used to hold cord for corded buttonholes.

After the first column of stitches is made, the foot rides on the narrow column of stitching so the two sides of the buttonhole are parallel.

Application: Unlike many other button-hole feet, this foot works well on light-weight fabrics because the needle is supported around all sides. However, because there is not a mechanism to ensure that all the buttonholes come out the same size (except on Memory Craft models, in which you can program the buttonhole length) mark the buttonhole length carefully before stitching. Also use this foot for couching over cord (see instructions for corded entredeux, page 198) and corded shell tuck (page 178).

D HEMMER

• Hemming Curves

• Hemming over a Seam Allowance

• Turning Corners

Sometimes referred to as a rolled hemmer, a hemmer is used to stitch the narrow rolled hems commonly found on shirttails. The top has a scroll-shaped feeder; the underside, a straight groove (Fig. 9.13).

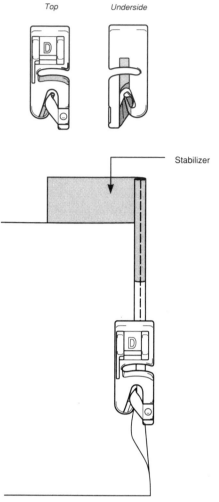

Top   Underside

Stabilizer

Fig. 9.13
The D hemmer has a scroll-shaped feeder on top and a straight groove the width of the finished hem on the underside. Move the needle position and stitch the narrow hem by guiding the fold to the inside edge of the curl.

The width of the groove on the underside of the foot determines the finished hem width (i.e., 4mm hemmer = 4mm finished hem). The hemmer can also be used with the zigzag stitch.

Sew-How: *To start stitching the rolled hem on the edge of the fabric, overlap a 2″ (5cm) square of tear-away stabilizer and stitch it to the raw edge of the fabric at the starting end of the hem. Start rolling the stabilizer into the hemmer by "sawing it" back and forth into the scroll. Stitch, then remove the tear-away after stitching.*

1. Roll and press a couple of inches of the hem to get started.

2. Set the needle in center needle position.

3. Feed the stabilizer into the scroll and begin sewing. With your right hand, hold the fabric up and slightly to the left of center, curling the edge of the fabric before it enters the scroll. Patti Jo Larson, a rolled hem expert from Sheyenne, North Dakota, says to watch that the curl on the left does not exceed the "ditch" in the foot or the hem will have extra fabric in it. Also watch that extra fabric on the right does not get caught under the foot.

4. Stitch slowly and carefully to finish hem. Remove stabilizer. **Note:** This takes some practice, so try it on a scrap first.

Hemming Curves

Another tip from Patti Jo:

1. Press a hem $\frac{1}{2}$–$\frac{3}{4}$″ (1.3–2cm) all the way around the curve.

2. On the wrong side, turn the fold into the scroll of the hemmer and stitch. The hem will turn only once this way. If the rolled hem needs to be altered, it is easy to do before trimming (Fig. 9.14).

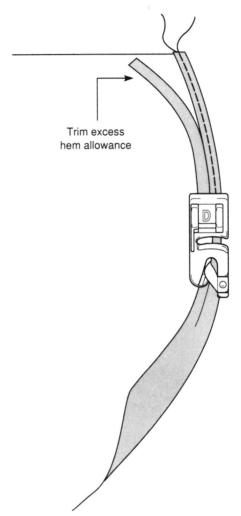

Trim excess hem allowance

Fig. 9.14
Press the curved hem. Turn the fold into the scroll and stitch the curve. Trim away excess hem allowance.

3. Trim excess fabric away from the hem after stitching.

4. When you get back to where you started, remove the hem edge from the scroll for the last two inches, and meet the stitches where you began.

Hemming over a Seam Allowance

Clip the seam allowance at the hem edge as shown (Fig. 9.15) to remove unnecessary bulk so the seam allowance rolls into the scroll smoothly.

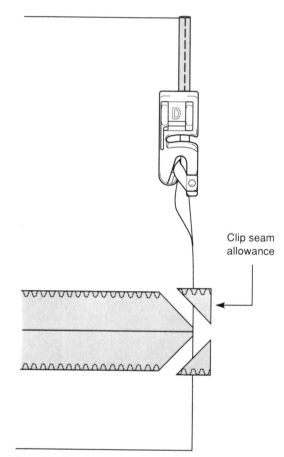

Clip seam allowance

Fig. 9.15
Clip the seam allowance at the hem edge to remove unnecessary bulk.

Turning Corners

1. Prepare and stitch hem as described above all the way to the corner. Stop and remove the fabric.

2. Stitch a small piece of tear-away stabilizer under the corner, then roll it into the scroll of the hemmer. Begin stitching on the stabilizer, then into the fabric. This way your stitching starts right at the corner. Pull thread ends to the back and tie them off.

Application: Roll shirt and ruffle hems. On tricot, use the hemmer and a 2–3 length zigzag to roll and shell tuck an edge at the same time. Use the scroll to guide cord, yarn, pearl cotton, or narrow trim for a corded edge finish.

F APPLIQUÉ FOOT

Sometimes referred to as a transparent appliqué foot, this foot is made of a clear synthetic material for better visibility—excellent for machine appliqué and embroidery. This foot also has an elevated heel so a satin stitch or satin stitch variation can be sewn and move smoothly under the foot without being flattened in the fabric. The elevated heel also helps when you are stitching around curves and corners (Fig. 9.16).

Top   Underside

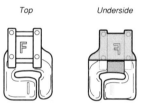

Fig. 9.16
The F appliqué foot is transparent and has an elevated heel so closed decorative stitches move smoothly under it. It also makes stitching around curves on an appliqué smooth and even.

Sew-How: *If the fabric is not feeding smoothly, lighten the foot pressure to 2.*

This foot also fixes to the shank like the E zipper foot; because it does not pivot on a hinge, it enables you to stitch with greater accuracy.

Application: Use this foot to appliqué and embroider on light and midweight fabrics because it provides more pressure and better maneuverability than the F satin stitch foot described in this chapter. Also, use this foot for appliqué and with decorative stitches.

G ADJUSTABLE BLIND HEM FOOT

The G adjustable blind hem foot has a flat underside with an adjustable guide on the right (Fig. 9.17). Use it for stitching close to and an even distance from the fabric edge—helpful for topstitching, edgestitching, staystitching, and making traditional pintucks. To use it, move the guide as desired, then butt the edge of the fabric against the guide in the foot and either adjust the guide or decenter the needle as far to the left of the edge as desired and stitch.

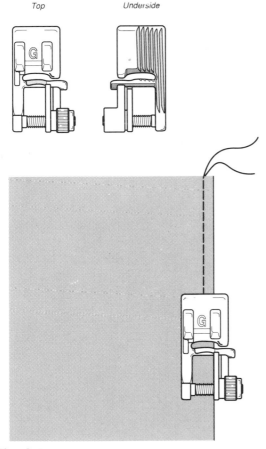

Fig. 9.17
The G adjustable blind hem foot has a movable guide. Use it for edgestitching, topstitching, or making traditional pintucks by snugging the guide against the edge of fabric fold. Then stitch.

The G adjustable blind hem foot can also be used to stitch-in-the-ditch (see Fig. 8.8), for blind hemming (see Fig. 8.38), and to join lace to fabric or fabric to fabric using the multiple zigzag (36, 7500; 18, 8000), or patchwork stitch (45, 7500; 25, 8000). This is called fagoting. To do this, simply butt the straight edge of one piece of lace or the folded edge of a piece of fabric against one side of the guide. Snug the straight edge of another piece of lace or folded edge of another piece of fabric against the other side of the guide and stitch. (You may have to move the guide slightly right or left so the stitch is centered between the two pieces of fabric.) The lace or fabric edges are next to each other so they will not overlap, and the join is strong and even.

Application: Edgestitch, topstitch, staystitch, or pintuck evenly from the fabric edge. Piece leathers, suedes, vinyl, and synthetic suedes and leathers for handbags and belts. Join straight-edge laces and trims.

H CORDING AND ONE-GROOVE CORDING FOOT

· Cording and Finishing Edges
· Couching Down Cord

This unusual foot has three channels in a clip to guide pearl cotton, fine yarn, or embroidery floss. The underside has four channels behind the needle and edges that flair out at the heel so that sewing around a curve is unimpaired (Fig. 9.18).

Fig. 9.18
The H cording foot has three channels in a clip to guide pearl cotton, fine yarn, or embroidery floss.

Use it to zigzag over a cord for even gathers (see Fig. 8.21), to cord an edge that will later be satin stitched, or to apply mini-cord as a topstitch.

The one-groove cording foot looks like the H cording foot but has only one groove in the center. Use it like the H cording foot for couching over cord in center needle position.

Cording and Finishing Edges

Use the H cording foot to cord and edge a placemat or tablecloth, then satin stitch over the cord for a raised look to the satin stitch. Also use it to cord hems and edges that will later be satin stitched and to couch down cord, yarn, and cordonnet for decorative treatments.

To cord and edge, lay a strand of #5 pearl cotton in the center groove in the clip. Couch it down with a 2.5 width, 1.5 length zigzag, guiding a presser-foot-width away from the cut edge. Trim excess fabric up to the stitch, then satin stitch over the cord (see Fig. 8.25).

Couching Down Cord

An easy way to outline an appliqué or to create your own designs is to couch down a strand of yarn or cord (Figs. 9.19, 9.20, 9.21).

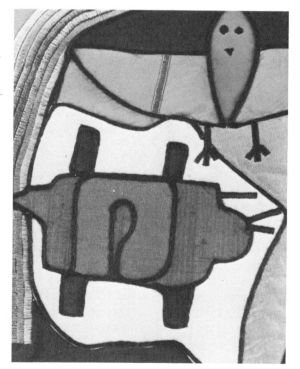

Fig. 9.19
Children's artwork enlarged and appliquéd as a wall hanging. The outline is done with black yarn and couched with a straight stitch using nylon monofilament thread top and bobbin.

Fig. 9.20
Embellish jackets or children's clothing and costumes with heavy yarn, cord, trim, or soutache braid.

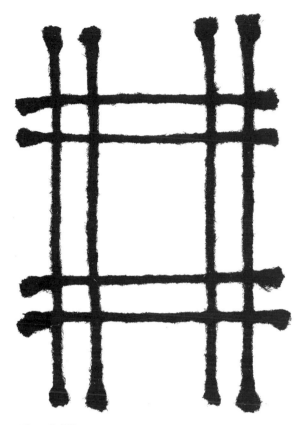

Fig. 9.21
Couch interesting yarn in a plaid, stripe, or scrolled design using the H cording or one-groove cording foot.

Machine Readiness Checklist	
Stitch:	center needle position straight (30, 7500: 2. 8000)
Length:	2.2–2.5
Width:	0
Foot:	H cording or one-groove cording
Needle:	11/75 Blue Tip
Thread:	nylon monofilament
Feed dogs:	up
Tension:	normal (auto)
Accessories:	#5 or #8 pearl cotton

1. Place the presser foot on the fabric where you want to begin.

2. Snap the cord in the center groove in the clip. Adjust needle position by pushing the width key so the needle stitches exactly in the middle of the cord.

3. Stitch around the edge of the appliqué or in the desired design. The cord follows in the groove under the foot so you can stitch in any direction without missing the cord.

Sew-How: For best results, don't pull on the cord while sewing.

Application: Cord an edge or around an appliqué, or create texture on a solid-colored fabric by couching over yarn or cord.

K CRAFT FOOT

• Covering Upholstery Cord

This foot came with the Memory Craft 6000 and has limited usage; it is designed to cover the cord used to edge upholstery and pillow seams (Fig. 9.22). It is made of transparent material for good visibility and has notched toes for a guiding reference. The underside of the K foot has two levels to accommodate the cording and the seam allowance. Although you can use the zipper foot for the same uses, the craft foot is more accurate. It can also be used to apply certain flat braids.

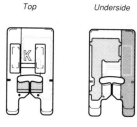

Top   Underside

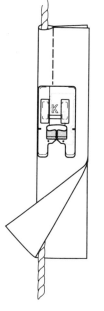

Covering Upholstery Cord

1. Cut the fabric on the bias the width of the cord plus $1\frac{1}{4}''$ (3cm), or unfold bias tape. Sandwich cord in the bias tape or fabric; then place it under the foot so the cord fits in the left groove of the foot.

2. Decenter the needle, so the line of stitching snugs up against the cording and stitch. To attach the covered cord or piping evenly, place right sides together, sandwiching the covered cord in the seam allowance. As before, decenter the needle so the foot snugs against the ridge created by the cord, then stitch.

Application: Make covered piping to cord yokes and pockets, tote bags, handbags, backpacks, pillows, hemlines, or upholstery projects . . . anywhere there is a seam. Make even lips for bound buttonhole and welt pockets.

L QUILTER

Do you have trouble sewing straight? The L quilter will help. It slips into the foot shank and adjusts out $2\frac{1}{2}''$ (6.4cm) to the right of the needle (Fig. 9.23).

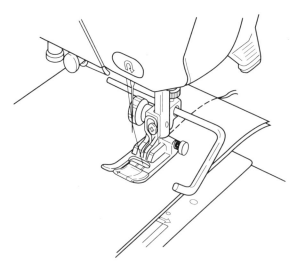

Fig. 9.22
The K craft foot has two levels on the underside and is designed to cover upholstery cord.

Fig. 9.23
The L quilter slips behind the foot shank and adjusts out to the right of the needle.

Use it as a seam guide, adjusting the guide to the right of the needle the desired width of the seam allowance. Use it as a quilting guide to help keep many lines of machine quilting straight and evenly spaced from one another (Fig. 9.24). Quilt your own fabric using the straight stitch, zigzag, multiple zigzag, or other decorative stitches.

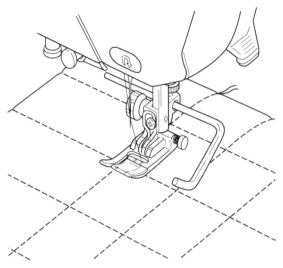

Fig. 9.24
Use the L quilter to keep many rows of quilting straight and even.

Sew-How: *If you are quilting many rows, the underlayer of fabric may pucker or come out shorter than the rest of the piece. You can prevent this by using the walking foot (see instructions Fig. 9.44), but then you can't use the L quilter. When using the walking foot, use movable transparent tape to mark your quilting lines.*

Application: Use the L quilter as a seam guide any time you are stitching farther from the edge of the fabric than what is marked on the needle plate. The L quilter also is helpful for stitching deep hems or cuffs and for topstitching and quilting.

M SPECIAL OVERCAST FOOT

This foot is designed for use with the special overlock stitch (40, 7500; 23, 8000) and works similarly to the presser foot on a serger (Fig. 9.25).

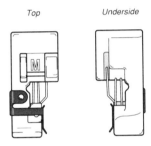

Top   *Underside*

Fig. 9.25
The M special overcast foot is designed for use with the special overlock stitch (40, 7500; 23, 8000). The stitch forms over the wires, including the wire on the far right, which is completely off the fabric, to prevent tunneling.

Snug the raw edge of the fabric against the black guide in the foot. The stitch forms over the three wires in the foot, including the one at the far right, which is completely off the edge of the fabric. This enables the stitch to pull off more thread so it will not tunnel.

Application: Overcasting a raw edge, $\frac{1}{4}''$ (6mm) seams on lightweight wovens and knits.

N AND R BUTTONHOLE SENSOR FEET

The N sensor buttonhole foot comes as standard equipment and presently can be used only with New Home 7000 and 7500 models (Fig. 9.26). The R buttonhole sensor foot works similarly but simply snaps onto the Memory Craft 8000. The advantage of the buttonhole sensor over the B or J buttonhole foot is that the machine and foot read the length of the buttonhole, log it into the memory, then make as many buttonholes as needed exactly the same size. Unlike many brands, the New Home buttonhole sensor feet measure the length of the buttonhole on the fabric rather than counting stitches. This way each buttonhole measures the same length regardless of the fabric weight, weave, or number of fabric layers.

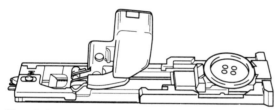

Fig. 9.26
The N and R buttonhole sensor feet automatically measure the buttonhole and memorize the length by use of a light-sensitive mirror. This way you can make one-step buttonholes the same length, time after time, regardless of the fabric weight or weave or number of fabric thicknesses.

Sew-How: *If necessary, use the − and + on the feed balance dial or length key to fine-tune or balance the stitch density of both sides of the buttonhole.*

Application: Use the N or R buttonhole sensor foot on all buttonhole styles.

P EMBROIDERY FOOT

The P embroidery foot is used for free-machine darning and embroidery to insure proper stitch formation, minimize skipped stitches and puckering, and protect your fingers while you move the fabric freely under the needle (Fig. 9.27). The P embroidery foot (not pictured here) for the Memory Craft 8000 has been simplified but serves the same purpose as the P foot for other Memory Craft models.

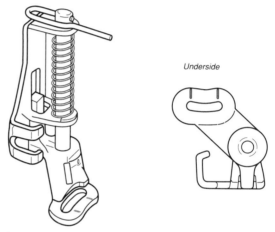

Underside

Fig. 9.27
The P embroidery foot is used for free-machine darning and embroidery to protect your fingers and to prevent skipped stitches.

To use the P embroidery foot, attach it to the needle bar and drop the feed dogs. When you put the foot down and the needle is up, the foot rests about $\frac{1}{8}''$ (3mm) above the fabric. When the needle is in the fabric, the foot rests on the surface during stitch formation. This prevents the fabric from pulling up and down with each stitch.

Application: Use the P embroidery foot to gain confidence when learning free-machine embroidery, for darning heavy or fine fabrics, and for basting (see page 195).

BIAS BINDER

Sometimes called a binder, this accessory is used for applying prefolded bias tape, binding, or trim and has a funnel to fold and guide the binding over the base fabric before it reaches the needle (Fig. 9.28).

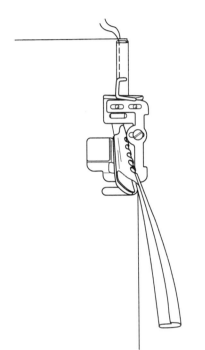

Fig. 9.28
The bias binder is designed to fold and attach bias tape or extra-wide double fold bias tape to an edge in one step. Thread bias through the funnel, then slip base fabric into slot in the center of the funnel and stitch.

This binder can be used with a zigzag or decorative stitch and is adjustable.

Machine Readiness Checklist	
Stitch:	straight (29, 30, 7500; 1, 2, 8000), zigzag (35, 7500; 4, 8000), or decorative
Length:	varies
Width:	varies
Foot:	binder
Needle:	11/75 Blue Tip or 12/80 universal
Needle position:	left, varies
Thread:	all-purpose
Feed dogs:	up
Tension:	normal (auto)
Fabric:	prequilted or medium to heavy woven
Accessories:	$\frac{1}{4}$" (6mm) (folded finished width) flat or prefolded bias tape

1. Unfold 3" (7.5cm) of one end of a length of bias tape and press flat.

2. On the pressed end, fold tape in half the long way and make a V-shaped cut so the point of the cut is at the fold.

3. With the binder off the machine, thread tape through the funnel so the point of the cut is to the right. **Note:** If you are having trouble threading the funnel, use a hand needle and doubled thread to stitch through the point of the V and pull the point through the funnel (Fig. 9.29).

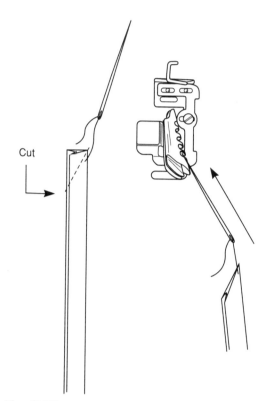

Fig. 9.29
The binder is also used for applying narrow prefolded bias tape, binding, or trim. With binder off machine, take a hand stitch through the V-shaped cut, then pull it through the first slot in the funnel.

Sew-How: Feed extra-wide bias tape through the large feeder at the front of the foot. Feed the narrow double-fold bias in the first slot in the feeder cone. (If tape feeds in easily, you are doing it wrong.) Because it is difficult to thread the narrow bias tape in the binder, leave a length of tape in the foot after completing a project. Then stitch the new tape to the end of the tape in the binder and pull it through.

4. Put binder on the machine and pull the feed end of tape so it extends about 2″ (5cm) behind the foot.

5. Slip the base fabric into the slot in the center of the funnel.

6. Adjust your needle position so the needle stitches inside the folded edge of the tape.

Application: Bind the edges of double-faced quilted fabric for placemats or an unlined jacket. Stitch on bias tape or Seams Great for a Hong Kong seam finish (see Sew-How) or hem.

Sew-How: Rather than finishing a raw edge with a stitch, try a Hong Kong finish. To do so, tape over the raw edge with bias tape or Seams Great for a clean, finished look to an unlined garment.

BUTTON SEWING FOOT

This foot has two bars that attach to the foot shank like the E zipper foot to provide extra stability for button sewing (Fig. 9.30). It also has a rubber sleeve so the button stays put under the foot. To create a shank between the garment and button, slip a needle into the groove of the rubber sleeve and stitch over it.

Top   *Underside*

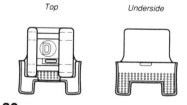

Fig. 9.30
Button sewing foot.

Machine Readiness Checklist	
Stitch:	zigzag (35, 7500; 4, 8000)
Length:	0
Width:	3.5–4 (test on button and adjust as needed)
Foot:	button sewing
Function order:	M/memory + M/memory + lock-off stitch + M/memory (7500 only)
Needle:	appropriate for fabric
Needle position:	left
Thread:	all-purpose
Feed dogs:	down
Tension:	top, loosen slightly; bobbin, normal
Accessories:	water-erasable marker, glue stick, liquid seam sealant

1. Mark button placement.

2. Dab glue stick on the back of the button, then place it on the fabric.

3. Stab the needle into the left hole and lower the presser bar (Fig. 9.31).

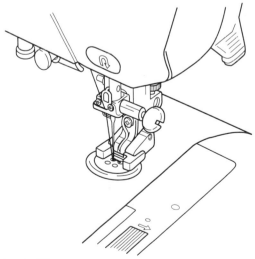

Fig. 9.31
Stab the needle in the left hole and lower the presser bar lever. Check needle clearance, then stitch.

4. Move the flywheel by hand to check needle clearance, adjust the stitch width if necessary, then stitch 10 to 12 stitches. If sewing a four-hole button, lift presser bar and move the fabric to stitch the front two holes.

Sew-How: If you have a Memory Craft model and have programmed your machine as described above, the needle will zigzag 12 stitches, then lock off automatically in left needle position.

---

5. Move the stitch width to 0 and stitch two to three stitches to lock them off. For the 8000, touch stitch 1, then the reverse/lock-off key.

Remove fabric by pulling off enough thread to wrap the shank between the button and fabric, then thread it through a hand needle. Wrap the shank (see Figs. 8.17, 8.18). Pull free ends through to the back of the fabric and tie them off.

Sew-How: To eliminate the need to tie off threads, bring threads to the back, snip them close to the back of the fabric, and dab them with a spot of liquid seam sealant.

Did You Know? Regardless of button size, 90 percent of the holes in buttons are the same distance apart. Why? Button manufacturers use the same equipment to make the holes in most buttons, whatever the diameter.

Application: Button sewing.

FLOWER STITCHER AND EYELET MAKER

This fun accessory attaches to the presser bar and enables you to make perfect decorative circles and eyelets (Fig. 9.32). The screw on the left loosens and adjusts so you can make circles of varying sizes. You can even use this accessory with twin needles.

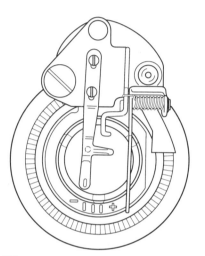

Fig. 9.32
Use the flower stitcher to create flowers and decorative eyelets for covered buttons, soft jewelry, or decorative effects down a placket or on a cuff.

Use it with the zigzag stitch to make an eyelet; use it with decorative stitches to create decorative eyelets or flowers. An instruction sheet comes with this accessory.

Sew-How: *For this accessory to work properly, make sure the bar on the right fits on the needle clamp and that the screw on the left is tightened into position.*

Application: Stitch decorative eyelets and circle flowers to decorate placemats or napkins, create your own designer labels, or make soft jewelry. Also make your own eyelet or embroidered fabric. For inspiration, make a sampler for your notebook using stitches 35, 36, 56–61 (7500) or 4, 18, 29–35, 37–44 (8000).

228

FRINGE FOOT

- Fringe Foot for Marking
- Fringe Foot for Chenille

Sometimes called a tailor-tacking or looping foot, the fringe foot has a blade in the front that sticks up, off the fabric (Fig. 9.33). When used with the zigzag stitch, the blade causes the thread to stand away from the fabric. The underside is open, which allows the thread loops to stand up once stitched.

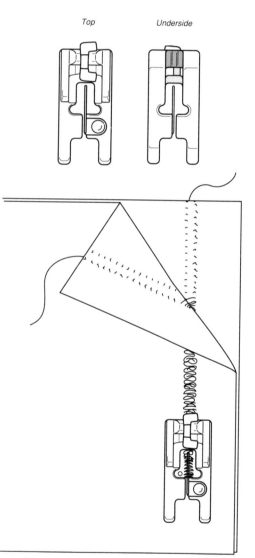

Fig. 9.33
The fringe foot, sometimes called a tailor-tacking or looping foot, has a raised bar in front which causes the thread to stand away from the fabric. The underside is completely open so the thread fringe passes smoothly under it. To mark a pattern piece, pull fabric apart so thread loops are between two layers of fabric, then clip the thread.

Fringe Foot for Marking

Machine Readiness Checklist	
Stitch:	zigzag (35, 7500; 4, 8000)
Length:	1–2
Width:	4–4.5
Foot:	fringe
Needle:	11/75 Blue Tip or 12/80 universal
Thread:	all-purpose or cotton embroidery
Feed dogs:	up
Tension:	top, loosened slightly; bobbin, normal
Fabric:	medium-weight woven or knit

1. Place fabric right sides together with the tissue pattern on top, and stitch where fabric is to be marked. Carefully pull off tissue pattern piece.

2. Pull fabric apart so the thread loops are between the two layers of fabric, then clip threads. The threads accurately mark both pieces of fabric.

Fringe Foot for Chenille

Make chenille fringe for flowers, eyelashes, or grass or to texture an existing piece of fabric. Use it also for appliqués or a freely embroidered design.

Set your machine as described above, but shorten the stitch length to 0.5. If you are covering a large area on one layer of fabric, fill it in faster by using two threads through the same needle and lengthen the stitch to about 0.8. You may have to iron freezer wrap to the wrong side of the fabric to prevent puckering. To make a circle or square, start in the middle and work out.

For another technique using the fringe foot, see Wide Cording (Rickrack) Stitch as a Decorative "Ladder" Seam (Fig. 8.56).

Application: Use for pattern marking, for making chenille fringe, for flowers, toys, and other decorative sewing.

GATHERING FOOT

This foot gathers light to midweight fabrics automatically while sewing. The underside is raised behind the needle, and the slot in front of the needle enables the user to gather and attach the ruffle simultaneously (Fig. 9.34).

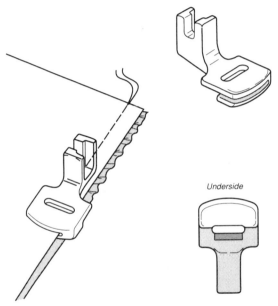

Underside

Fig. 9.34
The underside of the gathering foot is raised behind the needle and has a slot in front of the needle. To gather and attach a ruffle onto a flat piece at the same time, place ruffle under foot right side up. Slip flat piece into slot, right side down, and stitch.

To use it, set your machine for a straight stitch (or slight zigzag for knits). The amount the fabric gathers is determined by the weight of the fabric, stitch length, and upper thread tension. Use a fine fabric, a long stitch, and a tighter tension for a lot of gathers. Use a medium-weight fabric, a short stitch, and normal tension for finer gathers.

To gather and sew a ruffle onto a flat piece of fabric simultaneously, place the fabric to be gathered under the foot, right side up, then put the foot down. Slip the flat piece into the slot, right side down, and stitch. To prevent the top piece from slipping out of the foot, hold it with your right hand toward the right front corner of the presser foot.

Sew-How: Sometimes the stitching may not be straight and even, so you may prefer to gather the ruffle separately, then attach it to the flat fabric piece in a second step.

To determine how much gathering you need, stitch a test piece. Start with a scrap of fabric then stitch so you have the desired look to the gathers. Then cut a strip of fabric 10″ (25cm) long and gather. If the fabric gathers to 5″ (12.5cm), you know to use a 2 : 1 ratio. Thus you would use a 50″ (125cm) length of ruffle to attach to a 25″ (63cm) waistband. **Note:** A gathering foot should not be confused with a ruffler. Both accessories gather, but a ruffler can also pleat (see Fig. 9.39).

Application: Gather ruffles for children's clothing, curtains, dust ruffles, tablecloths, pillows, or blouses.

PINTUCK FOOT

• Pintucks
• Corded Pintucks

The pintuck foot is used with twin needles to create the multiple rows of pintucks found on dressy blouses or shirts, christening gowns, and French hand-sewn garments. The underside has either five or seven grooves. Use the 5mm (five groove) foot with models in the 2000 and 1500 series. Use the 7mm (seven groove) foot with Memory Craft models (Fig. 9.35).

Top   Underside

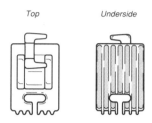

Fig. 9.35
The pintuck foot is used with twin needles to stitch multiple rows of pintucks. This foot has five grooves on the underside. After the first tuck is stitched, the remaining rows ride in one of the other grooves so each tuck is parallel to the first.

Use 2.5–3mm twin needles with the five groove foot. Use the 1.6–2mm twin needles with the 7-groove pintuck foot. The grooves of the foot make it easy to stitch all the rows parallel and evenly spaced from one another for a straight or curved row of tucks.

Pintucks

Machine Readiness Checklist	
Stitch:	straight (30, 7500; 2, 8000)
Length:	2.5–3
Width:	0
Foot:	pintuck
Needle:	twin
Needle position:	center
Thread:	100% cotton or all-purpose
Feed dogs:	up
Tension:	Top, tighten for pronounced tuck; bobbin, normal
Fabric:	light to medium-weight cotton, cotton blend, wool jersey, cotton T-shirt knit
Accessories:	vanishing marker or dressmaker's chalk, #8 or #5 pearl cotton, cocktail straw, transparent tape

1. Mark tuck placement with vanishing marker or dressmaker's chalk, marking the center of the row only.

2. Stitch the first tuck on the line marked in Step 1.

3. Stitch second row next to first, guiding the fabric so the first tuck rides in one of the channels of the foot. Stitch as many rows of tucking as desired, working from the center row out (Fig. 9.36).

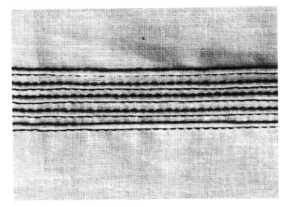

Fig. 9.36
Stitch multiple rows of tucks from the center out, and change sewing direction for every other tuck to prevent fabric distortion.

Application: Pintuck blouses, shirts, or children's clothing. Use this method to create texture on a solid fabric, matching the thread to the fabric.

Corded Pintucks

1. Set your machine as described above.

2. Cut a length of cocktail straw about $\frac{1}{2}''$ (1.3cm) long and tape it on the needle plate or hook cover plate to the center and in front of the presser foot.

Sew-How: If you plan to stitch a lot of corded pintucks, buy another needle plate or hook cover plate and tape the straw in place permanently for future use.

---

3. Thread pearl cotton through the straw, bringing it under and behind the presser foot.

4. Stitch tuck. When the straw is positioned properly, the cord will run under the tuck for a higher, sharper look.

Sew-How: If you plan a lot of tucks on a pattern that doesn't call for them, stitch rows of tucks first; then center the pattern on top of the tucks and cut out the project. This way the garment will not be too tight.

PIPING FOOT

This foot goes by a number of names—e.g., knit edge foot and cording foot. The underside has two wide, deep grooves designed to hold and cover cord used to edge upholstery and pillow seams (Fig. 9.37). It is also used to insert piping. Although you can use the zipper foot for either purpose, the piping foot makes it easier and the stitching is more accurate.

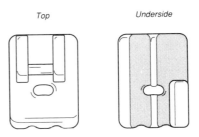

Top   Underside

Fig. 9.37
The piping foot has two wide, deep grooves on the underside to hold and cover cord used for upholstery, pillows, or slipcovers.

To cover cord, cut the fabric on the bias the width of the cord plus $1\frac{1}{4}''$ (3cm), or unfold bias tape. Sandwich cord in the bias tape or fabric; then place it under the foot so the cord fits in one of the grooves. Decenter the needle so the line of stitching snugs up against the cording, and stitch.

To attach the finished cord or piping evenly without catching it in the seam, this foot is a must.

Application: Cord yokes and pockets, tote bags, handbags, backpacks, pillows, hemlines, or upholstering projects— almost anywhere there is a seam.

ROLLER FOOT

The roller foot has rollers that roll against the fabric and act like the track on a bulldozer for sewing heavy fabrics (Fig. 9.38). The rollers move freely between the foot and feed dogs, so the foot rides easily over varying thicknesses.

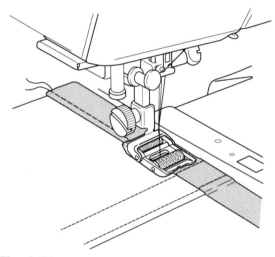

Fig. 9.38
The roller foot has rollers that roll against the fabric and act like a track on a bulldozer for sewing up and over heavy seams and uneven surfaces.

Application: Use this foot when sewing heavy fabrics such as denim, upholstery, and drapery fabrics. Use it also to sew sticky leather and vinyl.

RUFFLER

Rufflers haven't changed much from the days of the treadle machine (Fig. 9.39). They are adjustable and designed to ruffle or pleat the fabric to the desired fullness. Remember to stitch a sample first, because once stitched, ruffles or pleats are not adjustable.

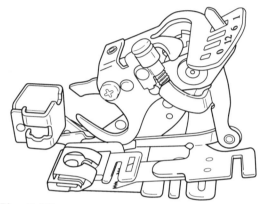

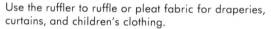

Fig. 9.39
Use the ruffler to ruffle or pleat fabric for draperies, curtains, and children's clothing.

There are four adjustment slots on the top of the ruffler that say 0, 1, 6, and 12. To use the ruffler, insert the fabric under the metal tongue so about 1" (2.5cm) extends beyond the tongue. Then sew. When set on 12, the ruffler pleats the fabric every twelve stitches. When set on 6, it pleats every six stitches; when set on 1, it pleats every stitch.

You can also pleat and attach a flat piece of fabric together simultaneously, as with the gathering foot. However, the flat piece of fabric is placed right side up under the ruffler, then the piece to be pleated is slipped right side down under the tongue.

When set on 0, the fabric will not ruffle or pleat at all. Use this setting when sewing napped fabric, such as velvet, to prevent the underlayer of fabric from coming up short. Place one layer of fabric under the foot, while the second layer is slipped under the tongue. Remember to place right sides together, and sew.

Janome makes a good ruffler, and there are generic rufflers available. However, I have found generic rufflers to differ greatly from one to another, and they may not work at all on your machine. Therefore, if you plan to purchase a generic one, take your own fabric and test it in the store before buying it.

Application: Stitch ruffles for square dance dresses, costumes, tablecloths, curtains and other home decorating projects, and children's clothing.

SIDE CUTTER

With the advent of the serger, New Home developed an accessory that will cut and sew a seam or finish an edge in one step (Fig. 9.40). Although not a replacement for a serger, the side cutter stitches the seam and finishes it with the overlock (2, 7500; 58, 8000), double overlock (13, 7500; 59, 8000), or overcast (38, 7500; 5, 8000) while cutting the excess fabric off next to the stitch. Instructions come with this accessory so I won't duplicate them here.

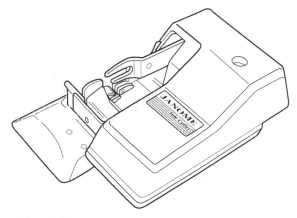

Fig. 9.40
The side cutter is designed to trim the seam allowance off after a seam has been stitched with one of the overcasting stitches.

Application: Use the side cutter for finishing raw edges, stitching and finishing ¼" (6mm) seams in one step, attaching bias binding, stitching French seams, sewing on lace edging, and staystitching.

STRAIGHT FOOT FOR CENTER NEEDLE POSITION

The straight stitch foot is often used on very fine or very heavy fabrics. The reason? It's flat on the underside to provide even pressure against the feed dogs, and it has a round needle hole to offer more support around the needle and thus prevent skipped stitches and puckering (Fig. 9.41). Note that because the needle hole is round, you cannot stitch wider than a 1 stitch width without breaking a needle. It also must be used in center needle position.

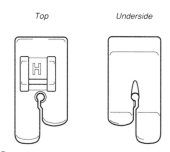

Top   Underside

Fig. 9.41
The straight stitch foot has a flat underside and a round needle hole for support around the needle to prevent skipped stitches and puckering.

Sew-How: It is not necessary to use a straight stitch foot when straight stitching provided you are using the appropriate needle for the fabric and the proper stitch length. (See Table 1.1.) To achieve similar results, use the A zigzag foot with the needle decentered to the left or right. Also, use a fine needle and short stitch length for fine fabrics; use a heavier needle and longer stitch length for heavier fabrics.

Application: Use this foot if you have tried everything else and are still experiencing skipped stitches, puckering, or uneven stitching. Also use it to topstitch difficult fabrics such as fine silks and cottons, handkerchief linen, denim, heavy duck cloth, canvas, leathers, and some vinyls. (If the vinyl you are working with sticks and you experience uneven stitching, use the Teflon foot described below instead. Then use a 3–4 stitch length to prevent tearing and perforation.)

Sew-How: *If your fabric puckers, shorten the stitch length. If your fabric waves out of shape, lengthen the stitch. This rule works with the straight stitch, zigzag, or other stitches available on your sewing machine.*

TEFLON FOOT

I consider this a "problem-solving" foot. It is made of white Teflon with a smooth, nonstick underside (Fig. 9.42). It also has a slight indentation behind the needle so it can be used successfully with both forward cycle and open reverse cycle stitches.

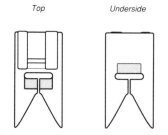

Top   Underside

Fig. 9.42
The Teflon foot has a smooth, flat underside, which allows the foot to move smoothly over sticky leathers and vinyls without the underlayer coming up short. Also use this foot for difficult, slippery fabrics.

Use the Teflon foot for sewing slippery silks, stretchy knits, or sticky leather, vinyl, or synthetic suedes to prevent the underlayer of fabric from coming up short. Also use it if you are experiencing puckering.

Application: General garment construction—seaming, staystitching, topstitching on fine, stretchy, or sticky fabrics.

TRICOT FOOT

The tricot foot is designed to keep soft slippery fabrics from sliding and to keep seams smooth and pucker-free. When the needle is in the work during stitch formation, the rubber pad holds the fabric firmly. Then when the needle is out of the work, the bar that rests against the needle clamp picks the pad off the fabric, releasing it to make another stitch (Fig. 9.43).

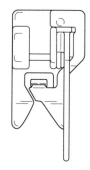

Fig. 9.43
The tricot foot grips slippery fabrics to prevent seams from puckering.

Application: Use this foot with a straight stitch (29, 30, 7500; 1, 2, 8000), the (outline) stretch stitch (33, 7500; 16, 8000), or other reverse cycle stitches to seam slippery fabrics such as tissue faille, acetate and polyester lining fabrics.

WALKING FOOT

Often referred to as an even-feed foot, the walking foot has a top set of feed dogs to feed the fabric without shifting or slipping to keep the underlayer from coming up short (Fig. 9.44). It works with the straight stitch; however, it can be used with other stitches, because the needle hole is wide enough to accommodate the swing of the needle. Make a machine-quilted sample for your notebook using the multiple zigzag stitch (36, 7500; 18, 8000), scallop (47, 7500; 27, 8000), or the patchwork stitch (45, 7500; 25, 8000).

Application: Use the walking foot for matching stripes and plaids and sewing napped and slippery fabrics. Use it when sewing long seams and hems for draperies and curtains. It's also wonderful for quilting.

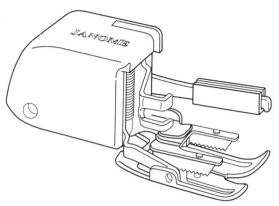

Fig. 9.44
The walking foot has a top set of feed dogs to prevent fabric from shifting or slipping and the underlayer from coming up short. Use the walking foot for matching plaids and stripes, for quilting, or sewing long drapery seams and hems.

SOURCES OF SUPPLY

The following source list tells where you can find or write away for information on New Home sewing machines, threads, and other sewing supplies you may not have at your local sewing store. For an extensive list and specific sewing needs, see *Sew, Serge, Press—Speed Tailoring in the Ultimate Sewing Center*, by Jan Saunders (Chilton, 1989), *Innovative Sewing* and *Innovative Serging*, by Gail Brown and Tammy Young (Chilton, 1989).

NEW HOME INFORMATION

The New Home Sewing Machine
  Company
100 Hollister Road
Teterboro, NJ 07608

New Home distributes educational materials too numerous to list here. Check with your local dealer.

KEY RING KITS

Showcase Keychain
Prime Arts Ltd., Inc.
Cincinnati, OH 45236

THREADS

Ask your local retailer or send a preaddressed, stamped envelope to the companies below to find out where to buy their threads.

Extra-fine

• Assorted threads
Robison-Anton Textile Co.
175 Bergen Blvd.
Fairview, NJ 07022

• DMC 100% cotton, Sizes 30 and 50
The DMC Corp.
107 Trumbull Street
Elizabeth, NJ 07206

• Dual-Duty Plus Extra-fine, cotton-wrapped polyester
J. & P. Coats/Coats & Clark
Consumer Service Department
P.O. Box 1010
Toccoa, GA 30577

• Iris 100% rayon
Art Sales
4801 W. Jefferson
Los Angeles, CA 90016

• Iris 100% silk—see Zwicky

• Janome Embroidery Thread #50, 100% acrylic
The New Home Sewing Machine Company
100 Hollister Road
Teterboro, NJ 07608

• Madeira threads
Madeira Co.
56 Primrose Drive
O'Shea Industrial Park
Laconia, NH 03246

• Mettler Metrosene fine machine embroidery cotton, size 60/2; long-staple polyester
Swiss-Metrosene, Inc.
7780 Quincy St.
Willowbrook, IL 60521

• Natesh 100% rayon, lightweight
Aardvark Adventures
P.O. Box 2449
Livermore, CA 94550

• Paradise 100% rayon
D & E Distribution
199 N. El Camino Real #F-242
Encinitas, CA 92024

• Sulky 100% rayon, sizes 30 and 40
Speed Stitch, Inc.
3113 Broadpoint Drive
Harbor Heights, FL 33983

• Zwicky 100% cotton, size 30/2; white
and black darning thread
V.W.S., Inc.
11760 Berea Rd.
Cleveland, OH 44111

All-Purpose

• Dual-Duty Plus, cotton-wrapped polyester—see Dual-Duty Plus Extra-Fine,
above.

Also Natesh, heavyweight, Zwicky in cotton and polyester, Mettler Metrosene in
30/2, 40/3, 50/3, and 30/3, and Metrosene
Plus. See addresses above.

Metallic

YLI Corp.
45 West 300 North
Provo, UT 84601

Troy Thread & Textile Company
2300 W. Diversey Ave.
Chicago, IL 60647

MACHINE-EMBROIDERY AND SEWING MACHINE SUPPLIES

(marking and cutting tools, hoops,
threads, patterns, books, etc.)

Aardvark Adventures
P.O. Box 2449
Livermore, CA 94550
*also publishes "Aardvark Territorial
Enterprise"*

Clotilde, Inc.
1909 S.W. First Ave.
Ft. Lauderdale, FL 33315
assorted sewing notions, and books

Craft Gallery Ltd.
P.O. Box 8319
Salem, MA 01971

D & E Distributing
199 N. El Camino Real #F-242
Encinitas, CA 92024

June Tailor, Inc.
2861 Highway 175
Richfield, WI 53076
*tailor boards, hams, mits, press cloths,
etc.*

Nancy's Notions
P.O. Box 683
Beaver Dam, WI 53916
assorted sewing notions and books

National Thread & Supply Corp.
695 Red Oak Road
Stockbridge, GA 30281

Patty Lou Creations
Rt. 2, Box 90-A
Elgin, OR 97827

Sew-Art International
P.O. Box 550
Bountiful, UT 84010

Sew/Fit Company
P.O. Box 565
LaGrange, IL 60525

Sewing Emporium
1087 Third Ave.
Chula Vista, CA 92010

Speed Stitch, Inc.
3113 Broadpoint Dr.
Harbor Heights, FL 33983

The Fabric Carr
P.O. Box 32120
San Jose, CA 95152

The Perfect Notion
566 Hoyt Street
Darien, CT 06820

Treadleart
25834 Narbonne Ave.
Lomita, CA 90717

MISCELLANEOUS

Applications
871 Fourth Ave.
Sacramento, CA 95818
release paper for appliqué

Berman Leathercraft
145 South St.
Boston, MA 02111
leather

Boycan's Craft and Art Supplies
P.O. Box 897
Sharon, PA 16146
plastic needlepoint canvas

Clearbrook Woolen Shop
P.O. Box 8
Clearbrook, VA 22624
Ultrasuede scraps

Folkwear Patterns
The Taunton Press
63 South Main Street
Box 5506
Newtown, CT 06470-5506
timeless fashion patterns

Kid Sew Patterns
1176 Northport Drive
Columbus, OH 43235
children's patterns and teaching materials

Kids Can Sew
P.O. Box 1710
St. George, UT 84771-1710
children's patterns and teaching materials

To Sew
P.O. Box 974
Malibu, CA 90265
beginning sewing kits for children of all ages

BIBLIOGRAPHY

BOOKS

Ambuter, Carolyn, *The Open Canvas*, Workman Publishing, New York, 1982.

Betzina, Sandra, *Power Sewing*, and *More Power Sewing*, Sandra Betzina, San Francisco, CA, 1985, 1990.

Bishop, Edna Bryte, and Marjorie Stotler Arch, *The Bishop Method*, W & W Publishing, Memphis, TN, 1966.

Brown, Gail, and Pati Palmer, *The Complete Handbook for Overlock Sewing*, Palmer/Pletsch Inc., Portland, OR, 1985.

Coffin, David Page, *The Custom Shirt Book*, David Page Coffin, P.O. Box 1580, La Jolla, CA 92038, 1985

Dodson, Jackie, with Judi Cull and Vicki Lyn Hastings, *Know Your New Home*, Chilton Book Company, Radnor, PA, 1987.

_____, *Know Your Sewing Machine*, Chilton Book Company, Radnor, PA, 1988.

Fanning, Robbie and Tony, *The Complete Book of Machine Quilting*, Chilton Book Company, Radnor, PA, 1980.

Griffin, Barb, *Petite Pizzazz*, Chilton Book Company, Radnor, PA, 1990.

_____, *St. Nick's Knacks*, Country Thread Designs, 1988.

Habeeb, Virginia, *Ladies' Home Journal Art of Homemaking*, Simon & Schuster, New York, 1973.

Hazen, Gale Grigg, *Owner's Guide to Sewing Machines, Sergers, and Knitting Machines*, Chilton Book Company, Radnor, PA, 1989.

Jabenis, Elaine, *The Fashion Director*, John Wiley & Sons, New York, 1972.

Maddigan, Judy, *Learn Bearmaking*, Open Chain Publishing, Menlo Park, CA, 1989.

Palmer, Pati, Gail Brown, and Sue Green, *Creative Serging Illustrated*, Chilton Book Company, Radnor, PA, 1987.

Reader's Digest, *Complete Guide to Sewing*, The Reader's Digest Association, Inc., Pleasantville, New York, 1976.

Saunders, Janice S., *Illustrated Speed Sewing*, Speed Sewing Ltd., Centerline, MI, 1985.

_____, *Sew, Serge, Press: Speed Tailoring in the Ultimate Sewing Center*, Chilton Book Company, Radnor, PA, 1989.

Shaeffer, Claire B., *The Complete Book of Sewing Shortcuts*, Sterling Publishing, New York, 1981.

_____, *Claire Shaeffer's Sewing S.O.S.*, Open Chain Publishing, Menlo Park, CA, 1988.

_____, *Claire Shaeffer's Fabric Sewing Guide*, Chilton Book Company, Radnor, PA, 1989.

Simplicity, *New Simplicity Sewing Book*, Simplicity Pattern Company, New York, 1979.

Simplicity, *Simply the Best Sewing Book*, Simplicity Pattern Company, New York, 1988.

Singer Instructions for Art Embroidery and Lace Work, foreword by Robbie Fanning, Open Chain Publishing, Menlo Park, CA, 1989.

Bibliography

Singer, *Singer Sewing Update 1988*, Cy DeCosse Inc., Minnetonka, MN, 1988.

Vogue, *The New Vogue Sewing Book*, Butterick Publishing, New York, 1980.

Zieman, Nancy, with Robbie Fanning, *The Busy Woman's Fitting Book*, Open Chain Publishing, Menlo Park, CA, 1989.

———, *The Busy Woman's Sewing Book*, Open Chain Publishing, Menlo Park, CA, 1989.

MAGAZINES

Aardvark Adventures
P.O. Box 2449
Livermore, CA 94550
> newspaper jammed with information about all kinds of embroidery, design, and things to order

Fiberarts
50 College Street
Asheville, NC 28801
> gallery of the best fiber artists, including those who work in machine stitchery

Sew It Seams
P.O. Box 2698
Kirkland, WA 98083-2698

Sew News
P.O. Box 1790
Peoria, IL 61656
> monthly tabloid, mostly of fashion garment sewing

Threads
Box 355
Newton, CT 06470
> glossy magazine on all fiber crafts

Treadleart
25834 Narbonne Ave.
Lomita, CA 90717
> bimonthly publication about machine embroidery

INDEX

Index